THE WAR CORRESPONDENTS

THE
ANGLO-ZULU
WAR

PROFESSOR JOHN LABAND
and IAN KNIGHT

Bramley Books

First published in 1996 by
Sutton Publishing Limited

This edition published in 1997 by Bramley Books,
an imprint of Quadrillion Publishing

British Library Cataloguing in Publication Data

A catalogue record for this book is available from the British Library.

ISBN 1-85833-732-1

This book was designed and produced by
Sutton Publishing Limited · Phoenix Mill · Thrupp · Stroud · Gloucestershire

Typeset in 10/12 Times.
Typesetting and origination by
Sutton Publishing Limited.
Printed in Great Britain by
WBC Limited, Bridgend.

CONTENTS

ACKNOWLEDGEMENTS

In preparing this book we have received generous help from a number of institutions and individuals. The University of Natal awarded Professor Laband a grant from its Research Fund; he is also indebted to the University's Publications Committee and to the Research Incentive Fund administered by the Department of Historical Studies in Pietermaritzburg for financial support.

Invaluable research assistance was proffered by the staff of the Killie Campbell Africana Library, Durban; and in Pietermaritzburg by the staffs of the Natal Archives Depot, the Natal Society Library and the University of Natal Library. Special thanks are due to Mrs Bobby Eldridge of Killie Campbell and Mr John Morrison of the Natal Society Library.

Ms Cynthia Wortley, secretary to the Department of Historical Studies in Pietermaritzburg, accurately and cheerfully transcribed passages from the colonial newspapers onto disk. Ian Castle skilfully produced crisp maps from our tangled instructions, and Keith Reeves and Rai England allowed generous access to their extensive private collections of newspapers and illustrations.

John Laband
Ian Knight

INTRODUCTION

NEWS FROM THE FRONT:
WAR REPORTAGE IN THE ANGLO-ZULU WAR

Under strong criticism from his government for what it considered the 'indefinite prolongation' of the Anglo-Zulu War of 1879, the commander of the British forces in the field, Lieutenant-General Lord Chelmsford, wrote to the Secretary of State for War on 10 June 1879 defending his conduct of the campaign. He concluded his long and querulous letter with the bitter reflection that it was 'more than probable with such a large number of newspaper correspondents in camp, that many false impressions may be circulated and sent home regarding our present operations either intentionally or ignorantly'. Chelmsford undoubtedly resented the unwelcome presence of journalists whom he petulantly regarded as 'always ready without sufficient data for their guidance to express opinions on every conceivable military subject ex cathedra'.[1] Yet he could scarcely banish them from his side, for by 1879 they were a standard (if predatory) presence with any British army on active service.

Victorian war correspondents and artists, in their dashing wide-brimmed hats and riding boots, slung about with military-style paraphernalia and flaunting foreign decorations, formed a glamorous, self-conscious elite among journalists. Known respectively as 'special correspondents' and 'special artists', they brought news of the frequent colonial wars of the British Empire vividly home to an insatiable public. By reinforcing the romantic images of these far-flung conflicts they contributed to the more favourable image of the army and boosted the reputations of its successful commanders. They instilled vicarious patriotic pride in ordinary people at home, and inflamed popular imperialism.

All editors knew that war news greatly increased sales, so they were prepared to bear the heavy costs of supporting special correspondents with their hugely expensive telegraphed reports. Smaller and provincial newspapers who could not afford special correspondents, and were therefore out of the costly race to get the news home before competitors, made do with reprinting the despatches that appeared in the major papers. But the general result was that news of campaigns was published in the fullest detail. Comment on the way they were being conducted was also trenchant and sometimes highly critical, but was the inevitable consequence of a free press in Great Britain and her colonies. Military concerns at the potential security risks of uncensored reporting were brushed aside, not least because Britain's enemies in her colonial wars were hardly equipped to pick up their intelligence from the English press.

William Howard Russell of *The Times*, who so ably reported the Crimean War, established the credibility of the war correspondent, and set the pattern for those select British journalists who followed his example. Few were primarily war correspondents, and many had no previous military experience. But they soon learned the ropes. Those who made the reporting of imperial small wars their speciality were regularly thrown together in uncomfortable corners of the globe. They inevitably found themselves members of a select band, bound together in camaraderie by their shared wartime dangers and hardships, yet driven into hectic competition by their dauntless efforts to bring the news to their own newspapers ahead of their rivals.

Sending despatches home was an arduous business. The introduction of the telegraph line meant that news could now travel faster than horse or even train, but unfortunately for special correspondents covering colonial wars, telegraphs were seldom close to hand. In the case of those reporting the Anglo-Zulu War, the nearest extremity of the international telegraph system was in Madeira, where the trans-Atlantic cable, which had been laid from Brazil to Europe in 1874, touched land. The weekly mail steamer took sixteen days – if the sailing was good – between Cape Town and the island. Charles Norris-Newman's report of the disaster at Isandlwana on 22 January 1879, which he wrote up once he reached Pietermaritzburg straight from the battlefield after an exhausting ride, and which was then telegraphed from the Natal capital to Cape Town, where it was put on board the *Dunrobin Castle* for Madeira, only reached London on 11 February – twenty days after the event had taken place.

After the Isandlwana debacle, action was taken to improve communications. A cable already existed from London to Bombay via Aden. A new link was established down the east coast of Africa from Aden via Zanzibar and Delagoa Bay to Durban, and thence, via the internal South African network, to Cape Town. But the link-up was not completed until the end of 1879. This meant that news from the Zulu front still had to be taken by despatch rider (who, like Archibald Forbes, might be the correspondent himself) to the nearest local telegraph station for transmission to Cape Town and the mail steamer. Special artists' drawings had to be carried to Durban and the first ship sailing for England. When Melton Prior, the special artist of the *Illustrated London News*, worked through the night to ensure that his was the first illustrated paper to print authentic pictures of the death of the Prince Imperial of France in Zululand on 1 June 1879, it was still only on 28 June (nearly four weeks after the event) that the paper was able to rush out its special supplement.

Not all the special correspondents were necessarily near the scene of action and confronted with potential front-page news, as were Norris-Newman or Forbes. Many, particularly those reporting for the local Natal newspapers, saw only the less dramatic sectors of the war. Perhaps it was because their stories were often so unavoidably mundane that they regarded the hardships endured in transmitting them scarcely worth the effort. A special correspondent with the *Natal Witness* wrote on 19 June 1879 from the Lower Thukela on the border between the Colony of Natal and Zululand ruefully describing 'a war correspondent's difficulties':

. . . [T]o enthusiastic persons, the position of War Correspondent may be a very pretty one; to rove at will among armed camps; to witness with feelings of awe the vast preparations made for an engagement; to look on the serried ranks, of infantry, cavalry, and artillery, as they push forward to encounter the enemy; but above all the terrific grandeur of looking on at an engagement when the cannon belches forth its deadly fire, rockets whizzing on their mission of death, and the sharp ring of the rifle is heard on all sides. Then to sit down on the victorious field, collect thoughts, and rapidly dash off an account of the whole affair which you will know will be earnestly read by thousands. It is a very pretty picture, no doubt, but a little practical experience of such work will rub off a great deal of its gloss. Difficulties beset a correspondent when following the regular troops at every turn, and he often finds himself encountered by serious troubles where least likely to be found. Take for instance, a little adventure of my own on last evening. Having learned authoritatively that the troops were to march forward on Friday, I at once hurried off and scribbled in my note book the piece of intelligence, and . . . went in quest of the post office. . . . Though the hour was early (7 p.m.), the night was dark, and once away from the light of the camp, I found myself completely lost. I

Melton Prior's sketches of the adventurous life of the 'special' in Zululand: thrown by an ant-bear hole; sketching under fire; and setting fire to a Zulu homestead. (Ian Knight)

had to go down some hills, and up others, to cross streams overflowing with stagnant water, the whereabouts I only discovered after a 'header'. . . . The lights from the Kafir fires beside the out-spanned wagons only got me into a maze of leather thongs, chains, desselbooms, and bullocks' horns. Guided by a solitary light on the pontoon bridge which now crosses the Tugela, I found myself wandering by the banks of that river, and trembled for what the results of a false step may produce. With difficulty I got over the bridge, condensing my proportions as much as possible for the passage of mules that appeared in the highest state of madness, kicking in all directions as they were vigorously led over the bridge by a 'fore-looper,' helped in his work by a Kafir in the rear, who energetically applied his whip to their ribs. This, and an upturned wagon . . . were the only obstacles I encountered at the Zulu side; but in Natal they became far worse. Roads seemed to be cut in all directions on the side of the hill, leaving in some places a wall some four feet in height – climbing from one road to another, and creeping up a hill to the right of Fort Pearson, I was, after a little direction, able to grope my way to a solitary tent on the summit of the hill, outside which, after playing the old game of 'blind man's buff,' I discovered something, judging from the sense of touch, resembling a soap-box, and after diligent search in this box, I discovered a hole which seemed to be placed so as to give the greatest amount of trouble to any one who may require it. Into this I dropped my letter, and was fortunately able to get down the hill, cross the pontoon bridge, and find myself once more in Zululand with only half-a-dozen falls. . . . And what was the gain of all this two hours' hard labour? Simply half-a-dozen lines which perhaps may be stowed away in some corner of the *Witness*. Little did those who read them dream of how they came there, or through how many pools, holes, and corners they were dragged, though safely stowed away in a breast-pocket, before they reached Maritzburg.[2]

Those correspondents who succeeded – regardless of cost and despite the myriad impediments of the sort described above – in getting their news to England ahead of their rivals, were puffed up into heroes by their own newspapers who made capital of their extraordinary pluck and energy. Indeed, war correspondents and their employers did their best to create a romantic mythology about their occupation. Kitted out to look the part on campaign (and for publicity pictures and the photographs that accompanied their highly-coloured memoirs), they sported paramilitary clothing, campaign ribbons, revolvers and aggressive moustachios. They tended to decorate their homes with suitable trophies and military items, and made a point of appearing dressed for the part at self-advertising public lectures.

Nevertheless, although this breed dominated the reporting of colonial wars, they never monopolized it entirely. They had to accommodate all sorts of interlopers. Those they most particularly resented were serving officers employed as correspondents who, complained the professionals, could not provide the necessary impartial reporting and criticism. However, newspapers often favoured them because they were generally only paid for copy received and this meant a considerable saving. The exhaustive coverage of the Anglo-Zulu War provided in the Natal newspapers regularly emanated from colonial Volunteers and officers serving with the various columns.

War correspondents identified with the British army and its ethos. They prided themselves on the soldierly qualities of bravery, toughness and competitiveness they felt called upon to exhibit. Since they enjoyed an ill-defined quasi-officer status on campaign, often being honorary members of officers' messes, they tended to relate closely to the officers with whom they mixed, and usually had little individual contact with the ordinary soldiers. They consequently shared the officers' attitudes, not only to war as a professional and glorious

The correspondent militant: F.R. MacKenzie of the London *Standard*, with notebook in one hand and carbine in the other. (S.B. Bourquin)

occupation in which they revelled, but also towards the contemptible 'lesser breeds' against whom they fought. This meant they seldom entertained doubt as to the justice of the British cause, and stoutly believed that once defeated their dusky and stereotypically savage foes would learn to appreciate the inestimable benefits of British rule.

Since war correspondents valued their close association with officers, they tended to praise them when they could, and brought particularly successful ones to the public eye. However, ever since Russell's revealing despatches from the Crimea, the correspondent's mission had also included critical comment on all aspects of the way in which a campaign was being conducted. This is not to say that in order to preserve the honour of the army and the public's faith in it a correspondent was not above some self-censorship over discreditable incidents. Yet where a correspondent felt that the public interest would be served by revelations of defective weaponry, inadequate supply and transport arrangements, negligent medical care and deficient military planning and leadership, his reports home could have a salutary and ultimately beneficent effect.

Naturally, relations between officers and war correspondents tended to depend on the extent to which the latters' reporting was unfavourable. Ambitious officers like Sir Garnet Wolseley cynically cultivated war correspondents to ensure he received a laudatory press and caught the public's imagination. In return, he cooperated fully with them. Yet, when subjected like Lord Chelmsford to Archibald Forbes's stinging criticisms of his conduct of the Zulu campaign, officers could respond with hostility and non-cooperation. When, as in Chelmsford's case, the debate became a public one, the military establishment was not above closing ranks and branding the war correspondents as insolent and ignorant upstarts.

What sold newspapers, though, was not exchanges of correspondence between aggrieved military men and bumptious war correspondents over elements of strategy, but graphic, exciting accounts of battles that scooped competitors and caught the mass readership's imagination. The best of such accounts conformed to all the requirements of effective reportage. This depends on the vivid, eye-witness, on-the-spot record, the use of telling detail, and the sense of the heat and rush of events that are still in flux. Victorian special correspondents, however, were also expected by their avid readers to depict imperial wars and battles as grand, glorious and justified. And since the required emphasis was on adventure, heroism, glory and noble death, preferably selflessly offered up for a comrade, they habitually did not dwell on the horrors of the battlefield, and certainly not on British corpses. It was permissible to praise the bravery of a noble adversary like the Zulu, but not to write about the horrible mutilations inflicted on them by Martini-Henry bullets. Circumlocutions were designed to neutralize and conceal disturbing or unseemly details. For war was the business of stern warriors in service of the queen against her generally rather despicable foes, and the often terrible price of victory did not have to be dwelt upon. Besides which, if newspaper reports of slaughters in exotic places were read by many people rather as if they were imaginative literature removed from daily and mundane realities, then the purpose was to provide them with reassurance in their own apparent invulnerability. There was no point in puncturing that self-satisfaction, especially since it sold newspapers.

Victorian special artists similarly sanitized their subject, and, in keeping with the conventions of war illustration of the time, dwelt on the dramatic, heroic and picturesque while suppressing the ugly and disturbing aspects of war.

The term 'special artist' was first used of the artists commissioned by the pioneering illustrated newspaper founded in 1842, the *Illustrated London News*, to cover the Crimean War. The illustrated papers depended on pictures of wars to boost their circulation, and an international troop of artists was constantly on the move around the world to meet the demand. Special artists had to have the intuition of the journalist in knowing where to be and what to draw, and to have the skill to make rapid and accurate drawings on location. Accoutred and equipped very much like special correspondents, and likewise dodging bullets, avoiding capture or arrest as spies and shaking off disease, they carried, in addition to the normal kit, sketchbooks, pencils, brushes and other necessary artistic equipment. Their problems in getting their material back to impatient editors from inaccessible battlefields was as great as that of special correspondents. Melton Prior, for example, had to entrust his detailed sketch of the battle of Ulundi to Forbes, who was riding off with his own despatch, for posting in Durban.

It was fortunate for special artists that the invention of the photo-mechanical reproduction of photographs was still far in the future, and cameras were not yet efficient or easily portable. By the 1870s a dry plate or gelatin emulsion process enabled plates to be stored ready for many months, and did away with the need for special vans in which to develop the glass plates before the sensitizing chemicals dried. The real breakthrough in photography only came in 1888 when the celluloid roll film appeared. Until then the fragile and bulky equipment necessary could only be transported gingerly to the area of operations, usually after military activities had ceased. Then only laboriously posed pictures were possible because of the slow exposure time – invaluable for the record, but quite static. This meant that only the quick hand of the experienced draughtsman could capture action and movement. Thus, in 1879, the special artist was still effectively a human camera.

That in itself was often a frustration for the special artist, condemned to produce over-literal sketches against the clock. There was seldom time to embellish these into finished drawings. They were sent off as they were, scribbled over with helpful descriptions, for the staff artists in London (sometimes working as a team) to complete and redraw for engraving. Inevitably, this work transformed the original sketch to conform to the conventions of war illustration, dramatizing it, altering its composition, and subtly metamorphosing faces, plants and animals into forms familiar to the untravelled and

Eurocentric staff artist. The illustration was then traced in reverse on to a boxwood or cherry wood block, engraved, and a facsimile in copper then made for printing. To expedite the process for large pictures, a number of wood blocks were bolted together, the picture was traced on and the blocks were then disassembled for distribution to a number of engravers. Even if few changes were made to the original drawing supplied by the special artist, the wood-engraving process inevitably coarsened its essential quality and spontaneity, and blunted the often sensitive draughtmanship of the artist in the field.

At the time of the outbreak of the Anglo-Zulu War in January 1879, the outcome seemed so inevitable that only one of the influential London dailies thought it worth its while to send out a special correspondent. William H. Mudford, the *Standard*'s shrewd editor, despatched Charles Norris-Newman, who also acted as a stringer for the *Times of Natal* and the *Cape Standard and Mail*. Norris-Newman wrote of himself in the preface to his popular reminiscences of the campaign, *In Zululand With the British Throughout the War of 1879*:

> I was the first and only officially appointed special correspondent that was in the field with the troops during the early days of preparations and our first entry into Zululand. . . . Having been sometime previously residing in Natal I knew something of the country, and of the native language and customs; and throughout the whole campaign I was constantly about with the different Divisions of our force. Thus I was able to get a more general view of the whole conduct of the war than if I had attached myself to any one Division throughout.[3]

Norris-Newman was never the only correspondent in the field, however. The local Natal newspapers took a close interest in the movements of the British troops and eventually in the involvement of the colonists themselves. The *Times of Natal* had enlisted Norris-Newman's services, but he could not be everywhere. Like the *Natal Witness*, *Natal Mercury* and *Natal Colonist*, it had to look beyond its own full-time correspondents and to draw on reports from British officers, colonial officers and volunteers serving with the forces, colonial officials and ordinary settlers living in the towns and villages affected by the war. These correspondents were never named in the columns of the colonial newspapers, and their names are consequently lost. They are the source, nevertheless, of the extraordinarily detailed and vivid accounts that make the colonial press such a vital source for historians.

The Isandlwana disaster on 22 January 1879 ensured that neither Norris-Newman nor the local correspondents could any longer have the war to themselves. The war was now international news and the pride of Britain was at stake. Consequently, when the reinforcements the badly shaken Lord Chelmsford urgently requested sailed for Natal at the end of February, they were accompanied by a small flock of professional war correspondents from the leading English newspapers. They included Francis Francis of *The Times* (later fishing editor of *The Field*), W. Peace who represented the *Daily Telegraph* until Phil Robinson arrived from Afghanistan, F.R. MacKenzie of the London *Standard*, and Archibald Forbes of the *Daily News*. M. Deleage of *Le Figaro* came out to South Africa more to follow the progress of the former Prince Imperial of France, who was an observer on Chelmsford's staff, than the war itself.

Archibald Forbes was the most successful and famous Victorian war correspondent after Russell (who recognized his great abilities), and surely the most decorated journalist ever to have lived. Born in 1838 in Morayshire, Scotland, the son of a minister, he dropped out of Aberdeen University, squandered his inheritance and enlisted penniless as a trooper in the

Royal Dragoons. Though his regiment never saw active service, Forbes applied himself, read deeply in military history and theory, wrote articles on the army under an assumed name, and rose to acting quartermaster-sergeant.

He was convinced that he had discovered a natural affinity for the glamorous business of soldiering. However, in 1867 he was invalided out of the army and became a struggling journalist in London. His break came when he was fleetingly employed as a war correspondent by the *Morning Advertiser* to cover the Franco-Prussian War. J.R. Robinson, the general manager of the *Daily News*, the leading organ of the Liberal Party, recognized Forbes's potential and snapped him up. Within a short space of time Forbes established his reputation as the top special correspondent of the *Daily News*, between 1870 and 1878 covering the Carlist, Serbian, Russo-Turkish, Afghan and Anglo-Zulu wars. His health then failed, and he supported himself until his death in 1900 through his lecturing and writing.

As a correspondent, Forbes wrote clearly and dramatically, emphasizing the heroic and picturesque – which is what his public demanded. His own daring-do escapades in acquiring his information under fire and carrying his reports over impossible terrain to scoop his rivals to London were newsworthy in themselves. They made him, the leader of the 'adventurous school' of war correspondents, a popular hero in his own right, comparable to the soldiers whose deeds he reported. His 'ride of death' from the field of Ulundi to bring the first word of the final victory of the Anglo-Zulu War to the anxious public at home, was his most famous exploit. The *Illustrated London News* eulogized his feat in the issue of 9 August 1879. On its front page it printed a dramatic picture of a galloping Forbes drawn by Caton Woodville, the journal's leading London-office artist, and fulsomely explained:

> The bold, unwearied, dauntless, solitary horseman, 'bloody with spurring, fiery red with haste,' who is represented in our front-page Engraving, is the renowned Special Correspondent of the Daily News, Mr Archibald Forbes. This gentleman, who has served in a cavalry regiment, is equally distinguished among those who follow military campaigns in the service of journalism, for his practical knowledge of warfare, his literary powers of description and spirited narrative, and his extraordinary feats of rapid travelling, through the roughest country and braving the most obvious personal dangers, to send off his letters or telegrams at the earliest possible moment. After the battle of Ulundi, which was fought, between eight and nine o'clock in the morning, on the 4th ult., Mr Forbes volunteered to convey Lord Chelmsford's despatch, for Major-General the Hon. H. Clifford at Maritzburg, announcing the victory, the news of which was to be instantly sent to England. The nearest telegraph station for the purpose of this important communication was at Landman's Drift, on the Buffalo River, the boundary which separates Natal from the Utrecht district of the Transvaal, a place situated nearly due west of Ulundi, and not less than a hundred and ten miles distant from it. Mr Forbes had to go there as quickly as he could in order to dispatch his own report of the battle to the Daily News, and Lord Chelmsford was glad to avail himself of so good a messenger for the conveyance of the official despatch to be forwarded by General Clifford to the War Office. It was a ride of the distance we have mentioned in fourteen hours, entirely alone, over a rugged and mountainous country without any proper roads, and with no small risk of being cut off by the straggling bands of the enemy dispersed all over Zululand after the rout of their main army, or probably still lurking about the British rear, and along the route of its communications, for the plunder of occasional convoys. Mr Forbes rode on all through the night, which was dark, with a thick fog, and he twice lost his way. He performed this valuable public service with such

intrepid courage and so much personal address that we trust he will receive from Her Majesty the Queen a suitable honorary distinction, at the request of the Secretary of State for War. If he cannot have the Victoria Cross, being a non-combatant, let him have the Order of St. Michael and St. George, which is usually bestowed on civilians for services rendered in any of the British colonies or foreign possessions.[4]

Nevertheless, Colonel F.A. Stanley, the Secretary of State for War, ruled categorically that war correspondents, as non-combatants, were not eligible for war medals. Forbes was deeply affronted, and contended in vain that his carrying of Chelmsford's despatch made him an official despatch rider.

Nor was this snub all Forbes had to bear. Settler opinion in Natal was considerably less impressed with his dramatic ride than was that in England, primarily because it was better informed as to the true circumstances. The *Natal Mercury* correspondent commenting from Utrecht on 1 October 1879 was particularly devastating:

. . . The Archibald Forbes' account of his ride from Ulundi with despatches has very much amused those who know the man, and the road he had ridden over, and the feat performed. Mr Forbes was not asked to carry despatches, he only rode with the news in the interest of his employers. There was nothing extraordinary about the matter, for unless he had been irresponsible for his actions he could not have missed the track left through the country by 600 ox wagons, 2000 cavalry, and 10,000 footmen, and travelling at a time when it was perfectly safe to ride from one fort to the next by easy short stages. What he brags so much about would have been done by any of our colonial volunteers had they been asked to do it as a part of their duty, without any extravagant boast or brag. If Forbes had cared to do it, the news could have been carried to the coast in eight or ten hours' ride with ease.[5]

Naturally, this report may to an extent have been coloured by a humble colonial correspondent's jealousy of the hyperbole surrounding the famous professional's perhaps not unduly remarkable exploit. But in any case, colonists were not the least enamoured of the dashing special correspondent on acount of his exceedingly unflattering 'honest opinion' of the Natal settlers expressed in the columns of the *Daily News*. The colonists, he declared, where entirely at odds with the army operating from Natal, shamelessly fleecing it at every turn. Not only were they squeezing every penny of profit out of a war being fought for their defence but, to add insult to injury, they were on the whole an unpunctual, insolent, lying, swaggering, drunken and generally cussed lot.[6] Not unnaturally, he was severely taken to task in the indignant Natal press. The *Natal Witness* grandly demolished the intemperate correspondent on 12 August 1879:

MR. ARCHIBALD FORBES has certainly not taken the trouble to be polite to Natal colonists. Speaking in haste and probably in a bad temper, he has fallen into the error of the psalmist, and said that all men in Natal were liars and all sorts of other bad things. . . . We have not the smallest intention of joining in the wild shriek of personal abuse that is being poured out against Mr. FORBES. It is quite enough to know that things are not as Mr. FORBES has represented them, and that Natal colonists have many more virtues than can meet the eye of a man galloping through the country at the speed which the work of a Special Correspondent requires.[7]

Forbes left the indignant colonists safely behind when he returned to England to embark

'The Ride of Death'. How the *Illustrated London News* depicted Archibald Forbes's dash to be first with the news of Chelmsford's victory at Ulundi. (Ian Knight)

on a series of public lectures recounting his adventures in Zululand. Lord Chelmsford, however, was more immediately to hand. As we have seen, from the moment Forbes arrived in Zululand Chelmsford had resented his unsympathetic presence, and was not taking kindly to the many criticisms Forbes continued to level publicly at his generalship. Forbes gleefully hit back and, in a letter of 27 August 1879 to the editor of the *Daily News*, rebutted Chelmsford's charges that 'party feeling and political bias' were behind his strictures. He then went on vigorously to defend the integrity of the special correspondents reporting from Zululand:

> If Lord Chelmsford has indeed been misrepresented by the correspondents accompanying his army, he has been misrepresented with a strange malignity and unanimity. . . .
> In the insinuation that in the late campaign journalists wrote with a view to lower him in the estimation of the force he commanded, Lord Chelmsford has allowed his impatience under criticism . . . to impel him to attribute base motives to men whose sole care was their honest duty. . . . [The] *army does its own criticism*; it knows too much to be swayed one way or the other by the lucubrations of a journalist. If a force . . . has formed an unfavourable opinion of its leader, it laughs to scorn the journalist who would have it believe that its commander is a capable chief; if it believes in its leaders, its anger rises at the writer who would make light of its idol. . . . I recognise a serious danger, under certain circumstances, in the full freedom of expression by war correspondents; but the intelligence bureau of the Zulus was not supplied with English newspapers. Lord Chelmsford's apprehension is a mere bogey.[8]

An even more famous war correspondent than Forbes was drawn to report the war in Zululand. As General Sir Garnet Wolseley prepared to sail at the end of May 1879 to bring the campaign to a speedy conclusion, William Russell himself – fifty-nine years of age and current editor of the *Army and Navy Gazette* – offered his services to *The Times*. He was refused. The *Daily Telegraph* then snapped him up to write reports on the general state of affairs in Natal and Zululand (Phil Robinson was covering day-to-day events in the field). Meanwhile, the *Telegraph* printed reports sent by Arthur Aylward, the editor of the *Natal Witness* in Pietermaritzburg. Russell eventually arrived in Natal too late to report on the campaign. Undaunted, he succeeded in stirring up quite a fierce controversy with Wolseley in the press over the embarrassing drunkenness and pillaging committed by the troops under his command.

Special artists, because of the medium in which they worked, were inevitably less controversial than special correspondents. The most renowned to illustrate the Anglo-Zulu War was Melton Prior (1845–1910) of the Conservative *Illustrated London News* of London, founded in 1842. First employed as a special artist to cover the Ashanti War of 1873–4, during his career he depicted no less than twenty-four colonial wars. Prior worked in black and white with soft graphite pencils, copiously inscribing his drawings to explain what was going on to the caption writer, studio artist (such as Caton Woodville) and engraver at home. He had a remarkable facility for grasping the sense of a battle, but the strains of his career and the necessarily long absences abroad were costly both to his marriage and his health.

Prior arrived in South Africa on 6 April 1879. He followed the 2nd Division into Zululand in an American-built ambulance which contained all the comforts of home. At the battle of Ulundi he lost his sketchbook out of his saddle holster and fell despairingly to the ground in tears. Fortunately, a passing officer gave him his own notebook in which Prior made duplicates as best he could from memory.

When publishing a page of engravings of Prior's Zululand sketches on 18 October 1879, the *Illustrated London News* informed its readers of the vicissitudes endured by their special artist:

> Travelling on horse-back over that rough country, where the holes of burrowing ant-bears, and other insidious ground traps, sometimes leave but an unsafe footing beneath the ragged herbage of the wilderness, he more than once got an awkward tumble. The first time he was thrown clear over the horses's head. . . . But on the second occasion, when horse and man fell together, the Special Artist lying undermost while his kicking steed rolled over upon him, it was a case of greater peril. The real injury, fortunately, did not amount to more than a painful complication of bruises, which were soothed by proper surgery and lapse of time. His friends of the 17th Lancers showed him much kindness when enduring this temporary affliction. Our Artist is an old campaigner . . . and his previous experiences in Bulgaria and Bosnia, and in the Ashantee War, had made him tolerably indifferent to the danger of being under an enemy's fire. This degree of self-possession in 'sketching under difficulties' was more than some of the combatant officers and soldiery had expected to find in a pacific civilian with a portfolio and case of lead-pencils. A friendly Zulu warrior of the Native Contingent would therefore be sent to warn him that fighting was already commenced on the neighbouring hill-side, of which Mr. Prior was probably quite aware, but too much intent on his drawing to mind the whiz of a stray bullet now and then above his head.[9]

Another noted special artist who recorded the later stages of the campaign was Charles Edwin Fripp (1854–1906) who came from a Bristol Quaker family of artists. In 1878 he began his highly adventurous life of constant travel reporting colonial wars for the Liberal *Graphic*, founded in 1869. He was of stern stuff, critical of military officiousness but an excellent draughtsman. He usually worked in small sketchbooks with an HB pencil, working up outlines into larger, more finished drawings in pencil and wash. He did not

THE ATTACK ON THE PRESS.
Another Defeat for Chelmsford.

Even after the war was over, Chelmsford's reputation continued to suffer in the press. 'I only went and gave Mr. Forbes a kick', complains the General to 'Grandpa' Disraeli in this *Fun* cartoon, 'and he's been and gone and hit me back again!' (Ian Knight)

much relish the Zulu campaign since the bravery of the Zulu and their fortitude in defeat uncomfortably impressed him. As he wrote in 1900 of the aftermath of the battle of Ulundi:

> The smoke of Cetywayo's burning kraal hung like a pall over the plain to conceal hundreds of dead warriors from the great moon which stood calmly and gloriously in the eternal heaven above. Whatever the rights or wrongs which brought on the war, these same brave Zulu died resisting an invasion of their country and their homes.
> Naked savages as they were, let us honour them.[10]

With special artists as with special correspondents, and the newspapers made use of suitably skilled serving soldiers to supplement the drawings of the professional journalists. One such was Dr Doyle Glanville (b. 1844) whom the *Graphic* employed. In 1871 he completed his medical training, which took him from London to Cambridge and finally to Edinburgh, and went on to serve as a military surgeon during the Ninth Frontier War in the Cape. During the Anglo-Zulu War he served with No. 2 Column until it was redeployed after Isandlwana, and then joined the Flying Column during the final advance on Ulundi. His often light-hearted sketches are quite distinctive.

The *Illustrated London News* in its turn tapped the talents of Brevet Lieutenant-Colonel John North Crealock (1837–1895) who was on Chelmsford's Personal Staff and served as his Military Secretary. Crealock was an accomplished artist in pencil and wash who, whenever the column halted, would sit down and depict the scene in his notebook. Several of his drawings (including the famous 'Our return to the camp of Sandhlwana (22 Jan 1879)' and 'The store at Rorke's drift – on return to it on 23 Jan 1879') were carried by the *Illustrated London News*, but the conventional artist who redrew them for reproduction lost the quality of the originals.

Photographers had not found it possible to take pictures of the actual fighting. Even those who actually accompanied the troops into the field had, in the main, to content themselves with static shots of individuals, groups, forts, camps, parades and landscapes.

The 'special artist' personified: Melton Prior of
the *Illustrated London News*. Prior almost always
preferred to be photographed wearing a hat, since
he was largely bald; he was known among his
colleagues as 'The Screeching Billiard Ball'.
(Ian Knight)

Most of these were taken in Natal or along the frontiers with Zululand rather than while on
campaign in enemy territory. But once hostilities had died down, and it was safe to travel,
some Natal professional photographers took to the rutted tracks to cash in on the war by
compiling albums of 'pictorial souvenirs' for sale.

There were no less than nine photographic businesses operating in Pietermaritzburg in
1879, and six in Durban. The most successful photographers of Anglo-Zulu War sites
were James C. Lloyd of Durban, who had been busy at the port since 1859, J.W.
Buchanan of Pietermaritzburg, who had taken the pictures of Cetshwayo's 'coronation' in
1873, George T. Ferneyhough of the same city, and Benjamin Kisch with photographic
studios in both towns. Kisch enjoyed the reputation of being exceptionally skilled. Since
1872 he and his brother Henry had been in partnership. Henry liked to do the travelling
while Benjamin stayed in Durban. Even successful photographers found it difficult to
make a living and, while Lloyd also worked as an artist, Benjamin Kisch had a general
outfitter's store.

The preparation of specialized albums was a considerable investment on the part of the
photographer, but one that provided excellent publicity and promised financial rewards.
Henry Kisch and his staff joined the troops concentrating on Zululand's western border
during April 1879 in order 'to supply the public with views of all the interesting situations
of the coming campaign'. George Ferneyhough, meanwhile, accompanied Wood's Flying
Column 'with every appliance for obtaining the many interesting and . . . historical
mementoes of the Zulu war'.[11] His 'truly beautiful series of Zulu war photos' was not
finally complete until the middle of 1880, when the *Natal Witness* gave them its
'unqualified commendation'. The newspaper's belief that they would enjoy 'a rapid sale'
showed that a year after the end of the conflict the local market still was not sated with
Anglo-Zulu War memorabilia.[12] Meanwhile, Lloyd's collection of war scenery
photographs had already enjoyed a considerable success. On 2 August 1879 the *Natal
Witness* enthusiastically reviewed his 'album of views':

Charles Fripp of the *Graphic*, who was clearly moved by the destruction inflicted on the Zulus at Ulundi, depicted himself in his own sketch showing a group of warriors cut down by volley fire during the battle. (Ian Knight)

Mr. Lloyd the well-known photographic artist of Durban, has just returned from a lengthened tour of professional operations in districts which have now been rendered famous by the stirring incidents of the Zulu war. . . . Leaving Maritzburg, Mr. Lloyd succeeded in getting some capital . . . views of Fort Durnford, Estcourt, Colenso, and Newcastle [and] also some very interesting scenes showing the daily routine of life in the military laager at Utrecht. It will, though, be on the photographs which bring before us so realistically all the neighbourhood of Rorke's Drift and Isandhlwana that the spectator will linger. . . . They certainly take us back to the terrible 22nd of January last, but the gloom of the retrospect is lightened as we gaze on the monument at Rorke's Drift of one of the most brilliant instances of British heroism which adorn the pages of history. The mealie bags which formed the hastily-contrived retrenchments are gone, but the photographs bring clearly before us, near and distant views of the house in which the handful of gallant Britons kept the Zulus at bay. By the aid of these beautiful sun pictures, the spectator pursues the mental journey from the present camp at Rorke's Drift, across the river in the direction of Isandhlwana mountain, which can be seen – memorable landmark – in the distance to the eastward. One picture shows us the punt crossing the Buffalo at Rorke's Drift, and really the manner in which Mr. Lloyd has succeeded in firing the exquisite sheen of the placid river surface on his plate, stamps him as a rare artist indeed. We follow in imagination the windings of the Buffalo, and are silently transported before the white stone cross which marks the last resting place of those brave heroes, Lieuts. Melville and Coghill. . . . Making our way by the famous Fugitives' Path, we have now some very fine photographs of the whole vicinity. Sad tokens of the awful slaughter with which the surrounding scenery is so bitterly associated lie in the foreground of several views, which have as an imposing background the lofty mountain or crag of Isandhlwana, while the empty wagons which lie dotted here and there remind us of the long unavenged spoliation of Cetywayo's hordes. . . . Among the incidental pictures with which Mr. Lloyd embellishes his most complete album of war scenery photographs, are 'counterfeit presentments' of Oham,

James Lloyd, one of the leading photographers in
Durban, whose photographs produced some of the
most enduring images of the war. (Bryan Maggs
Collection)

his chief indunas and galaxy of wives, while some charming landscapes – all
possessing considerable attractions – go to make up what will undoubtedly prove the
most interesting pictorial souvenir of the Zulu war which the public will have the
opportunity of obtaining.[13]

The special correspondents, special artists and photographers, both British and colonial,
left a rich legacy of first-hand written reports and images of the Anglo-Zulu War. It is our
hope that those selected for inclusion in this volume will provide some indication of their
extraordinary diversity, depth and vividness. Historians have long tapped the many official
despatches and reports, private letters, diaries and reminiscences dealing with the Zululand
campaign. They also know that it is essential to consult the newspaper reports too. This is
particularly the case when less familiar sectors of the war are under consideration, notably
the frontier zones along the Natal, Transvaal, Swazi and Zululand borders, and the districts
in Natal behind the front line. Reflecting this consideration, the editors have chosen not
only items dealing with the main campaign, but have included a considerable number of
entries that throw light on the situation in those areas usually left in the shadows.

John Laband
Ian Knight

NOTES

1. J.P.C. Laband (ed.), *Lord Chelmsford's Zululand Campaign 1878–1879* (Stroud, Alan Sutton for the Army Records Society, 1994), p. 194: Chelmsford to Colonel F.A. Stanley, Camp on the Upoko River, Zululand, 10 June 1879.
2. *Natal Witness*, 19 June 1879: special correspondent, Lower Tugela, 13 June 1879.
3. C.L. Norris-Newman, *In Zululand With the British Throughout the War of 1879* (London, W.H. Allen, 1880), p. v.
4. *Illustrated London News*, 9 August 1879.
5. *Natal Mercury*, 14 October 1879: Utrecht correspondent, 1 October 1879.
6. See the *Times of Natal*, 11 August 1879.
7. *Natal Witness*, 12 August 1879.
8. Archibald Forbes to the editor of the *Daily News*, 27 August 1879, quoted in the *Natal Colonist*, 30 September 1879.
9. *Illustrated London News*, 18 October 1879.
10. C.E. Fripp, 'Reminiscences of the Zulu War, 1878', *Pall Mall Magazine*, 20 (1900), p. 562.
11. *Natal Witness*, 12 April 1879.
12. *Natal Witness*, 12 June 1880.
13. *Natal Witness*, 2 August 1879.

SOURCES FOR INTRODUCTION

Bensusan, A.D. '19th Century Photographers in South Africa', *Africana Notes and News*, 15, 6 (June 1963)
———. *Silver Images: History of Photography in Africa* (Cape Town, Howard Timmins, 1966)
Benyon, J.A. 'Lines of Power: The High Commissioner, the Telegraph and the War of 1879', *Natalia*, 8 (December 1978)
Brown, R.A. (ed.). *The Road to Ulundi: The Water-colour Drawings of John North Crealock (The Zulu War of 1879)* (Pietermaritzburg, University of Natal Press, 1969)
Bull, M. and Denfield, J. *Secure the Shadow: The Story of Cape Photography from its Beginnings to the End of 1870* (Cape Town, McNally, 1970)
Carey, J. (ed.). *The Faber Book of Reportage* (London, Faber, 1987)
Hogarth, P. *The Artist as Reporter* (London, Gordon Fraser, 1986)
Laband, J.P.C. (ed.). *Lord Chelmsford's Zululand Campaign 1878–1879* (Stroud, Alan Sutton for the Army Records Society, 1994)
Norris-Newman, C.L. *In Zululand With the British Throughout the War of 1879* (London, W.H. Allen, 1880)
Spencer, B. 'Notes on Photographers in Natal' in Verbeek, Jennifer and Alistair, *Victorian and Edwardian Natal* (Pietermaritzburg, Shuter & Shooter, 1982)
Stearn, R.T. 'War Correspondents and Colonial War, *c*. 1870–1900' in MacKenzie, J.M. (ed.), *Popular Imperialism and the Military, 1850–1950* (Manchester, Manchester University Press, 1992)
Wilkinson-Latham, R.J. *From Our Special Correspondent: Victorian War Correspondents and their Campaigns* (London, Hodder and Stoughton, 1879)

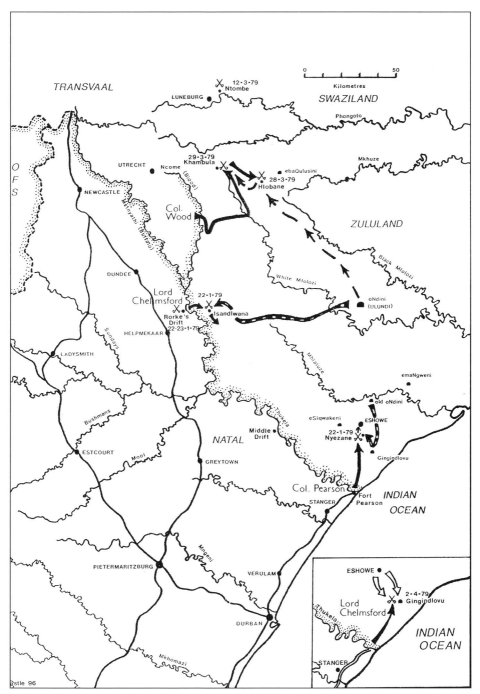

The first British invasion of Zululand, and the Zulu response, January to March 1879.
Inset: the Eshowe relief expedition, April 1879.

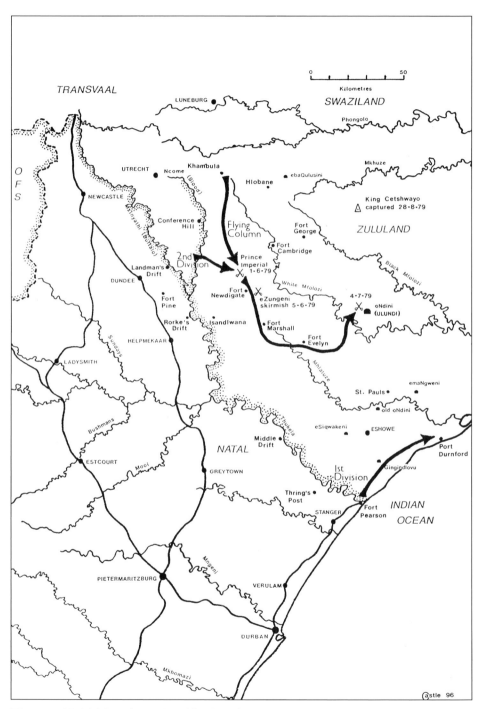

The second British invasion and pacification of Zululand, May to September 1879.

The Unfolding Crisis

The Anglo-Zulu War of 1879 was engineered by Sir Bartle Frere. He arrived in South Africa in March 1877 as British High Commissioner with instructions to create, under the British Crown, a confederation of the white-ruled states of southern Africa. Such a confederation, the British government intended, would enhance imperial security while cutting down on its cost. At the same time, it would enhance the economic prospects of the region. Frere quickly came to the same conclusion as most local administrators that the independent but unstable black polities abutting the states earmarked for confederation constituted a major obstacle in the way of the successful consummation of his mission. None was a more apparent obstruction than the militarily powerful Zulu kingdom, which Frere and his advisers perceived as a standing threat to its neighbours and as the centre of a far-flung black conspiracy to overthrow white supremacy in southern Africa.

The relative ease with which the General Officer Commanding in South Africa, Lieutenant-General Sir Frederick Thesiger (who was to succeed his father as the second Baron Chelmsford in October 1878), had brought to an end the Ninth Frontier War of 1877–8 in the eastern Cape against the Ngqika-Gcaleka Xhosa misled Frere into imagining that it would be possible similarly to neutralize the Zulu for the price of a minor campaign. Conceivably, it was feasible to draw the Zulu lion's teeth through diplomatic pressure. But Frere believed that only a crushing military defeat would guarantee the dismantling of the Zulu state and its permanent elimination as a potential threat to British South Africa. What Frere required was an excuse for war that would satisfy his government in London, which desired at all costs to avoid an expensive and unnecessary campaign.

The long-standing boundary dispute in the region of the Ncome (Blood) and Mzinyathi (Buffalo) rivers between the Zulu kingdom and the land-hungry Boers of the South African Republic made Frere's interference in Zulu affairs legitimate and even necessary. Britain inherited the boundary dispute when it annexed the former Boer republic in April 1877 as a step along the road to confederation. Frere wanted to settle the dispute in the new Transvaal Colony's favour in order to demonstrate the advantages of British rule to the many Boers who remained unreconciled to having become subjects of the queen. The attempts of the administrator of the Transvaal, Sir Theophilus Shepstone, to negotiate with the Zulu proved fruitless, since they would not give up their counter-claims to the Disputed Territory, as it was known.

Frere and Shepstone were hardly dismayed that the dispute seemed clearly to be moving towards the violent solution they were more than prepared to risk, but the Lieutenant-Governor of the Colony of Natal, Sir Henry Bulwer, wished to forestall a war which might spill over into his territory. In December 1877 he offered to mediate. The Zulu king, Cetshwayo kaMpande, accepted with relief, and Frere could not do otherwise but acquiesce. Bulwer's Boundary Commission began its sittings on 17 March 1878 at Rorke's Drift, a Swedish mission station on the Natal bank of the Mzinyathi River which divided the colony from the Zulu kingdom. The commissioners completed their hearings by mid-April 1878. It was clear that the evidence had gone against the Transvaal, and the *Natal Witness* correspondent reported the disquiet of the Boer delegation and the corresponding cockiness of the Zulu:

> The Border Commission have brought their labours to a close, and we think it very probable that more harm than good will result from the costly comedy. . . . The Natal Commission, with its eighteen tents, its Police escort and Union Jack, put the Transvaal in the shade, with its humble encampment of three tents. . . . The Zulu representatives, as a rule, insulted every witness who gave evidence by calling them liars, until it became unbearable. . . . The Zulu Chiefs persisted in repudiating the existence of any boundary in the district of Utrecht, with the exception of the Buffalo River. . . . They refused to accompany the Commissioners to inspect the disputed boundary, saying it would amount to an admission on their part that there was a line in existence, which they were instructed not to admit.[1]

The commission's scrupulous report by no means conceded every Zulu claim. Yet it was sufficiently disadvantageous towards the Transvaal for Frere, who received it on 15 July 1878, to see that it would have an explosive effect on the Boers and would ill serve the cause of confederation. Frere consequently delayed making the commission's findings public until he had consulted widely and found a means of neutralizing its likely repercussions.

Meanwhile, the white settlers along the exposed frontiers with Zululand, whether on their isolated farmsteads or in the scattering of embryo towns that served as administrative and commercial centres, became increasingly alarmed at the prospect of a violent Zulu incursion. The colonial authorities had no contingency plans in the event of a Zulu raid other than to advise the colonists, with their livestock, wagons and servants, to take refuge in the various government laagers. These were no more than stonework enclosures, some still under construction. The govenment bore the expense of those built in the villages; but if farmers wished to erect laagers in the countryside, it would only bear half the cost of those it deemed essential. The balance was borne by the local settler community, who elected a committee to supervise the building. A typical case was that of the Rietvlei Laager in Umvoti County, south-west of Greytown. A *Natal Witness* correspondent reported:

In consequence of the growing feeling of uneasiness and insecurity prevailing in this part of the country, on account of the doubtful position of affairs on the Zulu border, it was considered absolutely necessary that a Laager should be erected to serve as a place of refuge for the families, and for defence against any Zulu raid in Wards No. 2 and 3, County of Umvoti.

The Government Surveyor, Mr. A. Singleton, having reported that Riet Vlei – both from its situation on the main road, midway between Greytown and Weston, and from the number of families living in the neighbourhood – was a proper and suitable place for the erection of such a Laager, a meeting was therefore called, on June 1st. . . . Mr. P. Norton proposed the following resolutions, which were duly seconded: . . .

> That the Laager . . . to be built of dry stone, sixty yards square, with two flanking bastions; the walls to be nine feet high, loopholed every six feet at a height of six feet six inches from the ground; walls to be three feet six inches at the base, tapering to one foot six inches at the top. . . .
>
> That a Subscription List be at once opened to meet the require expenses. . . .

This last clause would appear, at first sight, rather a hard one, but was rendered necessary by many people being only too willing to take advantage of the benefit of the Laager without contributing either to the trouble or expense of the erection.[2]

Despite the erection of laagers, the settlers remained apprehensive and suspicious of Zulu intentions, as a report of 30 May from a correspondent from the Biggarsberg between Newcastle and Ladysmith made very clear:

> At present everything is quiet in this part of the colony, but it is difficult to say how long this will last, for, to judge from what we see and hear, a row with our black neighbours cannot be staved off much longer. Small parties of Zulus have been roaming through this district lately; they pretend to be selling mats and skins, but owing to the small number of articles they have for sale, and the great difficulty there is in striking a bargain with them, we are led to believe they have other motives in view. They are suspected by more than a few to be spies sent by Cetywayo to see and report on our state of defence. Be this as it may, I feel it is wrong that Zulus can cross the Buffalo River and pry into our affairs without any restriction whatever. . . .[3]

To help defend themselves in the laagers, or to patrol the countryside in between, the colonists had only the feeblest of forces available. The Natal Volunteer Corps, first raised in 1855, consisted of one artillery, three infantry and eleven mounted corps averaging only about thirty men each. They were drawn predominantly from English-speaking colonists. The Mounted Burgher Force, operative since 1863, consisted of volunteers bound to respond if called out by the field cornets of their wards. This system was similar in form to the traditional Boer commando, and was favoured by the Dutch-speaking settlers of Natal and those living in the districts of the Transvaal abutting Zululand. Only the small force of Natal Mounted Police, created in 1874, could lay any claims to professional discipline and training.

Despite the widespread apprehension at the prospect of war, many settlers nevertheless felt that their future security depended upon the destruction of Zulu military power, and did their best to be positive about the limited military preparations that were being made. As a correspondent from the Biggarsberg expressed it:

> . . . The Zulu power, as it exists at present, with a tribal organization under a supreme chief, with a standing army always held in the leash and ready to slip upon defenceless people in the country, such a power is, and as long as it exists will be, a standing menace to the peace of this colony and the Transvaal, as bordering territories. A war, therefore, just now, when we are as much prepared for it as ever we can be, will find the people more ready to engage in it, because everyone feels that until the Zulu power is broken and the warlike organization of these people entirely destroyed, danger will perpetually haunt us, and prevent the peaceful occupation and development of the contry. Until Zululand is proclaimed British territory, and a disposition of the people and territory made, as in the Old Colony, under proper officers, appointed by the Government to rule the country, we cannot expect to live in peace.
>
> The Government have commenced building a laager [Fort Pine], within which, in due course, a barracks is to be erected for a number of the mounted police, who are to be stationed in these parts. At present they will erect and complete the four walls pierced for musketry, and these are to be completed in five months, at the furthest. . . .
>
> The Buffalo Border Guard has been reduced in number by the resignation of a number of the young Dutch farmers belonging to it. The older members of the corps have beaten up a few recruits, and we hope they will be able to hold the corps together. . . . Mr Kisch, the photographer, who is up here, will take a picture of the corps, if he can, before he leaves. . . .[4]

The most volatile border region during 1878 was that of the undefined frontier between north-western Zululand, Swaziland and the Transvaal. The Zulu were spilling northwards over the Pongola River in search of grazing where they came into competition with both white settlers and the Swazi. Confrontation during mid-1878 centred on the successful little German settlement of Luneburg, established in 1869 by the Hermannsburg Mission Society just north of the Pongola. To stake his claim to the region, King Cetshwayo encouraged the abaQulusi people to establish their homesteads nearby, and their hostile presence greatly disquieted the Luneburgers, as the following report shows:

> From a gentleman just returned from Luneberg . . . I hear that the Zulus have come there in great numbers, and have made about forty new kraals, without asking leave of the owners of the farms in any way. He himself counted over twenty, many of them within shot of the church. The German settlers there are, of course, in great terror, and know not where to fly; their homesteads are invaded and their flocks at the mercy of these free-booters. The situation is now such that without war it is impossible to see how there can be any peace. The

The impressive stone walls of Fort Pine, built on the heights between the village of Dundee and Helpmekaar, to protect the settler population of the Mzinyathi valley. (Ian Knight)

Zulus have evidently made up their minds to have the country as far as it suits them. The temptation is immense. At the present time and until the spring sets in, and cattle can return to the 'high-veld,' there are enormous herds of sheep and oxen in winter quarters under the mountains, close to their hand. Not less than 150,000 head are at this moment situated in this precarious position. . . .[5]

Meanwhile, those settlers actively involved in the Natal Mounted Volunteers went on manoeuvres to prepare themselves for the approaching fray. In Greytown the Natal Hussars were joined in mid-June by the Natal Mounted Police, as a local correspondent reported:

The muster of the Natal Hussars last week appeared to be quite a success. The camp was pitched on the south side of the village [Greytown], snugly sheltered from the strong north wind that prevails at this season. Thirty-two troopers assembled out of a total muster-roll of forty. . . .
. . . Many troopers had long distances to ride; pitching tents, hunting up camp equipage, and a general shake into camp life occupied the day. . . . The officers' tent was very comfortable; green baise lining, camp-table, chairs, and hospitality, made the visit a pleasant and prolonged one. . . . The other tents in the encampment were . . . threadbare – but respectable even in their seediness. . . .
[T]he Mounted Police stationed here joined with the Hussars for squadron drill on the racecourse. . . . The various evolutions of this large (for Greytown) body of men were watched by many with great interest, and appeared to be very creditably carried out, the skirmishing and blank cartridge firing causing

considerable amusement as well, for not a few of the horses did not like the smell of powder a bit a first; doubtless, like other recruits, they will mend with practice. . . . It is no compliment to say they [the Natal Mounted Police] were smarter than the Volunteers for it is their business to be so; lookers-on thought they might well have been smarter than they were. It is essential that a cavalry trooper should sit up straight in his saddle. . . .[6]

For Sir Bartle Frere, contemplating the unsatisfactory Boundary Commission's report and pondering how best to proceed against the Zulu, incidents along the tense frontier were a godsend, for they provided a vital justification to the reluctant Colonial Office for taking firm action against the incorrigibly aggressive Zulu. Threats against white farmers like the Luneburgers was one thing; an actual violation of British territory was another. When Mehlokazulu, the son of Sihayo kaXongo, the Qungebe chief, crossed the border near Rorke's Drift to punish two errant wives of his father, he did more than greatly alarm settler opinion. He provided Frere with an excuse for issuing an ultimatum to the Zulu government. Not that the incident, which the *Natal Witness* headlined 'The Zulu Outrage', was not lurid in itself:

A very sad case happened here the other day. On Friday, the 26th ultimo [July], two of the wives of the Zulu Chief Sirayo eloped with two young men. They crossed the Buffalo River, and one pair came to a native police kraal near Mr. Field-cornet J.S. Robson's farm; the other to a kraal on a farm which formerly belonged to the late Mr. James Rorke, and which is commonly known as 'Rorke's farm.' Shortly after the arrival of the runaways, or, to be more punctual, about ten o'clock a.m., on Friday, a large body of Zulus, some on foot and some on horseback, crossed the Buffalo and surrounded Mr. Robson's police kraal. Some went into the huts and, after discovering [her], dragged out the woman, while the others kept the men of the kraal at a distance, pointing their guns at them and holding their assegais ready to stab them if they interfered. They seized the woman, knocked out all her front teeth, tied reins to her neck and wrists, and so dragged her away about 500 yards along the ground. They had brought two horses, placed them close together, and laid the woman across their backs; in this way they brought her through the river. A short distance on the other or Zulu side of the river a son of Sirayo killed her, and threw the body in a ravine or 'dinga' that happened to be near the place where the foul deed was comitted.
    From what I hear, there must have been about 300 of the Zulus. They marched in column of companies. First were eighteen men on horseback, armed with guns; then a company of young men, also armed with guns; then a company of young men, armed with shields and assegais; and next was the rear company, Kehlas [older men], armed with guns and assegais.
    On the Sunday morning they acted in the same way by the woman who was at the kraal on 'Rorke's farm.' They surrounded the kraal early in the morning, dragged the woman out, took her across the river, and shot her dead. The murderer, in both these cases, was Meshlu-ka-Zula, a son of Sirayo. The Zulu leaders were three sons and a brother of Sirayo. I should think, after this, the

Zulus must be put down with a strong hand; if not, we had better all clear out of this part of the country as soon as possible. Our lives, to borrow a phrase from Mr. Boshoff, M.L.C., are not worth a 'snap of the fingers.'[7]

Inflamed settler cries that 'the Zulu must be put down' were fuelled by the urgent and informed communications by old Zulu hands who, like 'Rufus', presented a grim picture of a Zulu army of 20,000 effectives, well supplied with fire-arms and activated by hate of Europeans:

. . . When I first visited Zululand, in the year 1872, I was struck with the gentle and modest behaviour of the natives. They were a quiet, peaceable, and unoffending lot of men, just in their dealings with traders, and a quarrel with a white man was a thing almost unheard of. . . . At that time there were not more than 200 guns of any description in the country, and those who possessed them were considered by their friends to be something above the average of ordinary human beings, the majority of them being afraid to come near a rifle, let alone to touch one. Gradually, however, and by almost imperceptible degrees, as trader after trader brought in his one, five, or ten guns, this feeling of awe died away, and the idea that to carry a gun was a sign of manliness and equality with the 'Abelunga,' or white man, took its place. Umpande [King Mpande] ordered that every chief or captain should at his earliest convenience become the possessor of an English fire-arm, not that it would be of any use to him, but as a mark of distinction. This favour was soon after conferred on captains' sons and petty indunas [headmen]. No sooner, however, had the young blood of the land got to understand the use of them, as proved in the killing of a buck (by accident) now and then, than they wished to carry them instead of their native weapon, the assegai. This, however, was discovered by the king, who strictly forbade it on pain of a severe penalty, saying that they were too dangerous a weapon to be handled by 'Abafana,' or boys. It was about this time that one or two traders from Delagoa Bay made their first appearance, their whole stock-in-trade consisting of a few second-hand condemned Prussian muskets, a few pounds of inferior powder, and a few boxes, or, strictly speaking, packets of caps. These they disposed of to great advantage, realizing for every outlay of 5s. about £15. The cattle received in exchange for these articles were brought into Natal, sold, and the men returned overland to Lourenço Marques, where they purchased fresh supplies, and made a second trip, which, as the gun mania was increasing, proved even more successful than the former. European residents in the country, seeing that money was to be made at it, entered heart and soul into the trade. Wagon after wagon arrived from Natal, each one bearing one or more of the smuggled weapons, which were to fill their purses with gold. The number of stand of arms, although on the increase, was not alarmingly so until the year 1875–6, when, from having about 500 guns, rifles, and pistols, they had increased to 5,000. It was then a monthly occurrence to see a trader arrive, not from Natal, but Delagoa Bay (where the trade in fire-arms is not restricted) with on an average 100 guns, mostly consisting of cheap muskets, bought from the Portuguese for about 18s. a piece, and an inferior imitation of Enfields. Since then the number has been steadily increasing, and Zululand is now in possession of twenty thousand (20,000) stand of European fire-arms. . . .

. . . I estimate the whole population of Zululand at 250,000, out of which number Cetywayo [Cetshwayo] can send into the field 20,000 fighting men, fairly equipped for war, with arms and ammunition sufficient to carry on a campaign for six months.[8]

Such information confirmed Frere in his inclination to take action against the Zulu. By September his military and naval commanders, who had preceded him to Natal, were preparing on a contingency basis for hostilities against Zululand. Earlier in the year regular troops had been moved up from the Cape to the Transvaal. They were deployed to act against Sekhukhune, the Pedi chief, whose war against the South African Republic the British had inherited when they annexed the territory, and also to guard against a Boer rebellion in the reluctant new colony. Between September and November 1878 most of these troops and further reinforcements were redeployed in a steady trickle to the Zulu border. By mid-September the Zulu were feeling endangered by the British military build-up along their frontiers, and were thinking increasingly in terms of having to defend themselves. Harassed white traders scurrying back from Zululand confirmed that the Zulu were in a bellicose and aggressive mood:

. . . A trader, who has just returned, reports the Zulus as very insolent, and . . . [they] state that the Queen of England has no troops, as she has been obliged to send for coolie soldiers to fight her battles. They also state that if they make an inroad into Natal, they will spare the sugar planters, so that they can grow and manufacture sugar for them; so there is a future and a good chance for the planting interest. . . .[9]

With the noose tightening around the Zulu kingdom, Frere arrived in Natal to take close personal supervision of affairs as they developed. He still had not entirely made up his mind precisely how to move, and to the disappointment of the colonists remained non-communicative regarding his plans. General Thesiger was much more open on the need for effective colonial defence in the face of a looming conflict, and on 10 September persuaded the Natal government to set about devising appropriate security measures. Frere's and Thesiger's contrasting approaches to the settler public were expressed very clearly at a banquet in Durban on 27 September:

The banquet to Sir Bartle Frere, . . . was a very successful affair. . . . Those who attended . . . naturally looked forward to the speech of Sir Bartle Frere in the earnest hope, . . . that he would give some faint idea of what policy he intended to adopt, as regards this colony and the Transvaal. In this, however, disappointment awaited them, for His Excellency . . . merely told his audience he came to learn what was wanted. The various speakers who followed were not slow to take the hint, and if Sir Bartle Frere can remember one half the complaints, suggestions, and recommendations given, he will have a wide field before him to operate on. From what I heard, I am inclined to think the expression of his truly intellectual face betokened that he felt not a little bored. . . .

General Thesiger spoke at much greater length, and . . . considered it much the best plan to speak his mind, an observation which was greeted with cheers. The General admitted that with thirty or forty thousand men upon our borders 'under irresponsible governments,' we could not but feel a little anxiety, but in no way conveyed the impression he experienced it himself. He urged a more extended organization among the colonists for their defence, and gave a pretty hard hint that they must not think, because a large number of British troops were here, that they must not therefore be prepared to do something for themselves. . . .[10]

A few days later, on 5 October, as a correspondent reported by electric telegraph to the *Natal Mercury* in Durban, Sir Bartle Frere opened up rather more and made very explicit at a banquet in Pietermaritzburg his philosophical justification for subduing the Zulu kingdom. It was Britain's exalted mission, he proclaimed to the assembled leading residents of the city, to spread the civilizing influence of Christian government, to eradicate barbarous institutions and to guide Africans up the ladder of evolution:

. . . Replying to the toast to his health, the High Commissioner said, though there might be occasional rivalry between this colony and the Cape, they were at one in feeling they were brothers belonging to one race, destined to carry out high obligations in this distant part of the world. He said his long experience of native races led him to conclude that there was every reason to hope that they were capable of being raised from the state of barbarism in which they are at present; especially when we remember how ten centuries had raised us from a similar state to the state of civilization we now enjoy. We cannot expect the kafirs to advance at a rate much greater than that [at] which we ourselves proceeded. . . .[11]

Threatened by the growing concentrations of British troops along his borders, in late September King Cetshwayo took provocative though necessary action to show that he was prepared to defend his territory. He called up several *amabutho*, or age-grade regiments, to stage great hunts along the Natal border as a show of strength. The poor season and lack of supplies meant that by early October they had temporarily dispersed home again. But it was clear that the Zulu were seriously mobilizing for the war they saw would soon be unleashed against them, even if most wished still to avoid it if possible:

From the attitude and behaviour of the natives on the border, there is no reason to believe that this hunt was meant as a demonstration; though who can tell?
. . .There is little doubt that the Zulus live in as great an uncertainty as we do. They know there is something coming, but expect it from our side. They say they don't want to fight, but can plainly see that the English are determined to do so . . . [and] watch us narrowly and don't trust us. Our supplies of troops and ammunition, and the military movements in Natal and the Transvaal have created a state of anxiety and excitement. . . . The want of food in the country

and the distressing state of the crops will all increase the feeling of discontent and restlessness. Not seldom you hear the opinion given that this drought is only due to the whiteman, and that we want them to starve, so that they might have no strength to fight.[12]

'Up-country', as the journalist called it, on the volatile and undefined north-western frontier of Zululand, the situation continued inflammable. Mbilini kaMswati, a renegade Swazi prince whom the Zulu kings had allowed to settle in the region, lived as a freebooter at the expense of his Boer and Swazi neighbours, often acting as Cetshwayo's covert instrument. In October he launched a series of raids which panicked the local settlers and compelled the dynamic Colonel Evelyn Wood, who commanded the troops stationed at Utrecht, to dispatch two companies of infantry to take up position at Luneburg, where they built Fort Clery. Wood's determined action certainly caused Cetshwayo to repudiate Mbilini's activities and to attempt to defuse the situation. The settlers of Utrecht were as impressed by Wood's effective initiative as they were by the band of the 90th Light Infantry:

Saturday and Sunday [2 and 3 November] were epochs in the history of this rustic and becornered little village. Eighteen months ago no one ever dreamt of seeing so much activity, bustle, and amusement. The arrival of the band of the 90th was the wonder of the day, as very few of our inhabitants had ever heard a band, or were capable of forming any idea of how it was constituted, or anything else about it, further than supposing it to consist of a lot of German concertinas and a few fiddles. After a seven hours' weary tramp, the troops marched into town without exhibiting any signs of over-fatigue, but, as was to be expected, very dusty and travel-stained. . . . The stationing of troops at Luneberg, thus outflanking the Zulus by taking up a strong position in their rear, is bringing Cetywayo to his senses. He now denies having made any claim to the land known as the 'disputed territory' . . . and that it was his desire to live in peace with the white man. . . .[13]

Imperial troops continued to move up to the border, their normally laboured progress made even worse by the prevailing drought conditions. Two companies of the 2/3rd Regiment (The Buffs) were stationed at the strategic lower drift across the Thukela, where during November they threw up and garrisoned the earthwork Fort Pearson. Their hostile presence overawed the Zulu across the river:

. . . A worse country for marching troops in can scarcely be conceived than that which lies between Maritzburg and the Tugela, and none save those who have followed troops in their march can form an idea of the difficulties they have to contend with, nor the stubborn firmness with which they face them. Look at the troops heavy accoutred, plodding their way, under a broiling African sun, over interminable hills . . . and then when arrived at a halting place, where a plentiful supply of water was expected, to find the bed of the river dried up, and a few slimy vermin wallowing in the rank weeds on the bank. The whole face of the country looks parched, and cattle greatly impoverished. . . .

The springboard for invasion: Fort Pearson, on a knoll overlooking the Lower Drift on the Thukela River. (Killie Campbell Africana Library)

It was through such a country as this and under such circumstances that 'The Buffs' were, after a very short stay at Greytown, ordered to the Tugela. . . . [A]lmost immediately, under the supervision of an Engineer officer, a fort was commenced to be created just opposite the Lower Tugela Drift. The men are still occupied in its erection, and it is expected the work will be completed in a few days. . . . The site selected for the fort is an admirable one, giving, as it does, full command of the drift, and able to clear the river several hundreds of yards at each side. It is on the summit of a large hill overlooking the Tugela, is reached by a gentle slope from the main road, but is almost inaccessible from the river side. When completed, 200 men within it would be able to withstand any force that could be brought against them by the Zulu King.

The Tugela is at present fordable, water in some parts only reaching above the knees, but I may mention since the arrival of the troops renewed energy seems to have been given to all while the Zulu gentlemen who hitherto used to parade the banks of the river with a most bombastic swagger are nowhere to be seen. Zulus, like a good many more civilized of their brethren, have a most salutary fear of the red coats. . . .[14]

During November British reinforcements of different varieties steadily arrived in Durban. They ranged from the seasoned imperial regulars of the 1/24th (2nd Warwickshire) Regiment, through the equally salted men of the Naval Brigade to the hardened colonial irregular horsemen of the Kaffrarian Vanguard (or Kaffrarian Rifles). All had seen recent service on the Cape eastern frontier in the Ninth Frontier

Preparations for war: military supplies being unloaded at the Durban wharf. (Killie Campbell
Africana Library)

War. In addition, there were white officers and NCOs intended to command Wood's
Irregulars, drawn from Swazi in the south-eastern Transvaal, and the seven battalions
of the Natal Native Contingent being drafted from the Natal Native Reserves. These
black auxiliaries fell under Imperial, rather than Colonial command. The colonists
had been unwilling to arm the local Africans for fear of an uprising in support of the
Zulu, but military necessity had prevailed. The NNC were earmarked particularly for
garrison and convoy duty upon which it was not intended to disperse the valuable
and numerically limited regular troops:

> During the past week [the third week of November] Durban has been enlivened
> by the arrival of large reinforcements of men to supplement the British military
> strength in this colony and the Transvaal. Altogether, over 900 men have landed
> on our shores, composed of naval, military, and Volunteer contingents. The first
> to arrive was the

Kaffrarian Vanguard
This picked body of men, raised in Kaffraria by Commandant Schermbrucker,
arrived in the C.R.M.S. *Courland* on Monday [18 November] morning, and,
after a short stay in Durban, started for the City [Pietermaritzburg], where they
will be mounted and equipped, proceeding hence to Luneberg, where they will
relieve Colonel Wood and his detachment of the 90th L.I. They number three
officers, ten non-commissioned officers, and one hundred men. Most of these
have served in the Old Colony war, and many received their 'baptism of fire'

during the Franco-German troubles. There are about forty Englishmen among them, the remainder being from the Fatherland. Their full dress is plain, but serviceable, being made of black corduroy, and being good shots and bold riders, will prove a valuable auxiliary force. Three hundred more men for this corps are to come up from the Cape Colony.

The Naval Brigade

The announcement that the Naval Brigade would land from the *Active* on Tuesday morning [19 November] caused quite a rush at the Point, and every available space in the vicinity of the landing-place was covered with spectators. The *Adonis* arrived first, bringing the Armstrong and Gatling guns, rocket tubes, ammunition, stores, &c. These were in charge of one or two officers and about twenty stalwart Kroomen [African seamen from the Liberian coast], whose naval uniform and English speech seemed to puzzle the Kafir bystanders, who made some curious remarks with regard to them. The three Gatling guns were objects of much interest; they are furnished with ten distinct muzzle barrels, like an old-fashioned revolver, and can pour forth a rain of shot at the rate of 230 rounds in seven seconds, taking effect at a range of 1,800 yards, or more than a mile. The Brigade is supplied with ammunition enough for a Russian campaign. Shortly before one o'clock the *Somtseu* was seen rounding the spot, and was soon alongside the wharf, the blue-jackets swarming out of her with alacrity and forming into line. They were received with hearty cheers, to which they responded in a very effective manner. The men were mostly youngsters, but their sturdy, thick-set forms, tanned faces, and resolute bearing are proofs of very serviceable qualities.

. . . They were four months in the field in the Cape frontier, and did good work, while they got hardened and seasoned there. Within a few minutes of their landing they marched to the station, where a special train was in waiting to take them to the Saccharine Estate, beyond the Avoca [on the Natal north coast]. Cheer followed cheer as the train moved out of the station, and all along the route the same interest was excited. . . . The Brigade, which numbers (exclusive of Marines) 174 officers, non-commissioned officers, and men, are under the command of Captain Campbell. . . . The Marines number 40 men and two sergeants, and are under the command of Lieutenant Downing.

The First Twenty-Fourth Regiment

As soon as the Naval Brigade had been landed, the *Somtseu* set to work to bring ashore the first battalion of the 24th Regiment, which arrived by the transport *Tyne* on the same morning from Kingwilliamstown, *via* East London. They number twenty officers and 443 rank and file, under the command of Colonel Glyn, and are as fine a body of infantry as will be found under the colours. They have had many months of hard field work at Kaffraria and the Transkei, are thoroughly inured to camp life and bush fighting, and are capital shots. On landing they were loudly cheered by all those assembled to welcome them, to which they responded in an equally hearty manner. They brought on shore with them their travelling equipments and rifles, which were at once sorted out to

Major Farquhar Glennie and men of the 24th Regiment, whose battalions formed the backbone of Chelmsford's Centre Column. (Ian Knight)

them while drawn up in front of the Port Office, whereupon, headed by their splendid band, they marched out to the camp and took up their temporary quarters. They started for this City yesterday.

Commandant Lonsdale's Volunteers
Yesterday evening the U.R.M.S. *Nubian* arrived from East London, bringing Commandant R. La Trobe Lonsdale and 180 officers and non-commissioned officers, who are destined to fill up appointments in connexion with the native and Zwasie levies about to be raised. Commandant Lonsdale, formerly of the 'Black Watch,' has seen sharp service on the Cape Frontier, and his companions are all tried men, having passed through the hardships and vicissitudes of a campaign against the Gaikas and Gcalekas.[15]

Colonial mobilization was also progressing. The three corps of Colonial Volunteer Infantry and the Durban Volunteer Artillery were required for the defence of the larger towns in the colony, but Lord Chelmsford, who was painfully short of mounted troops for reconnaissance and patrol work, urgently required the services of the Natal Mounted Police and the Natal Mounted Volunteers. The latter, as volunteers, could not be required to serve beyond the borders of Natal unless they agreed to do so. Almost all did, the response of the Maritzburg Rifles on 21 November being typical:

A general meeting of the members of this Corps took place on Thursday evening [21 November] at the Drill Shed, Captain Matterson in the chair. Between seventy and eighty were present.

The CHAIRMAN explained that they had been called together in order to obtain their feeling relative to the crossing the Border should they be ordered out on active service, and should it be necessary. . . .

A long discussion ensued, the matter of the amount of pay engaging consideration. . . .

Ultimately Lieutenant Scoones proposed a resolution to the effect that the Corps is quite willing to cross the Border in the event of its services being required.

This was put to the meeting and carried, with but one dissenting, amid loud cheers.[16]

As war-fever mounted in Natal, a *Natal Witness* correspondent on the Lower Thukela commented on 24 November with considerable complacency (and not a little excitement) on the noose that was tightening around the apprehensive Zulu kingdom:

About one hundred and sixty men of the *Active*, under the command of Captain Cameron, arrived here to-day from Stanger, and at once pitched their tents opposite Fort Pearson, lately erected by 'The Buffs'. . . .

For the past three days we have had a regular downpour, which must produce the most beneficial results. The Tugela, which had run down to a mere stream, has again swelled, and is at present impassable. The mouth of the river is again getting choked up, and the water spreads from bank to bank.

. . . Of one thing you may rest confident, the Zulu King will show no hostile move in this direction until an attack is made on him; and it is plain to see from the various movements of the troops that things are not yet ripe enough for that.

The 'thin red line' is spreading, and day by day the Zulu King is getting more surrounded, and it requires no great foresight to see that things at the Front cannot much longer remain as they are. Exciting news may be looked for in a short time.[17]

To the accompaniment of considerable emotion and ceremony the Natal Mounted Volunteers began to move up to the border. On 29 November the Natal Carbineers rode out of Pietermaritzburg:

. . . They mustered on the Market Square at nine o'clock. . . . During the forenoon there was a great amount of interest – it can scarcely be called excitement – exhibited in the City as the Carbineers went around to bid their relatives and friends good-bye. The Corps represents all the principal families in the place, and their movements – their successes or reverses – are a matter of personal interest to nearly all of us. At two o'clock they again mustered in front of the Market House. There was a very large number of spectators present to witness their departure. Mr Wheeler, with characteristic foresight, had had a platform erected for the ladies, who turned up in large numbers. The Carbineers mustered on this occasion forty-six. . . . At about 2.30 General Lord Chelmsford arrived, and Captain Shepstone having drawn up his men in columns, His Excellency said that he regretted he had not previously had an opportunity of seeing the Corps, but from what he had heard of it he felt perfectly confident that should it ever come into action it would behave in a manner worthy of the reputation it had obtained and the City where it was raised. . . . The men were then placed in line, and shortly afterwards His Excellency the High Commissioner and His Excellency the Lieutenant-Governor arrived with their respective staffs. Their Excellencies rode along the line, in front and rear, and shortly afterwards the band of the 1–24th arrived to play them out. The order was given to form fours, and about three o'clock they left, to the strains of the military band and amid hearty cheers. The men are all well mounted and appeared a most serviceable Corps. . . . We understand that a daily post has been established between Maritzburg and Greytown, so that the relatives and friends of the members will have increased opportunity of communicating with them. . . .[18]

During late November, along the exposed Mzinyathi River frontier with Zululand, the settlers could not help expressing their anxieties at the march of events. The drought had broken and the arrival of men of the Natal Mounted Police provided some sense of security. But the local farmers knew how Colonel H. Rowlands' unsuccessful campaign during September/October 1878 against Sekhukhune and the Pedi was being construed in Zululand, and could take little comfort from reports of dissension in the king's council over responsibility for the mounting crisis. As one wrote:

Since my last to you, we have had several good showers of rain, and grass, which for months past has been quite dry, is now beautifully green, and there is almost enough of it for cattle to live comfortably on. As it is, stock of all kinds are improving in condition. The rain has also enabled farmers to do something in the way of ploughing and getting in their summer crops; although the season is far advanced, there is yet time for the mealies, should the weather now prove favourable for their growth.

The Mounted Police arrived in this district on Monday last [18 November]. Some of them, I am told, are to be stationed at Rorke's Drift, the remainder at Fort Pine; their arrival, together with rumours that are floating about, has caused no little wonder in the minds of our Kafirs, consequently there are no end of questions such as, What are the soldiers to do etc.

Usirayo [Sihayo], the Zulu Chief, whose kraal is near Rorke's Drift, is at present at the King's kraal, and I am informed that during a sitting of the King's counsellors, he was both insulted and assaulted by a son of Muyamani [Mnyamana, the Buthelezi chief and Cetshwayo's chief councillor], and told that he was the sole cause of the English soldiers being placed on the Zulu border; the King, however, administered a sharp rebuke on the young man, and said that Usirayo should live and die with him.

Had the Sekukuni campaign ended differently to what it has done, the Zulu difficulty would have been more easily settled; the Zulus are taunting our Kafirs by saying that the English were not beaten at Sekukuni's but that they were afraid to fight, and thought it best to run away, and they cannot understand that after being afraid to engage Sekukuni, who is only an *Umfogozani* [chief], they can dare to think of waging war with Cetywayo, who is an *Inkosi Omkulu* [king] . . .[19]

NOTES

1. *Natal Witness*, 27 April 1878: *Natal Witness* correspondent, Utrecht, 14 April 1878.
2. *Natal Witness*, 6 June 1878: Rietvlei correspondent.
3. Ibid.: Biggarsberg correspondent, 30 May 1878.
4. *Natal Mercury*, 10 June 1878: Biggarsberg correspondent.
5. *Natal Witness*, 11 June 1878: Newcastle correspondent, 5 June 1878.
6. *Natal Witness*, 29 June 1878: Greytown correspondent.
7. *Natal Witness*, 8 August 1878: Biggarsberg correspondent, 3 August 1878.
8. *Natal Witness*, 22 August 1878: 'Rufus' to the editor, Ladysmith, 15 August 1878.
9. *Natal Mercury*, 16 September 1878: Lower Tugela correspondent, 11 September 1878.
10. *Natal Witness*, 28 September 1878: Durban correspondent, 27 September 1878.
11. *Natal Mercury*, 7 October 1878: Maritzburg correspondent, 5 October 1878.
12. *Natal Colonist*, 8 October 1878: Lower Tugela correspondent, 4 October 1878.
13. *Natal Witness*, 12 November 1878: Utrecht correspondent, 4 November 1878.
14. *Natal Witness*, 19 November 1878: Tugela correspondent, 14 November 1878.
15. *Natal Witness*, 23 November 1878.
16. Ibid.
17. *Natal Witness*, 30 November 1878: Lower Tugela Drift correspondent, Sunday evening, 24 November 1878.
18. *Natal Witness*, 30 November 1878.
19. Ibid.: Biggarsberg correspondent, 20 November 1878.

Ultimatum

By 14 September 1878 Lieutenant-General Thesiger had already resolved upon his strategy for the invasion of Zululand. Since an advance would leave his own frontiers inadequately protected, and since slow-moving and vulnerable supply-trains would limit manoeuvrability and the number of troops they could support, he resolved to send in five relatively small columns to converge on oNdini, Cetshwayo's chief residence in the heart of the Zulu kingdom. He reckoned that not only would these smaller columns move with greater speed, but they would support each other in engrossing more of the enemy's territory, reduce the chance of being outflanked and hopefully discourage counter-blows against the frontiers thinly held by inadequate colonial troops. These columns would either progressively drive the Zulu into a corner or – the preferred alternative – tempt them into attacking one or more of the columns. If they did so, all the advantage would lie with properly trained troops and their devastating, concentrated firepower, and the campaign would swiftly be concluded with a decisive battle. Since the planned campaign was being undertaken specifically to overthrow a militarily powerful state, victory in the field was in any case necessary to assert British ascendancy conclusively. Frere was convinced by his military advisers that the campaign would be rapid, decisive and therefore cheap. Sir Theophilus Shepstone assured him that under the strain of war existing internal divisions within the Zulu kingdom would widen to fragment resistance and hasten victory. Thus, for the price of a minor campaign, Frere would settle the problems of southern Africa and consummate confederation.

With the possibility of Zulu raids in mind, Thesiger selected invasion routes in sectors considered vulnerable to attack. No. 1 Column under Colonel Pearson would advance across the Lower Thukela and protect the coastal plain; No. 3 Column (or the 'Centre Column') under Colonel Glyn would cross the Mzinyathi at Rorke's Drift and cover central Natal; while No. 4 Column would march across the Ncome River and shield the Transvaal. No. 5 Column under Colonel Rowlands was to support Wood's left flank, though in the event Chelmsford decided to keep it in a defensive role on account of the still unpacified Pedi.

No. 2 Column, under Colonel Durnford, was initially supposed to cross the Thukela through difficult terrain at Middle Drift. During early December the three battalions of the 1st Regiment, Natal Native Contingent, and several troops of the Natal Native Horse took up position at Middle Drift below the heights at Kranzkop. Their situation, as described by a correspondent who was with them, was hardly pleasant:

A striking study of unidentified members of a unit of the Natal Native Horse. Most of the men appear to be carrying Snider carbines – although the man on the left has a Martini-Henry rifle – as well as a quiver of traditional weapons. Their only uniform is a white armband and red rag wound around their hats. (Ian Knight)

> The 1st and 2nd battalions have moved down to the Tugela, to be ready for any emergency. We expect to be here for two or three days yet. This is an awful place for mist, which is not very agreeable now one has to turn out every morning at three o'clock. I see the 3rd battalion is just coming in with a large number of kafirs out for target practice yesterday, and the shooting was very good, especially that of the Edendalites. We have 300 men altogether – Edendale troop, Hlubi troop, Jantje troop, and three troops of Sekuli's men. There is a good deal of sickness amongst the kafirs, caused, no doubt, by eating so much meat. A few of the officers suffer from dysentery. . . .[1]

The Natal government, on 26 November 1878, had divided the colony up into Colonial Defensive Districts for the better organization of its defence. The district commanders were named on 3 December, but they had precious few men at their disposal outside the laagers. Thus it became necessary to raise a scratch field-force of black levies to hold the border between the various columns. Unlike the NNC, which had been recruited as imperial troops, these border levies were maintained by Natal and were only to be activated in the event of a Zulu raid. A small standing reserve of black Border Guards was also established to hold strategic points, such as drifts across the border rivers. In Colonial Defensive District No. VI, between No. 2 and No. 1 Columns, the District Commandant, Captain G.A. Lucas, did what he could (in the disdainful words of an occasional correspondent) in

The White Rock Border Guard, which protected one of the drifts on the Thukela, between the Middle and Lower Drifts. (S.B. Bourquin)

> . . . getting a force of Natives commanded by Europeans to guard the several fords of the Tugela. This force it is said will only muster 500 natives, although it was formally proposed to be 2,000 strong; so many are to be placed at each drift, with two white men in charge, who are to live in tents, and armed with Sniders. These said white men all refused to go alone, so that they had to put two together to give them courage poor fellows, with 25s. a day, I doubt the courage of these men if this is a start. . . .[2]

Such defensive preparations as there were along the lower Thukela came none to soon. At the end of November Frere and Bulwer had finally devised an ultimatum whose terms, they felt sure, were so stringent that the Zulu problem would be finally solved, no matter whether the Zulu king accepted them or fought to resist their imposition. Either way, it would be the end of the Zulu kingdom as it had existed.

In order to facilitate Chelmsford's military preparations, they decided to present the ultimatum as soon as possible. The fateful document was read to Cetshwayo's representatives on 11 December 1878. It was cynically tied up with the Boundary Commission's long embargoed report, so that the Zulu delegates' initial satisfaction turned to horrified incredulity as the terms of the ultimatum became apparent:

> . . . On the appointed day, therefore, Wednesday, December 11th – the date fixed some time ago – the meeting took place. It was an occasion fraught with the highest political and historical interest. On one side were Her Majesty's Commissioners, Mr. Brownlee, Mr. J. Shepstone, Colonel Walker, and Mr. H.

Fynn; on the other were fourteen elderly, and in many cases grey-headed, natives, chosen from amongst the most venerable and trusted elders of the Zulu nation – men of acknowledged rank and distinction amongst their people. They had about forty attendants with them. At their head was Uvumandaba [Vumandaba], commander of the Umtubsazwi [uMcijo] Regiment, and a leading general, Mandule [Muwundula], who commands the Inkulutyaise [uMkhulutshane] Regiment, and was one of the Boundary Commissioners, a man of very superior intelligence and judgment, was also one of the party; so was Gebule [Gebula], who was also present at the Rorke's Drift Enquiry, and who, it may be remembered, was one of the bearers who brought in the message complaining of the Boer encroachments during Governor Scott's time, in 1864. Very remarkable was the keen and ceaseless attention paid by this wiry little Zulu to every word that was uttered. Mr. Dunn also accompanied the deputation, in an unofficial capacity.

The scene itself was interesting. On the Natal side stood forth the bush-clad bluffs by the river, which stretches below to where it enters the sea, three or four miles off. On the other side were the treeless slopes of the hills, one of which near the sea is famous for its ruddy crown; the small patch of forest near the water's edge, seaward; the horizon being closed in by the blue hills of Zululand. Within sight, and close by, are the scenes of the fight with Mr. Biggar's little force, forty years ago, and of the Umbulazi [Mbuyazi] massacre, in 1856, when the blood of three thousand slain reddened the river; and although the present meeting was a peaceful one, suggestions of war were manifest in the camp of the Naval Brigade, overlooking the river, and the presence on the spot of a small party of blue-jackets and of about twenty mounted Volunteers.

The Zulu deputies, having been brought over by boat to the Natal side of the river, were duly received by the Commissioners. Mr Fynney Border Agent, acted as interpreter, and rendered most faithfully every word of the two documents, which had been printed in both English and Zulu. The Award was first delivered. . . . [A]lthough the Zulus claim the whole of the territory, through which all rivers flowing westward pass, and although the claim was reiterated by the messengers, they seemed, on the whole (as well they might), to think that a satisfactory termination of a troublesome dispute had been arrived at. Mr. Shepstone explained most carefully the line as laid down by the High Commissioner. . . . [N]early the whole of the disputed territory has been handed over to the Zulus. . . .

After the award had been made known, a sense of relief was manifest on the countenances of the deputies. They evidently thought that a satisfactory termination had been found to a troublesome business; in other words, they had got more than they expected. An hour's adjournment then took place, and, on resuming the conference, the ultimatum was interpreted to them. A change then passed over the Zulu faces – those faces got longer and longer. This was a very different matter to the other, and they did not attempt to disguise their consciousness of the gravity of the demands made upon them. . . . [T]he stipulations in regard to military disbandment, covering, as they do, the permission to marry, were deemed to be a serious interference with the

Rather to their disquiet, the photographer James Lloyd took this picture of the Zulu delegation listening to Bartle Frere's ultimatum at the Lower Thukela on 11 December 1878.
(S.B. Bourquin)

Sovereign's prerogative, one which would require more time than a month to consider. Why should any time, indeed, be fixed, they urged, in a matter of such great importance? Why should they not be allowed to keep up an army when the English Government kept up one on its own side?

The Commissioners, however, said distinctly that all they had to do was to make known the High Commissioner's decision, without entering into any argument upon the terms of it. These were the last word of the Government, and these would be abided by.

The Zulu deputies evidently regarded the proposed change to the marriage system as the most serious item in the programme. They appeared anxious to enter into a discussion of the subject, but they were told that controversy was out of the question . . . and that if any explanations were desired they must be specially asked for. They replied that they fully understood the tenor of what had been conveyed to them, and they admitted they were able to communicate to the King exactly the words of the Government.

Throughout the whole of the conference, the demeanour of the Zulus was dignified, becoming, and respectful. There was no indulgence in any sort of threat, boast, or anger. It was noticed that the younger – and more warlike – portion of the nation, was not apparently represented. We understand that Umnyame [Mnyamana], Cetywayo's prime minister, was to have accompanied the deputation, but he appears to have changed his mind at the last moment, and was absent 'one of his wives being ill.' The only appearance of anything like disquietude displayed by the deputies, was when Mr. Lloyd, our photographic artist, levelled his camera at the group. The spectacle of this strange three-legged instrument, with its polished tube, directed seemingly at himself, caused Uvumandaba the portly leader of the party to nudge his neighbour, as though telling him to 'look out.' Mr. Brownlee assured him that there was nothing to be alarmed at, but though the sable ambassador succeeded in maintaining his native composure and continuing the conversation, he nevertheless kept his eyes fixed upon the mysterious piece of mechanism in front of him. . . .[3]

Cetshwayo indeed was left with no alternative but to resist. Nevertheless, even though he began to muster his *amabutho* in earnest for the struggle, he persisted in attempting to find a negotiated settlement. But Frere was not interested in his stream of messengers and their half-concessions. With the goal in sight, Frere exercised his wide discretionary powers as High Commissioner and manipulated the slow and inadequate lines of communications with London to push forward with a war which his government was actually eager to avoid. Once successful – as he had little doubt he would be – he confidently anticipated that a grateful government would readily condone his questionable initiatives.

The ultimatum was due to expire on 11 January 1879. At the depots of the various columns, where the troops were concentrating for their imminent advance, camp life followed much its normal course. This encompassed the usual excesses too, and a *Natal Witness* correspondent reported that at the Utrecht camp of No. 4 Column 'drunkenness is very prevalent here at present. Men are being tried by court-martial and flogged nearly every day.'[4] In a subsequent report he described the more acceptable aspects of camp life at Utrecht, such as the comings and goings of military units, entertainments and improving addresses. He also drew attention to the nigh panic of the inhabitants of the little village at the prospect of being left to defend themselves once No. 4 Column advanced:

The town defence meeting was a failure for want of unanimity on the part of members; only 16 out of 60 could be got to sign their names to an agreement to stay and defend the Laager, should the Zulus make a raid. The Landdrost explained to the meeting that it was called up to suggest and advise on the best means to adopt to protect the families and properties of the inhabitants in the event of a war with the Zulus. At this stage of the proceedings, the Landdrost was asked to see Colonel Wood, and learn how many troops would be left for the protection of the Military Hospital and Commissariat stores. The Colonel replied that not a man fit for active service would be left for that purpose. This was like a thunderbolt to the funky portion. Fieldcornet Schuer said that he would not remain in the town unless 200 troops were left for its defence. . . . There is no doubt that there will be an exodus as soon as the troops move, or at least it is fully anticipated. . . . Wagon-loads of supplies are daily arriving; forty-two wagons came in yesterday with military stores.

The Carrington Horse arrived on Thursday [12 December], looking very weather-begrimed and somewhat tattered and torn after their twelve months' hard service. The officers were not bronzed, but so sun-burnt that the skin of their faces peeled off, but they do not appear to have suffered in health from the rough life they have been compelled to live. The horses are in very poor condition, from the hard work that they have done.

On Friday [13 December] the Kaffrarian Rifles arrived, and were played in by the band of the 90th Regiment, and were heartily cheered by the red-coats. They are as fine a body of Volunteers as I have ever seen; their uniform and equipments are very appropriate for Rifle Volunteers. They formed camp alongside the Carrington Horse, giving Utrecht a very martial appearance.

Our Kafirs begin to express some astonishment at the arrival of so many troops and wagon-loads of stores; they were also greatly surprised at the bursting of the shells at the Artillery practice, and also the distance and precision with which the Artillery fired. There were constant exclamations of 'Oh, Cetywayo won't stand against that long!'

On Thursday the Dramatic Club of the 90th gave a vocal and instrumental entertainment to the public. The Court-house was so crowded that the officers who courteously gave up their own seats for the accommodation of the ladies were jostled out. Major Rogers contributed to the entertainment by singing 'Auld Roekio' in Rob Roy costume; he also sang 'Hearts of Oak' with great applause. Lieut. Biggs, R.A., Lieut. Lomax, Sergt. Gill, and Master Taylor (servant) gave some splendid songs and comic recitations. The Band-Sergeant played a solo in excellent style on the cornopean, and the brilliant pianist, Bandsman Banks, gave several airs on the piano. The Christy Minstrels kept the audience in a constant roar of laughter. On Friday there was another entertainment for the officers and non-commissioned officers, when Colonel Wood gave an instructive lecture on Zulu history, manners, customs, mode of warfare, and a geographical description of the country, and the precautions that the troops would have to take when invading the country. With the exception of trifling historical errors, the lecture proves that the gallant officer has taken great pains to collect information on Zulu matters. He seems well aware of the difficulties and obstacles that he would be called upon to encounter in commanding operations against the Zulus. If we have to fight the Zulus we can depend upon the troops maintaining their traditional honour as British soldiers. . . .[5]

The Natal Mounted Volunteers gamely did their best to adjust to the privations of camp life, and units at Potspruit between Greytown and the Thukela frontier were reported to have spent a jolly, if damp, Christmas day. Elements of the Natal Native Contingent and Natal Native Horse were at the same time moving up through Greytown to join No. 2 Column, which was concentrating between Potspruit and d'Almaine's farm:

The Volunteers had a fine time of it on Christmas Day at Potspruit camp. The Durban Mounted Rifles received a wagon-load of everything needful for the occasion, whilst the Greytown folks attended to their little company of Volunteers by sending a cart loaded with provisions, &c., for the Natal Hussars.

Almost all civilian goods in colonial Natal were transported by ox-wagon. Lacking sufficient military transport, Lord Chelmsford was obliged to hire huge numbers of such wagons, often at inflated prices. (Ian Knight)

They invited the Alexandra Mounted Rifles to join them in the attack, that was successfully made upon Christmas Day. The A.M.R. have travelled so far from their homes that the little comforts of the season could not readily be sent to them by their friends.

Potspruit appears to be about as damp and misty a spot as could be found in Umvoti County, or perhaps in Natal; lately the sun has rarely been visible, so no wonder that all stationed there hail with pleasure the prospect of being soon removed to Krantzkop, or elsewhere. The General has pointed out to the Colonial Government the necessity of supplying the Volunteers with waterproof sheets. There must have been an extraordinary lack of forethought on the part of some one that this want was not supplied long ago. In the service the health of the camp always receives earnest consideration.

Native levies, both mounted and on foot, arrive here daily; the village is crowded with people of all colours, and in all sorts of uniforms, from scarlet with gold lace down to the easy and elegant mutya [umutsha or loin-covering] of cat-skin; all seem eager to be moving forward. 'Moving forward' reads very easy, but I daresay the Transport and Commissariat Departments could tell a different tale, for the wet weather of late has played sad havoc with the roads, wagons are sticking fast daily. I was lately a few miles from Greytown, and noticed where a wagon had been dug out, leaving a large hole in the centre of the road, – doubtless the digging out was a necessity, but the person in charge of the wagon should not proceed without filling in the hole he had made. . . .[6]

When war was but twelve days away, Chelmsford inspected his troops massing along the Thukela frontier. He addressed a parade in the pouring rain at Thring's Post on

Settler society's contribution to the war effort: the camp of the Natal Volunteers at Thring's Post. (Killie Campbell Africana Library)

30 December 1878, sententiously impressing on the sodden men (and the *Natal Witness* correspondent) the virtues of coolness, vigilance and discipline:

> . . . The day was a miserably wet one, and completely annulled the arrangements for a field day, in which 'The Buffs,' Royal Artillery, and Stanger and Victoria Mounted Rifles were to take part. . . . However, as the General was anxious to see 'The Buffs' and the Royal Artillery, a parade was held about four o'clock amidst the pelting rain. The General rode down, accompanied by his staff and Colonel Pearson. . . . After the parade, being formed up, General Thesiger . . . wished to say a few words, especially as many before him were young soldiers who up to the present were not engaged in actual warfare. It was quite possible that in a few days – it may be two or it may be ten – the men under his command may have to cross the Tugela into the Zulu country, which should then be considered the enemy's country, and what he wanted to impress upon the men above all was to be cool under all circumstances, and to preserve their discipline. On no account should they get flurried, for though some large numbers of the enemy may have to be met – though they may come down in crowds – it should still be remembered they are but an undisciplined mob, and armed as British troops are with the Martini Henry rifle, they need have no fear of any enemy they may have to encounter among the Zulus. He was aware of the discipline of the troops before him, and he had the fullest confidence in them. Let them be said and led by their officers, in whom he had the greatest confidence, and all their efforts would be crowned with success. It all depended

upon coolness and taking steady aim. When in Zululand they should remember they are in the land of the enemy, and should act with the greatest circumspection. Troops should ever be on the alert and keep their eyes and their ears open. They should especially be on the alert for a night attack, and it would be an eternal disgrace to the man who should be lax in any way in his duty – his ears should be open in the night as his eyes should be in the day. He expected to see the same caution and attention on the part of the men whatever stay they may have in the country, as they were sure to show when they first enter it and their minds are fresh. They could not be too watchful, especially when on piquet. Men on outlying duty could not be too careful, and each should be most anxious to give the earliest intimation of the approach of the enemy. Discipline was everything, and, as he had said before, he had the greatest reliance in the officers and would impress on the soldiers to obey them implicitly. He had no doubt but all would do their duty, as all would participate in the glory and honour which he firmly felt was in store for the men under his command. . . .[7]

Unhappily, discipline was precisely what some of the imperial troops landing in Durban lacked. During 3 and 4 January men of the 99th (Duke of Edinburgh's) Regiment came on shore from the *Walmer Castle* and *American*. Many of these young, untried, soldiers had little experience with hard liquor and were soon incapably drunk. The dismayed military authorities were constrained to issue an order on 8 January warning troops of good character against the lethal effects of 'a most poisonous liquor sold at Durban, under the name of rum and Cape smoke'.[8] The *Natal Witness* correspondent reported the incident (which might have lent itself to entirely sensational and moralizing comment) in a particularly responsible manner, drawing attention to the shortcomings of the Commissariat Department, the lack of facilities for troops in Durban and the irresponsible rapaciousness of its publicans:

> . . . [S]cenes of debauchery were witnessed in this town last Friday and Saturday evenings among the soldiers. . . . I do not think I can do better than reproduce our Superintendent's report to the Town Council on Friday with respect to the matter. . . . He says:–'I have the honour to bring to your notice the sad scenes I witnessed in our streets on Saturday evening last. There were at least, from my own observation, about eighty young soldiers lying in West Street, totally insensible from liquor obtained from our local canteens. Two of these men were in such a dangerous state the next morning, that they were not expected to live, and they are still in a dangerous state. There were at least about 200 men on Saturday night incapable of walking to their camp. The men landed strangers to the Colony. They had little or no food that day, and had been worked hard. When let out in the evening their first move was for something to eat and drink. No place was open for them but public-houses, where they found *no food*, and all liquors *fit* to drink too expensive for the little they had to spend. Publicans were anxious to sell what gained *them* the most profit, knowing well what would be the result, for the lads had scarcely drunk the liquor before they were falling outside the doors like rotten sheep. The Police did their best to warn the

soldiers against drinking this vile liquor called Natal rum (*new*) for this is what was served to them. Although they are not blameless, they ought not to have been driven to it. 1st. By the Commissariat not providing them food and wholesome food at their own camp, which would have been done at cost price. 2nd. By the town not having a single eating-house or coffee-room open after six p.m., or any place for refreshments other than canteens and hotels, except that suppers are laid out in some of the billiard rooms which is only temptation for gaming. 3rd. The Government are greatly to blame, for they indirectly furnish the means of destroying half the constitutions in the Colony by allowing new rum just off the still to be sold for retail. The stuff is very strong, and will stand adulteration, therefore it is cheap to the publican, no matter how poisonous or unfit for consumption, it is sold to him, and he must retail it to others. . . . As for some of our canteen-keepers, and the part they took on Saturday evening – let their own conscience be their accusers.'

Since the day referred to I have heard that three soldiers have died in camp from the effects of the debauch, a result that may well appal the community; yet I very much question if the intelligence of these three lives being lost under such circumstances produces anything like the effect it would were it made known that they had fallen in fight against the Zulu King. Yet, indeed, it should fill us with grief and indignation to think that in a peaceful land, within an hour or two after setting foot upon its shores, these soldiers of the British Queen – men who had served her well in foreign lands and assisted to uphold the honour and dignity of her Empire throughout the world, men in the prime of their manhood, who would scorn the imputation of ever turning their backs upon a foe – come here to die a death worse than that of a dog. . . .[9]

Build-up for invasion: British troops camped at Durban. (Killie Campbell Africana Library)

While the chastened men of the 99th Regiment proceeded up the coast from Durban to join No. 1 Column concentrating at Fort Pearson, the various elements of No. 3 Column were coming together on the heights at Helmekaar overlooking the valley of the Mzinyathi. The *Times of Natal*'s special war correspondent, Charles Norris-Newman, was with them. He reported not only on Lord Chelmsford, the British regulars and the Natal Native Contingent, but on the Border Guard levies who were to hold the border once the column advanced into Zululand:

> . . . [I] reached Greytown just in time to accompany Col. Degacher and the 2–24th on their way up here. . . . Mooi River was reached that afternoon, and after much hard work the wagons were all got through the drift; the men being punted over. As it was a fine night and Major Black wanted to get on quickly we bivouaced in the open, and we were very comfortable. At daybreak next morning we proceeded, and reached the Tugela in five hours. We again bivouaced, but on this occasion, were not so lucky, as a heavy thunderstorm came on in the evening, and wetted us all through thoroughly. The men were walking about all night trying to keep warm, and then at daybreak we resumed our trek. Our next halt was at a spruit about 9 miles on, where breakfast was served out. At this place I left the 2–24th, as I wished to push on so as to reach Rorke's Drift in time to cross over with the 3rd Regiment N.N.C., and I was accompanied for the rest of my journey by Mr. Cooke, of Estcourt, who was proceeding with the final batch of Kafirs for Commandant Lonsdale's Regiment.

An unusual photograph of the Border Levy at Thring's Post, with the men formed up in companies, screened by skirmishers, and the earthwork fort on the skyline. (Killie Campbell Africana Library)

It is really astonishing how these Kafirs can march. Very few horses can walk
with them, and it is capital fun marching with a lot, as they are not only amusing
in their manners and speech, but are also constantly enlivening the march by
war songs extempore and otherwise. We got to the place where the 3rd
Regiment, N.N.C., had been encamped for some weeks, Sand Spruit, in a very
short time and made a halt for feeding purposes. While here, I noticed a lot of
over 300 Kafirs being marched off towards the border, and, on enquiry, found
that these men were part of the reserves being called out, to act as a border
guard, and were going on to the Buffalo to be distributed along its banks as
sentries. I found that this system is extended from Helpmakaar right down to the
Tugela, so that those who are in fear of a Zulu invasion, need not be afraid of
not receiving timely notice. These reserves are placed in parties of 300, under an
officer who speaks the language, and comes from the same district. The scheme
is one that recommends itself, and adds another to the many proofs (if needed)
of the careful and skilful manner in which this expedition is being carried out by
His Excellency the General and those under him. We were constantly on the
alert on this part of our journey between Sand Spruit and the camp, as a dense
fog prevailed all the way, and our Kafirs were rather apprehensive of meeting
any large body of Zulus who might perhaps be prowling about. When we
arrived here we were given quarters and rations, and then had to do the best we
could for ourselves. The cold during the night was intense, and all we suffered
from was the want of sufficient blankets. Great changes have been made here. . . .
The headquarter-staff camp is pitched to the right of all the others, almost in the
centre as you walk from one end to the other. The Union Jack flies in front of
the tent of the General, and his mule-wagons are placed in position behind,
otherwise there is nothing to show the difference between it and the other
camps. His Excellency is much liked, and in every way sets a good example to
the men under him. He rises at daylight, and when on the march assists in
striking and pitching his own tent. His manner is exceedingly affable to all, and
seems to have the happy knack of thoroughly understanding at once what is
meant to be conveyed to him, although it may be wrapped up in eloquence or
long-windedness. His love of punctuality is well-known throughout the camp,
and of course leads to the same system in others. . . .[10]

At the Lower Thukela Drift the men of No. 1 Column were busily engaged on
7 January in throwing a pontoon across the river preparatory to an advance:

. . . The work in connection with the pontoon, which is being done by the crew
of the *Active*, is most energetically carried out, difficult as the job is, especially
when it is remembered the river to be crossed, which runs over six knots an
hour, and from the early morning till late at night the sound of the hammer and
saw are to be heard by the side of the river, while the sailors like so many ants
are to be seen in the small boats rowing with all their might, bespeaking the
earnestness of the work, and the desirability of its early completion. While thus
employed active watch is being kept both from Fort Pearson, and by the piquet
on the opposite bank, to prevent such a thing as a surprise to the working party

by the enemy. The chances, however, of such an occurrence are very remote, as the land for over a mile at the opposite side is pretty low, and would not afford concealment from the sentry on Fort Pearson. . . .[11]

Upstream, at his camp at d'Almaine's farm, two days before the war began, Colonel Durnford put the mounted NNC officers of his No. 2 Column through some exercises preparatory to meeting the Zulu who, as a means of terrifying their enemies, usually rattled their spears against their shields. *The Times* correspondent facetiously noted the ludicrous consequences:

> We have had several very exciting scenes in camp to-day; at early parade, the natives were told by the Commanding Officer to make a charge on the officers who were mounted, as usual, to accustom the horses to the noise of their shields. The effect was perfectly miraculous; officers were to be seen shooting through the air in a horizontal position, like meteors, riderless horses covered the face of the earth for miles, and the earth was filled with the groans of the thrown. List of casualties:- One nose slightly skinned; several shoulders sore; two natives run over, but not seriously injured; numerous horses lost; no deaths.[12]

On the same day as Durnford's officers were being ignominiously thrown sprawling, No. 3 Column moved down from Helpmekaar to Rorke's Drift and into sight of KwaSokhexe, which was to be its first military objective once it crossed into Zululand. KwaSokhexe was the stronghold of Chief Sihayo of the Qungebe whose sons' foray into Natal in July 1878 had furnished Frere's main justifications for his ultimatum. The scene recorded by the *Natal Witness*'s special war correspondent was one to delight an artist's eye and to divert attention away from the fell purpose of the advancing column:

The African population of Natal offered the British a fertile recruiting ground, which was largely squandered through poor planning and lack of resources: an unidentified battalion of the Natal Native Contingent, possibly Major Harcourt Bengough's 2nd Battalion, 1st Regiment. (Ian Knight)

. . . [Y]esterday all the troops at Helpmakaar were moved down into the valley of the Buffalo, close to the drift. I was on the hills above, which overlook Rorke's Drift and Usirayo's stronghold, while this movement was taking place, and could see the long dark line of cavalry, artillery, infantry, and baggage as it wound down the valley. It was a scene worthy of a painter's brush, the masses of moving troops, edging the gleaming curves of the Buffalo, which the eye can follow for many miles above; the white tents of the Native Contingent and the other troops already stationed close to the drift – beyond, Zululand with its sharply defined peaks, and the great Nqutu hill looming darkly over the river. There was especial interest in looking at it, knowing as we did that there is Usirayo's stronghold, where our first fighting may be expected. The day, though not particularly favourable for reconnoitering – owing to the haze – was nearly perfect from a painter's point of view, the lights and shades being quite lovely, gleams of sunshine alternating with misty showers, and occasionally dark clouds crossing over the country. . . .[13]

NOTES

1. *Natal Mercury*, 13 January 1879: Krantz Kop correspondent, 7 December 1878.
2. *Natal Witness*, 15 January 1878: Stanger occasional correspondent, 8 December 1878.
3. *Natal Mercury*, 16 December 1878.
4. *Natal Witness*, supplement, 21 December 1878: Utrecht Camp correspondent, 15 December 1878.
5. *Natal Witness*, 24 December 1878: Utrecht correspondent, 15 December 1878.
6. *Natal Witness*, 7 January 1879: Greytown correspondent, 29 December 1878.
7. *Natal Witness*, 4 January 1879: Thring's Post correspondent, 30 December 1878.
8. *Natal Colonist*, 11 January 1879.
9. *Natal Witness*, 11 January 1879: Durban correspondent, 9 January 1879.
10. *Times of Natal*, 8 January 1879: special war correspondent, Helpmakaar Camp, Sunday evening, 5 January 1879.
11. *Natal Witness*, 14 January 1879: special correspondent, Lower Tugela Drift, 7 January 1879.
12. *Natal Mercury*, 20 January 1879: *The Times* correspondent, Dalamen's Farm, 9 January 1879.
13. *Natal Witness*, 14 January 1879: special war correspondent, Helpmakaar, 10 January 1879.

Invasion

As the deadline for the expiry of Frere's ultimatum approached with no sign of a Zulu response, a thrill of excitement passed through settler society. The editor of the Durban-based *Natal Mercury* was moved by a sense of history in the making to travel up the coast to the Lower Thukela Drift, to see Pearson's No. 1 Column, 'the most conveniently accessible',[1] actually cross into Zululand and begin hostilities. It was not a comfortable trip, for the bad weather which had plagued the build-up of forces continued unabated, and the *Mercury* began its extensive report with an account of the discomforts suffered by its august editor:

> I write this in the homely and very comfortable road-side inn kept by Mr. and Mrs. Wassink, near the Nonoti. Rain is pattering on the roof, thunder and lightning are in the air, and depressing thoughts are suggested of greasy roads and swollen rivers on the morrow. . . .[2]

The *Mercury's* interest was fuelled by the fact that among the Colonial troops who accompanied Pearson were the Durban Mounted Rifles, and the editor was secure in the knowledge that his readers were hungry for news of 'Our Lads'. Indeed, so close were the links between the mounted Volunteer units and settler society that many men in the ranks supplied anonymous reports of their adventures, which the papers in both Pietermaritzburg and Durban were eager to publish. As a result, the early stages of the war were exhaustively reported in Natal, but scarcely noticed in Britain, where Frere's notification of hostilities did not reach London until after the fighting had begun. The local reports covered in almost tedious detail the difficulties which beset Pearson's column in the last few days before the ultimatum expired. So great were the problems of marshalling both men and supplies at the Lower Thukela, indeed, that Pearson was not ready to begin the invasion on 11 January, the specified date. In fact, the crossing did not begin in earnest until the following day, although this did not dampen the enthusiasm of the *Mercury's* editor. For him, the war began on a note of high patriotism, full of hope for the triumph of British civilization over African barbarism:

> It is my good fortune to witness a scene which is one of a series which must ever be memorable in the history of South Africa. I have seen an army of British troops – Imperial and colonial, white and coloured – cross in perfect order, and without a hitch or halt, the frontier which divides the civilised domains of Queen VICTORIA from the savage domains of King CETYWAYO. I have seen the

bare, green hills of Zululand enlivened by the white tents, and the red or blue uniforms of men who have been gathered there to vindicate the just cause of an offended civilisation, and to assert the outraged authority of the British Crown. I have seen the climax of a policy which must end in the undisputed supremacy of British rule over all the native tribes that live south of the Limpopo. It is impossible – for me at any rate – to write of such an event without some degree of special enthusiasm, or to refrain from seeking to communicate to my readers some of the emotions that have been generated by the scene.

Up to the the very moment of our reaching the boundary of the Tugela, the exact time of crossing remained uncertain, and many remarks heard along the road rather encourged a belief that the actual passage would not be attempted until the week was well advanced. . . .

When, however, a turn in the road, after a wearisome struggle through horrible quagmires, brought the river itself within sight, a glance across the further shore set all doubts at rest. There, on the gentle slope of a grassy hill might be seen two or three thin red lines, which, when examined through a glass, resolved themselves into ranks of British infantry, standing at ease, while their remaining comrades were being brought over to join them. The 'crossing' had already taken place, and Zululand was virtually in the possession of British arms.

Dawn, on Sunday the 12th January, had barely made its approach perceptible, when a large and roomy 'punt' was hauled over slowly but surely from the southern to the northern shore. The square and clumsy looking vessel was filled by the men who had constructed and fixed it, and who were now to work it, belonging to the Naval Brigade. In the dim light these were taken over, and set

A rare photograph of an unidentified auxiliary unit – possibly the Natal Native Pioneers – in a camp outside Pietermaritzburg, with the men wearing old British army greatcoats and forage caps over traditional dress. (Ian Knight)

ashore; and as soon as the punt had been hauled back again, it returned with a party of the Native 'Pioneers', under the able command of Lieut. Beddoes. The passage of these men, from bank to bank, was viewed with intense interest and anxiety by the thousands of onlookers from Fort Pearson and the hills around. Would the enemy presume, upon the feebleness of the light and the fewness of their preliminary invaders, to resist by a sudden onslaught their attempt to land? Was an armed horde of Zulus lying in wait behind the ridge of the slope to pounce down upon the rash aggressors upon Cetywayo's soil? But no enemy appeared. Time went on; the day brightened; distant objects became clearly distinguishable, and nearer scenes were in full view, but all was still and lifeless on the Zulu shore. After the native pioneers went four companies of the Buffs, who at once took up position around Pearse's solitary homestead about a quarter of a mile above the river. Then came some from their camp above the well disciplined ranks of the Victoria Mounted Rifles, to which body, as the senior Volunteer corps, attached to the first column, belonged by right the privilege of being the first to enter Zululand. Under the command of their leader, Captain Saner, the V.M.R. marched down to the drift, and on to the punt, and in their turn were taken over. When they were across they at once proceeded to plant themselves along the brow of the hill above, where they did patrol and vidette duty throughout the whole of the long and anxious day.

The same process continued without interruption until nightfall, when, thoroughly tired out by their strenuous and unremitting labours, the Naval Brigade were ordered by the commanding officer, Captain Campbell, to desist, until dawn next morning. The manner in which these men worked commanded the warmest expressions of admiration from all the bystanders. Operations at the drift were, of course the chief attraction to all the camp; but the whole scene

Officers of the same unit enjoying lunch; their uniforms have an improvised look typical of the auxiliary units. (Ian Knight)

was one of surpassing interest and excitement. The mingling of men belonging to so many services and races was itself a strange feature. Here were gathered together the redcoats of the line, and the blue-jackets of the navy; the many uniforms of the colonial volunteers from Durban, Victoria, Alexandra and Nonoti; the scarlet tunics of the native pioneers, and the naked forms of the native contingent. Around Mr Smith's inn, just above the river, the crowding and confusion were distracting. All day, from an early to a late hour, the bar and the dining room of this humble edifice were crammed by the customers clamouring to be served and helping themselves, and there was not a nook in the establishment that had not been invaded and occupied. When I say that by Sunday night not a drop of liquor remained on the premises, and that the store had been denuded of all its edible contents, the amount of business done by the proprietor during this eventful day will be well appreciated.

A walk about the camp disclosed all manner of characteristic features. Yellow-coated officers of the native contingent, apparently waiting for orders, lounged about everywhere, while parties of the contingent itself continually marched to their ground in the rear. One of the Gatling guns, surrounded by boxes of ammunition, stood in readiness for transportation. Two seven-pounders were posted in front of the hotel, with their mouths gaping towards the river; two more were placed on a most commanding neck of land, just beyond the fort . . . . Much curiosity was expressed throughout the day as to what the Victorians on the hill top [i.e. in advance of the British position on the Zulu shore] were seeing and doing. Their videttes were seen posted along the ridges, and now and then the main body of the corps would disappear from view, only to reappear at a further point, being evidently engaged in a reconnaissance. They did not, however, advance far into the country, though eager to do so. Towards noon, they descried a body of Zulus, apparently several hundred strong, and Captain Saner telegraphed for permission to 'engage the enemy'. He was, however, apprised that it would not be well to do so until Barrow's Horse had crossed. About the same time another report became current in camp to the effect that two large columns of Zulus, variously estimated at from 7000 to 15,000 had been seen on the hills behind, apparently approaching the river. As the day went on the numbers assigned to this force became so conflicting that all which could be reasonably inferred was that ten considerable columns of the enemy were undoubtedly hovering in the vicinity. Hills are opaque, however, and we do not yet possess the art of seeing round corners or over obstacles, so we have to content ourselves with surmises as to what our neighbours are doing.[3]

Indeed, for all the bustle of the invasion, the day proved something of a disappointment to the crowd of civilian settlers who had gathered on the Natal bank in the hope of seeing the war begin in dramatic style. Despite the rumours current around Fort Pearson, the only Zulus to be seen were small scouting parties, who kept away on the hills in the distance. Nor, indeed, was Pearson in a position to begin his advance immediately. His column consisted of more than 4,000 combat troops – chiefly from the 3rd ('The Buffs') and 99th Regiments, with a detachment of sailors put ashore from HMS *Active* and *Tenedos*, over 300 mounted men, artillery, engineers and over 2,000 men of the Natal Native Contingent – supported by nearly 400 wagons and carts, drawn by 3,128 oxen, 116 horses and 121 mules. Since the pont at the Lower Thukela Drift could only transport one company of infantry, a single wagon, or two or three spans of oxen across at a time, the process of crossing the river was a slow and laborious one. It was not until 15 January that the last of the troops were across, and the passage of supplies would continue for days thereafter.

Once in Zululand, Pearson's column established a rambling camp which stretched in a huge arc, with either end resting on the river. Before the start of hostilities, Lord Chelmsford had issued standing orders which directed that camps should be partly entrenched on all sides, but such entrenchments had seldom been necessary in the Cape Frontier campaign, and since Chelmsford himself failed to insist that troops directly under his command enforced such precautions, there was a remarkable laxness in this regard throughout the army as a whole. For several days, Pearson's camp was entirely indefensible, although on the 16th a party of Royal Engineers marked out the perimeter of a large earthwork surrounding Mr Pearse's abandoned house, and fatigue parties of infantry began to dig the entrenchments. This position, known as Fort Tenedos, was intended to guard the crossing, though it was indifferently sited, since it was overlooked by a low hill 300 yards away. Nonetheless, the building of the fort aroused a flicker of interest and speculation in the offices of the *Natal Mercury*, who were already showing signs of frustration at the lack of more exciting news:

> It will be seen by the telegrams that the garrison at Fort Pearson is to be transferred to the northern side of the river, where a new fort has been constructed. As the river will be even better commanded and covered from that side than from this, this movement is probably one of sound strategic value. It will, moreover, enable the upper drifts to be more effectively watched and protected, and will give a better base for the advancing column.[4]

The same issue contained a comment on the fighting ability of the enemy, which suggests just how complacent both the military and settler society had become in the aftermath of the uncontested crossing:

> So far, every incident goes to show that the Zulu military qualities have been greatly overrated, and that they possess less capacity of resistance than either the Cape or Transvaal kafirs.[5]

In fact, Pearson's column had been inside Zululand for four days, and still had very little idea of the enemy's whereabouts or intentions. Pearson's own objectives, as specified by Lord Chelmsford, were to advance to the KwaMondi mission station on the Eshowe heights, about thirty-five miles by track from the river. The mission had been established by the Norwegian Mission Society in 1860, but Christianity had not thrived among the Zulus, and the missionaries fled their post in the tense months before the war began. For the British, the mission's mud-brick and thatch buildings offered ideal shelter for the enormous stockpile of supplies that were needed to support each column in the field, and Chelmsford had ordered Pearson to occupy the post and convert it into a permanent depot. Pearson's subsequent movements would depend on the progress of the other two invading columns, but he was broadly expected to move from Eshowe towards King Cetshwayo's principal residence, which the British knew variously as Ulundi or oNdini. Even as Pearson secured his crossing, therefore, he sent his mounted troops – a mixture of regular mounted infantrymen and Natal Volunteers under the command of a major in the 19th Hussars, Percy Barrow – out to patrol his intended line of advance. The road to Eshowe, little more than an old hunters' track, meandered across undulating country, which was carpeted with tall grass, wet after the recent rains, and broken here and there by patches of bush. It was crossed at regular intervals by a succession of small rivers, most of which were in flood. The area was lightly populated by the Zulus, and although Barrow's men came across a number of *imizi* – homesteads – they were largely deserted, apart from a few old or infirm civilians. Now and then they encountered a few Zulu patrols, who were clearly watching the column's movements, but the Zulus showed little inclination to fight:

> We hear that there was only a party of two or three Victoria Mounted Rifles when the Zulus, who were taken on Monday, saw them. The latter jeered at the volunteers, saying 'What do you red-jackets want here in our country?'. They stopped when they saw the whole patrol come in sight. One man appeared to hold his gun in a rather threatening way, but when Captain Saner drew his revolver he changed his attitude. The guns taken proved to be very inferior and old fashioned muzzle-loaders, if not converted flintstocks, and though the prisoners had plenty of bullets their powder was very bad.[6]

> . . . We are inclined to think that a considerable Zulu force is lurking in the neighbourhood of the Lower Thukela though with what designs we cannot say. On Monday the Victoria Rifles when patrolling only saw twenty or thirty kafirs within a radius of 15 miles. Those that had arms gave up with little hesitation. A party of ten Zulus armed, gave in quietly to four volunteers.[7]

Pearson's column finally began its advance at dawn on the morning of 18 January. Even by that date news had begun to circulate that Zulu fighting prowess was not a complete myth: on the 12th, Colonel Glyn's Centre Column had defeated Chief Sihayo's followers after a brief skirmish. The news reached Pearson's men on the 16th, and his men began their march in eager anticipation of a fight. Partly because of the delays, Pearson had decided to split his column into two divisions: the first, which he commanded, constituted a 'flying column', and included just fifty wagons, but was accompanied by over half the column's fighting men. The second division, commanded by Colonel Welman of the 99th, was to bring up the remainder of the wagons a day later. Pearson hoped by this means to allow the road sufficient time to dry out between the passage of the two columns. Nevertheless, progress remained painfully slow, and the advance ground to a halt every time it reached one of the many rivers across its path. On the first day it made perhaps six or seven miles, and camped beyond the Nyoni River, while virtually the whole of the next day was taken up with crossing the Msunduze, just four miles further on. The overnight camps were made miserable by the rain, and by the jittery state of the young, inexperienced men of the 99th, who provoked several false alarms. By this time, reports of Zulu movements further along the border had encouraged a general feeling that the Zulus would soon oppose the advance. On the 21st, the column crossed the most serious obstacle so far, the Matigulu River, and Pearson despatched a force of 600 men to investigate a report that some 5,000 or 6,000 Zulus had moved into the kwaGingindlovu *ikhanda* (military homestead) a few miles away. To their disappointment, the *ikhanda* was deserted, and the column returned with just one rather pathetic prisoner:

> Near here was the district military kraal of about fifty huts, called Umgingindlovu. This was of course burnt, having been found deserted by all but a very old woman, whom the chaplain of the forces has brought on with him in his wagon. Many surmises have been made as to the old lady's age, and the general opinion is that 'she must be 100, at least'. The same gentleman heard that another old woman had been left in a kraal close by. He was told that she was probably dead; but he, thinking that she might be hiding, went to make sure, and found that she had been dead for some days. She must have been too feeble to accompany the rest of the family in their flight, and was consequently left behind. Plenty of food was found in the hut along with her.[8]

Pearson's column camped that night on a ridge known as kwaSamabela. Rumours were rife of a Zulu presence, and the sentries spent a wary night, calling off their numbers to one another to reassure themselves that all was well. The next morning brought no sign of the enemy, however, although some of the local volunteers noticed that large swathes of grass had apparently been trampled flat around the camp during the night. The column moved off early on the morning of the 22nd, towards the next natural barrier, the Nyezane River. Hitherto the country had been open and undulating, but beyond the Nyezane it rose in a series of ridges which stretched away towards Eshowe. Pearson, worried that the hills might conceal a Zulu *impi* (military force), ordered Barrow's horsemen to cross the river, and scout the slopes beyond. They did so, and returned to report that there were no enemy in sight, and that the flat ground immediately beyond the river, below the hills, offered the best place to halt the advance for breakfast. While the column came up and the first elements began to cross the river, Barrow's horsemen were allowed to dismount and eat their breakfasts. Ahead of them, the track wound up a spur, flanked on either side by bush-choked gullies, which gave way to further ridges. The highest point of the range was a domed hill to the right of the road, known to the Zulus as Wombane. At about 8 a.m., as the first wagons were dragged across the high banks of the Nyezane, scouts reported that a small party of Zulus had been seen on the track ahead. Pearson immediately ordered some of the Native Contingent forward to drive them off. The Zulus disappeared into the gully to the right of the road, then re-appeared on the flank of Wombane. The NNC followed them through the gully, and up the slope. The Zulus had disappeared, but the NNC men apparently heard the murmur of men concealed in the grass, and became nervous. The *Natal Mercury*'s special correspondent gave a graphic account of what happened next:

The natives, fearing a trap, did not wish to follow [their officers]; but the officers urged them on, and very soon they found themselves surrounded on three sides – in a regular trap. The native levies, when they saw this, fled; four of them were killed, and their officers not being able to get away so speedily as they did, and probably being more eagerly pursued than their black followers, no fewer than six of them fell victim to the enemy; two horses, six rifles, and their ammunition being taken by the Zulus. One poor fellow, an Englishman, was literally riddled with assegai wounds. The writer of this has a copy of 'Sacred songs and solos, sung by Ira D. Sankey', taken from his pocket. It is saturated with his blood, and has been pierced by an assegai in two places.[9]

The sudden encounter was a dramatic confirmation of the rumours of the previous few days. British scouts had noted that the border regions were denuded of fighting men, and had correctly guessed that King Cetshwayo had mustered his army at oNdini. Yet the king was reluctant to commit himself to all-out war, and it was not until he received news that British troops had actually crossed the border, and were attacking Zulu homesteads, that he began the necessary rituals to prepare the *amabutho* (age-grade regiments) for war. The force was a strong one – some 28,000 men – and it left oNdini on the 17th, the day before Pearson began his march. The main party of the army moved west, to confront the Centre Column, but some 3,500 men under Chief Godide kaNdlela spilt off, and marched south. Some men had, in any case, been ordered to stay in the coastal sector, to watch Pearson's movements but keep out of reach of the British patrols; these were men who lived in the local area, and whose *amakhanda* were situated nearby. By the time Godide had affected a junction with these local troops, the *impi* numbered close to 6,000 men. For several days it had been manoeuvring around Pearson; Godide had expected to find the British closer to the Thukela, and had moved to occupy kwaGingindlovu, but his vanguard had almost blundered into Pearson's foray coming in the opposite direction, and had retired without fighting. The Zulus had moved close to the camp on the kwaSamabela ridge that night, but Godide had been reluctant to attack, believing that the sentries' shouts indicated that the British were prepared for him. Instead, he retired north again, behind the Nyezane heights, hoping to catch Pearson's column on the march. Any chance of this had been ruined by the encounter with the NNC patrol, however, and as soon as the firing began, the *amabutho* concealed behind the hills moved forward to the attack. They deployed in three bodies in the traditional Zulu 'chest and horns' attack formation, the left horn streaming down Wombane, to Pearson's right; the chest moving down the centre spur, along the track itself; and the right horn moving out to occupy the spur to Pearson's left. As soon as the Zulus came into view, streaming rapidly down the slopes, Pearson ordered his men up from the Nyezane Drift, and took possession of a low knoll by the side of the road, half-way up the slope. The Zulu attack was already under-way on Wombane, and Pearson effectively faced his line to his right, along the road, while turning his left flank to secure it against the attack of the Zulu centre, which had moved forward to occupy a deserted *umuzi* (homestead) further up the road.

Battles are confusing and terrifying affairs for those caught up in them, and combatants seldom have a very clear picture of events outside their immediate vicinity; nevertheless, a correspondent with the Victoria Mounted Rifles provided a crisp outline of the fight to the *Natal Mercury*. Like many accounts in the colonial press, it stressed the role played by the local Volunteers and paid little attention to the British regulars:

> . . . over the hills came several thousand blacks, uttering their war-cry, and rushing down on the unfortunate native levies. It was here that the five white men of one company lost their lives. Major Barrow disposed of the force under his command most judiciously, and checked the advance of the enemy. The mounted infantry and hussars took the right of the road, and the Victoria and Stanger squadron the left. The Engineers moved to the right of the mounted infantry, on arriving at the spot. The two corps of the Buffs, the Royal Artillery, and the Naval Brigade, with rocket apparatus, were in the advance of the column, and were soon in action. The first shot was fired about 8 a.m., and by 9 the hottest fire was over, and the kafirs retiring. The blue-jackets plied the bush with rockets; the artillery shelled, and the rattle of the breach-loader was incessant. The knoll occupied by the Royal Artillery, the Naval Brigade, and Buffs was the most exposed position, but was admirably selected, as it commanded the whole battle field. It was at this point that all the casualties, except those of the Native Contingent European officers, and mounted infantry, occurred. The rattle of the breech-loaders was deafening, and volleys swept the ground in front of the Buffs. The mounted infantry behaved well, as did, in fact, all the troops engaged. The mounted volunteers kept up the credit of the colony; the Umvoti Hussars had a hotter corner than the Victoria Squadron, and the latter were ordered to protect a valley on the left of the knoll, and clear the kafirs away from a kraal near the road, where they were swarming in great numbers. This was done very successfully, and with a steady telling fire. The kafirs stood the fire for about three minutes, then made a clear bolt for shelter, leaving many dead around the kraal. The enemy retired, and the troops extended in skirmishing order in pursuit, driving the enemy before them.
>
> The ground was strewn with the dead and severely wounded. Guns of all shapes and patterns were picked up. . . . A loss of 300 is below the real number left by the enemy; over a large breadth of ground the bodies were to be found pretty thickly strewn.[10]

The brunt of the attack had fallen on Pearson's advanced division; the 2nd Division was several miles off to the rear when the fighting began, and although troops were hurried forward to support Pearson, they arrived after the battle was over. To his chagrin, the anonymous writer who styled himself the *Mercury*'s 'own Correspondent', was with the Durban Mounted Rifles, who formed the rearguard of the 2nd Division. Nevertheless, these were sent forward in time for the correspondent to leave a vivid account of how the battle looked at a distance:

> Not an hour and a half later, we, to our surprise and satisfaction combined, heard report after report of cannon shot ahead. The first one or two, it was hazarded, might possibly be blasting explosions; all doubt, however, was soon

set at rest, for some of our fellows distinctly heard the after or second report of explosion which so unmistakably indicates the firing of a shell; and, in addition, a walk to the brow of the hill put several of our men in sight of the scene of the action, the Inyezane river, about five miles ahead, where the smoke from musketry firing in skirmishing order could distinctly be seen.

The Durban Mounted Rifles had already received the order for boot and saddle, and were not long in carrying it out. Our position instead of being in rear of the column changed to the head of the second half of it. Obliged as we were to keep pace with the wagons, it may be easily imagined what a state of impatience we were in, and how, on the qui vive, straining our eyes and ears, and restraining ourselves as we neared the scene of the fight. Now we were in full view; there ahead on the spur of a hill sloping down into the valley of the Inyezane was the artillery in full play; all along the road we had heard shot after shot in quick succession, and now we could distinctly watch the course of the smoking shells, as they flew over the enemy's bush cover and exploded among the trees. Skirmishers, too, peppering away at a terrific rate, a perfect fusillade it seemed to us; infantry firing away, piff-piff, fast and faster still it went, and then a volley and another volley; not much indication of the enemy's whereabouts by return fire, but the proverbial 'thin red line' towards a certain part of the bush told only too well where they were. No sooner had we halted than we observed kafirs – some making away at the top of their speed over distant hills, and others walking slowly in groups, far away from the line of fire; from cover to cover we saw them in fifty and sixty squads. By this time the 99th, or a portion of it to speak correctly, had come up and were thrown out in skirmishing order in the direction of the retreating kafirs, but to no purpose, for they were far off. Cavalry alone would have had a chance of heading them off. We remained at the head of the column. In a little while, 'forward' was given, and we advanced slowly. By this time firing had nearly all ceased and our share of the battle or rather view of it, as the reserve, was over.[11]

The battle of Nyezane was the first pitched fight of the Zulu campaign, and the Colonial Volunteers – almost all of whom had been under fire for the first time – were well pleased with their own performance. Nevertheless, the battle had been a sobering experience; the Zulu position had been well-chosen, and the skill and tanacity with which they stuck to their attack had impressed even the British regulars. They had endured a veritable storm of artillery, rocket and rifle fire, and had their attack been better co-ordinated, Pearson might have been in serious trouble. As it was, only the left horn had deployed properly, racing down Wombane towards the river to cut the column at the drift. They had been driven back by steady fire, while the attack of the chest had been half-hearted, and the right horn had been driven back by a picquet of just eight men. Twelve of Pearson's command had been killed, and twenty more wounded. The Zulu casualties numbered as many as 400, many of them fearfully mutilated by shell-fire, burnt by rocket propellant, or smashed by the heavy-calibre Martini-Henry bullets. Hundreds more had probably been wounded, but had been carried away from the field by their comrades. Once the excitement of the moment wore off, many of the British side, particularly among the part-time soldiers in the Volunteer Corps, found themselves deeply moved by the plight of the Zulu injured and the sight of the dead:

> The Victorian videttes were on the battlefield after the column had passed on, and as they left, many of the wounded asked for water, and to be taken on with the force. They were duly cared for. Many of our men were very kind to the wounded, placing them in the shade of the trees and giving them water. The behaviour of all the troops was everything that could be desired. Regulars and volunteers alike were cool and calm. In skirmishing, when passing the Zulus, the mounted men came upon bodies of the dead and wounded all over the place; in some places in batches of sixes and sevens.[12]

The British casualties were buried in a pit hastily dug beside the road. It was not possible to bury the Zulus: Pearson allowed his men to stand down for two hours to rest, but as the sun grew hotter the proximity of the dead began to be unpleasant, and Pearson was, in any case, keen to continue his advance, to show the Zulus that they had not checked him in any way. At about 10 a.m. the column once more started up the track. As it crested the hill, parties of retreating Zulus could be seen retiring in the distance, several miles away. Nevertheless, when the column camped that night on a ridge beyond the battlefield, the Zulus made no attempt to interfere with it, and the next morning Pearson advanced to Eshowe, and secured his first objective of the campaign.

Arriving so soon after the excitement of battle, the Eshowe mission station struck many observers as an oasis in the wilderness. The buildings, which consisted of a mud-brick church with an iron roof and three thatched outbuildings, had not been touched by the Zulus, and everything seemed just as the missionaries had left it, as the *Mercury*'s correspondent in the Durban Mounted Rifles reported:

> Now something must be said about this place and the peculiar impression it gave one when we came in view of a church, houses, and gardens containing fruit trees of all descriptions. Fancy in the heart of Zululand, on the day after a battle with savages, riding through a garden – laid out grounds, containing splendidly grown orange trees, at least ten or twelve years old, peaches, limes &c., finely grown blue gum tree, clumps of bamboos, granadillas, &c., &c., in fact everything that one would find at a long established place on the Berea! This station, from what I can gather, will be fortified and made a depot; the church is to be made a store. The missionary house is the Colonel's quarters, and the church bell tolls the hours. The column remains here for some days – a week at least I believe – until supplies come up. Wagons left this morning to meet the advancing convoy, which the Alexandra Mounted Rifles are escorting. The Kranskop contingent, under Colonel Durnford, are encamped within view, and will probably join us here to-day.[13]

This last comment was unduly optimistic. As early as 25 January the *Natal Mercury* had published the bald fact that 'A heavy engagement has taken place ten miles from Rorke's Drift with Colonel Durnford's column'.[14] This was the very column which the DMR's optimistic correspondent had claimed was visible from Eshowe. Clearly it was not, for on the 26th the Natal press broke the news that Durnford had been

The ruin of war: the KwaMondi mission station, Eshowe, where Pearson's column was besieged from the end of January to the beginning of April, photographed after it had been evacuated by the British and sacked by the Zulu. (Ian Knight)

seriously defeated just a few hours after Pearson's action at Nyezane. Nevertheless, the full implications of this were lost both throughout the colony and on Pearson's men, since it was generally supposed that Durnford's column had been based at the Middle Drift. The assumption was that the battle had taken place in that vicinity, but that all other columns remained in the field:

> The events of the week fully bear out all that the oldest colonists have said and urged regarding Zulu tactics. In both cases they have attacked what they no doubt deemed the weakest columns. In the case of Colonel PEARSON's column they discovered too late their mistake, and fled. In the case of Colonel DURNFORD's convoy, they probably carried out their favourite methods of getting in the rear or outflanking; and we hope to hear that they also here will find their tactics foiled by the presence in their rear of Lord CHELMSFORD's main army, the two columns under Colonels Glynn and Wood. The first force cannot have been far in advance, and could scarcely fail to give a severe handling to the retiring Zulu army.[15]

On the 26th the news of Durnford's demise reached Eshowe, where the men had been preparing to secure the post as a supply depot. Fatigue parties had been cutting down the missionaries' fruit trees to clear the field of fire, and surrounding the buildings with a ditch and rampart. Pearson expected further orders from Chelmsford before continuing his advance, but the first indication that something was amiss came when some of the Volunteers on vedette duty, who spoke Zulu, claimed to have heard Zulu civilians shouting to one another across the hill-tops that they had won a great victory.

Pearson and his officers dismissed the reports, but that evening a runner arrived with a note from Sir Bartle Frere, who was then in Pietermaritzburg, confirming that Durnford had been killed. The news was disturbing – a defeat at Middle Drift offered the possibility that the border might be open to a Zulu thrust at Pearson's lines of communication – but was hardly devastating. The next day, however, the blow fell in all its horror; a runner brought a bleak despatch from Lord Chelmsford himself.

The news, as all Natal knew by that time, was far worse than Pearson's column had imagined. Durnford had not been defeated in isolation; his column had been moved to support the camp of the Centre Column at Isandlwana Mountain. On 22 January Chelmsford had taken half his force out of the camp to search for the Zulus, and while he was away a concealed Zulu army had attacked and overrun the camp, killing over 1,300 men, Durnford among them. Chelmsford's own command had fallen back to the border in disarray, and the intentions of the victorious Zulu army could only be guessed at. Chelmsford's despatch baldly informed Pearson that he was on his own, that he could not be supported, and that he might expect to be attacked by the full weight of the Zulu army at any time.

The news of Pearson's victory at Nyezane was overshadowed by the bombshell of Isandlwana which reached England before it. As Frere had intended, the British public were not made aware that they were at war with the Zulus until after the fighting began, but no sooner did the news break than they were confronted with the evidence of disaster. This had not been quite what either Frere or Chelmsford had had in mind.

NOTES

1. *Natal Mercury*, Zulu War Supplement, January 1879: reports written on 11 and 12 January 1879 by the editor.
2. Ibid.
3. Ibid.
4. Ibid.: report dated 16 January 1879.
5. Ibid.
6. Ibid.
7. Ibid.: report dated 17 January 1879.
8. *Natal Mercury*, Zulu War Supplement, February 1879: report 'From our Special Correspondent', dated 21 January 1879, sent from Eshowe on 24 January.
9. Ibid.: report dated 22 January 1879, sent from Eshowe on 24 January.
10. Ibid.: report by a member of the Victoria Mounted Rifles, dated 'Umsundusi River, Zulu Country, January 25th 1879'.
11. Ibid.: report 'From our Special Correspondent', dated 'Etshowe, Zululand, 1st Column, January 24th 1879'.
12. Ibid., see note 10.
13. Ibid.: report 'From our own Correspondent', dated 'Schroeder, or Oftebro's Mission Station, Zululand, January 23rd 1879'.
14. *Natal Mercury*, Zulu War Supplement, January 1879: telegraph dated 25 January.
15. Ibid., 25 January 1879.

Disaster

Charles Norris-Newman, the only professional British journalist in Natal at the outbreak of the war, had attached himself to the 3rd Regiment, NNC, which formed part of No. 3 Column, the centre thrust of Lord Chelmsford's three-pronged invasion plan. Norris-Newman had befriended the NNC by accident; on his way to Helpmekaar in the middle of December 1878, he had fallen in with one of its surgeons on the road, and when he arrived at their camp found himself a comfortable billet:

> . . . we were not long before we had quarters assigned to us, and every arrangement made for our comfort that was, under the circumstances, possible. The doctor had a tent to himself, and I shared the Commandant's, who, with his officers, was most anxious that I should remain with them throughout. Being pleased at what I had already seen, and naturally thinking that, wherever there was any fighting, the native regiments would surely be in the van, I promised that I would go with them; only stipulating that I had to ride back to Pieter Maritzburg for my Christmas dinner, and would rejoin them at once. This settled the matter. I sported the red puggaree, joined the senior mess, and in fact soon came to be looked upon as 'one of them'.[1]

The Centre Column assembled on the wet and windy heights overlooking the Mzinyathi Valley at the end of December, and descended to the border crossing at Rorke's Drift in the first week of January. It was marginally the strongest of the offensive columns, consisting of two battalions of infantry – the 1st and 2nd 24th – a battery of artillery, the 3rd NNC, and several of the best-established Volunteer units. It was nominally under the command of Colonel Richard Glyn of the 1/24th, but the presence of Lord Chelmsford himself effectively robbed Glyn of much of his authority. The central Zulu border was a remote spot, unsettled by whites apart from a few farms, and the hamlet of Dundee, thirty miles away to the north. Rorke's Drift was named after an Irish trader, Jim Rorke, who, in the 1840s, had built two thatched buildings beneath a hill which overlooked the best ford into Zululand for miles. For Chelmsford, the position was ideal, since the buildings were perfectly situated to serve as a supply depot, and the old hunters' and traders' track which crossed at the drift led all the way to oNdini. Furthermore, Chief Sihayo's territory lay directly across the river, and afforded Chelmsford the opportunity to make a quick demonstration of British resolve.

Norris-Newman returned from his Christmas dinner to watch the column cross into Zululand. Being further from the metropolitan centres of Colonial Natal, there were no crowds of curious onlookers as there were at the Lower Drift; nevertheless, Norris-Newman was no less impressed with the spectacle of a British army at war:

Reveillé sounded at 2 [a.m.]; tents were struck, and the different regiments in their places to cross at 4.30. The first battalion of the 3rd regt. N.N.C. were ordered to cross the drift itself, which at present is broad and deep, and with a strong current. There was a small island in the centre, which helped to ease the crossing. The entire cavalry brigade, under Lieut.-Colonel Russell, deposited their arms, &c., on the pontoons, and then rode back to follow the 2–3rd N.N.C. at the drift. The 1–24th regt., under Captain [William] Degacher, crossed on one of the ponts, and the 2–24th under Colonel [Henry] Degacher, C.B., on the other; while the 2–3rd N.N.C. crossed at a drift higher up the river. The Artillery, six guns, under Lieut.-Colonel Harness, were in a position of a slight rise in the camp to protect our crossing, and did not follow over until the next day. A thick fog came on just as we were ready to cross. I had previously arranged to accompany the 3rd Regt. N.N.C. throughout the campaign, and so had all along remained with them. This morning I went down to the drift with their column, and with Captain Krohn led the way over, arriving first on the

The gateway into central Zululand: Rorke's Drift on the Mzinyathi, seen from the Zulu bank. Probably photographed in June 1879, this view shows Fort Melvill on the Natal bank and, just visible on the left skyline, the fortified mission station. (Ian Knight)

other side, so that I may say, as far as our column was concerned, I was actually
the first man in Zululand after war was declared, and the troops moved over.

The crossing of the troops was executed under the eye of the General, who
was attended by numerous and brilliant staff, and it was most successfully
carried out; although several minor incidents occurred, neither horse nor man
came to grief. The water was up to the men's necks in places, and ran at the rate
of over six knots an hour; this, with a very stony bottom, will show how
difficult it must have been. . . . The two line regiments crossed alright on the
pontoons, and, with the 3rd N.N.C., took up a position on the opposite side,
ascending the hill in skirmishing order.[2]

The crossing was tense, since it was feared that the Zulus might use the mist to mask
an attack, but when it burnt off mid-morning, the Zulu bank proved to be deserted.
For the remainder of the day, the ponts worked to ferry No. 3 Column's baggage
wagons across the river, and by evening a large tented camp had sprung up on the
Zulu bank. Unlike Pearson, however, Chelmsford was not prepared to bide his time in
careful preparation, and he was no sooner across the river than he gave directions for
part of his force to advance up the road into the Batshe Valley and attack Sihayo's
kwaSokhexe homestead. The force assembled at dawn the next morning; one part of it
– four companies of the 1/24th, both battalions of the NNC, and the mounted troops –
was to attack any of Sihayo's followers who lingered in the Batshe, while the
remainder – the 2/24th – were to sweep through the valley destroying homesteads. For
Norris-Newman, it was a chance to witness the first shots of the war:

We started punctually at five, and rode about six miles with the Carbineers
thrown out in skirmishing order, and videttes on each flank. When we arrived
on the other side of the hill, where it begins to descend into the valley where
Sihayo's kraals are, we heard a war-song being sung, as it seemed by a large
body of men, and we could also distinguish moving forms on the top of the
hills opposite, and also among the rocks up a steep and stony kranz in front.
The lowing of cattle was also distinguishable, and proved to us distinctly that
these men, having doubtless heard of our having captured cattle on the day
previous, had driven their cattle up among the rocks, and established
themselves up there in caves, &c., determined upon resisting. This knowledge
served to redouble both our vigilance and eagerness to get at them. At the
bottom of the valley a small spruit divides it and we were halted on this side
while the General and Colonel Glynn made their observations, and consequent
plan of attack. Some little time elapsed before this was done, and then the
cavalry were first sent over to go round the hill on the right, and try to outflank
those that might escape, and also to get up to the top for the same purpose. The
main attack, made upon the centre of the kranz itself was conducted by the men
of the 3rd N.N.C., led by Commandant Browne, under the command of Major
Black, 2–24th, and four companies of the 1–24th, under Captain Degacher.
This force was immediately extended in line, with orders to advance straight up
that part of the ravine where the Zulus were hidden. This was done steadily,
although great difficulty was found in keeping the line unbroken, owing to the

rough nature of the ground, and several very awkward gullies intervening. As we approached to within about five hundred yards a voice was heard asking 'By whose order the white impi had come there, and whether they were enemies?' To this no answer was given, and we again advanced. Major Black, in the meantime, sent down for orders as to when to open fire. Permission was given to fire only after they first fired upon us. Shortly after, at about 7.30, the first shot was fired from behind a large rock, and injured a kafir belonging to the native contingent. After that a constant fusillade was kept up until the cattle were taken with a rush made by No. 8 company, under Captains Duncombe and Murray, led by Commandant Browne. The kafirs then got desperate and retreated to their covers, pouring a heavy fire from behind rocks. This had the effect of breaking our line, and many of our natives turned and ran. However, owing to the magnificent exertions of the European officers leading the first four columns, and notwithstanding the fact that some of the enemy began to throw down heavy rocks on the advancing men, they succeeded, after a desperate hand-to-hand fight, in shooting nearly twenty men, taking four others prisoners, as well as many women and children. . . . The loss on our side was two natives killed and eighteen wounded. . . .[3]

The action at 'Sihayo's stronghold' was little more than a skirmish, but as far as the British were concerned it was almost completely successful. About thirty Zulus had been killed in all, including one of Sihayo's sons, Mkhumbikazulu, and the rest driven out of a naturally strong position. The 2/24th, arriving after the fighting was over, set fire to kwaSokhexe, and the whole force then marched back to Rorke's Drift in high spirits. Yet the incident was to have unfortunate consequences in two respects. Firstly, although Chelmsford and his staff had been impressed by the courage shown by Sihayo's followers, they concluded that the Zulus were no match for British troops, and this exaggerated a dangerous sense of complacency which was already taking hold within the column. The attack had been deliberately provocative, intended to force Cetshwayo to realize that the British were in earnest, and it certainly did that; when the news reached oNdini, the king summoned his *amabutho*, and led them through the necessary rituals to prepare them for war. Furthermore, the skirmish persuaded the king that the Centre Column was the most aggressive of his enemies, and was a threat which needed to be checked.

If the Centre Column's campaign had begun on a high note, however, it was to be immediately frustrated by the poor weather. The road ahead was little more than a track, and the passage of Chelmsford's baggage wagons soon turned it into a quagmire. An advanced camp was built in the Batshe Valley to cover the operations of fatigue parties who did their best to make the road serviceable, but it was not until 20 January that Chelmsford felt able to advance. Beyond the Batshe the track crossed a stream, the Manzimnyama, then wound up over a neck of land, flanked on one side by a distinctive rocky outcrop known to the Zulus as Isandlwana. Beyond Isandlwana the country opened into a gently undulating plain, and the forward slope of the mountain commanded an open view for several miles towards oNdini. It was on this slope that Chelmsford resolved to establish his next camp, as Norris-Newman recalled:

... about fifty yards to our left rises abruptly the Insandhlwana Mountain, to the height of several hundred feet above the level of the hill we were on. It is entirely unapproachable from the three sides nearest to us, but on the further, viz., that to the north, it slopes more gradually down, and is then connected with the large range of hills on our left with another broad neck of land. We crossed over the bend, then turned sharp to the left, and placed our Camp facing the valley, with the eastern precipitous side of the mountain behind us, leaving about a mile of open country between our left flank and the hills on our left, the right of the camp extending across the neck of land we had just come over, and resting on the base of the small kopje. . . .

The camp was pitched during the afternoon in the following order: – Beginning with the extreme left we had the 2–3rd regiment Natal Native Contingent, 1–3rd Natal Native Contingent, 2–24th, 1–24th, Volunteer Mounted Infantry, and the Natal Mounted Police on the right. The wagons were all placed between the camp and the hill at the back, and behind them, immediately against its base, the headquarters tents were pitched, with their wagons beside them . . . notwithstanding the clear and distinct orders given and published in an official book called 'Regulations for the Field Forces in South Africa', not a single step was taken in any way to defend our new position in case of a night or day attack from the enemy, either by forming the wagons into a laager, or by erecting a shelter-trench around it. . . .[4]

Chelmsford's reluctance to secure the camp seems unpardonably careless with the benefit of hindsight, especially as there were already indications of a Zulu presence in the vicinity. As early as the 19th Chelmsford's spies had brought news that Cetshwayo had despatched his army from oNdini two days before, and that it had marched westwards, towards the Centre Column; given the legendary mobility of the Zulu army, it might already be close by. Nevertheless, at that stage Chelmsford had no reason to fear a Zulu attack; his experience on the Cape frontier had suggested that even the largest of African armies was unwilling to fight regular troops in a pitched battle in the open. Indeed, his greatest worry was that the Zulus would try to avoid a confrontation, and slip past his flank into the rugged Mzinyathi Valley downstream of Rorke's Drift, and thence into Natal. He was quite prepared to take the war to the enemy, to cut them off before they did so; furthermore, he expected to spend no more than a couple of days at Isandlwana, and many of his transport wagons were needed to go back down the road to collect the stockpile of supplies which had been assembled at Rorke's Drift. To entrench Isandlwana seemed unnecessary and impractical.

It was concern about his right flank which prompted Chelmsford's next move. From the foot of the mountain, the view towards oNdini – eastwards – was open for about ten miles. To the left – the north – it was shut in by the escarpment of a plateau, the iNyoni, just a mile away, but the top of the plateau was open enough, and could easily be patrolled. The greatest threat was to the right – the south-west – where the view was blocked by a chain of hills, Hlazakazi and Malakatha, which gave way to wild, broken country leading down to the Mzinyathi. A Zulu force, approaching from oNdini, could slip behind the far end of Malakatha, and strike across the border without Chelmsford even spotting it. On the 20th – the same day that the column arrived at Isandlwana – Chelmsford and his staff rode out to the far end of the Malakatha range, where a stream called the Mangeni had cut a deep gorge. The experience confirmed Chelmsford's impression of the danger from that direction, and he returned to camp to order a strong probe – both battalions of the NNC and most of the mounted men – to be ready to leave Isandlwana first thing on the 21st, to scour through the hills to see if they concealed the approaching *impi*. The reconnaissance was under the command of Major Dartnell of the Natal Mounted Police. Norris-Newman was delighted that the job had fallen to his hosts, the NNC, and he set out on the expedition excited at the prospect of an encounter with the enemy:

> How well I remember that morning, and the dejected aspect of those officers belonging to the four companies N.N.C. detained by duty at the camp! Young Buée, the assistant surgeon, started with us, but his pony went so lame that he was obliged to go back; unhappily, as it turned out afterwards, for he, too, was fated never to leave the camp alive again.[5]

The march was a difficult one, through wild and beautiful country, made mysterious by the absence of any apparent signs of life:

> After a march of three hours, we reached the banks of the Indawene stream, which flows from a kind of precipice waterfall in the middle of the hills, and the valleys on both sides of which are magnificently covered with foliage, dotted through which are kafir kraals and mealie fields. Upon arriving at the stream, the 1–3rd advanced on its left bank, up towards its source, in open skirmishing order; and, although no kafirs were seen, several head of cattle were taken at the second kraal we came to. The 2–3rd kept on the other bank, in the same direction, and when both battalions were a few hundred yards off the waterfall, the first was ordered to right turn, cross the stream, and ascend the steep height on the opposite side, and then proceed on the top of the mountains, right around the edges, keeping parallel with the 2–3rd, which was then wheeled back, and sent in skirmishing order around the base and sides to the right. In going round, we had some very difficult ground to get over, and it seemed to try the powers of the non-coms – who were not mounted – very considerably. In fact, it cannot be disputed for one moment that white men cannot keep up with a kafir in a day's march over stony and hilly country. . . . [6]

Between them, the NNC and mounted Volunteers scouted the Hlazakazi and Malakatha heights thoroughly, and by late afternoon had encountered nothing more than a few civilians, hiding in rocky caves. Then, just as all three groups were about to effect a junction at the far end of the range, the Volunteers ran into a small group of the enemy, who retired before them. The NNC were ordered up in support:

> After much grumbling, for the men were tired and hungry and a long way from home, we marched across the top of Malakatha to the other or north-eastern

edge, and could then see on the next range three miles off, a large body of
kafirs, about 1000, who were massing, and seemed inclined to come down and
attack the cavalry, which had gone down across the valley and were halted about
a mile from them. We waited very patiently and saw a small body of volunteers
detached and gallop up to within about eight hundred yards of them, when
instantly, and with beautiful precision, two companies of the enemy opened out
into skirmishing order, the flanks at a double, and tried to surround the party,
although they did not fire a single gun. Our men, acting up to their instructions
had seen enough, wheeled round, and joined their main body again. The kafirs
did not follow far. As it was now late, nearly six o'clock, Major Dartnell
deemed it advisable not to attack, and came back to us with orders to bivouac
that night where we were, and attack them first thing in the morning.[7]

Chelmsford had intended Dartnell's command to return to Isandlwana before
nightfall, but the encounter, coming so late in the afternoon, presented something of a
quandary. The Zulus had, indeed, been discovered exactly where Chelmsford had
feared they would be, and if they proved to be the vanguard of a larger army, it would
be unwise to allow them to slip away into the darkness. Dartnell sent several
messages back to Isandlwana, and at about 2 a.m. on the 22nd, rather than recall the
probe, Chelmsford gave orders that roughly half his remaining force – the 2/24th
companies and four of the six guns – should be ready to march at first light to
Dartnell's relief. Chelmsford left his baggage at the camp, but took with him his
ambulances; he was expecting to fight. In the camp he left a caretaker force consisting
mostly of the 1/24th, two guns, and elements of the mounted corps and NNC, under
the command of Lieutenant-Colonel Henry Pulleine. At the last moment, Chelmsford
scribbled a note to Durnford, whose column had been moved from the Middle Drift to
Rorke's Drift a few days before, ordering him up to Isandlwana. Once Durnford
arrived, there would be some 1,700 men guarding the camp.
     Out on the Hlazakazi heights, Norris-Newman spent an uncomfortable night, as
the presence of a Zulu force in the darkness made the NNC nervous:

I was trying to sleep in the centre, near the Commandant at the time, and we
were both dozing off, when the first thing I remember was being trod upon by
some horses, when a hoarse shout arose, and several dusky forms naked and
with brandished weapons rushed over me, at which, waxing wroth, and very
naturally supposing the Zulus were come, I [rose] up with my rifle and clubbed
one man down, and then went to try and find my horse, which I did not do for
some time. I was coming back with revolver in hand, prepared for anything,
when I recognized the red strip on some of the men's heads, and then knew they
belonged to the contingent. I had, however, had enough of them that night, and
afterwards went and lay down among the mounted police and carbineers. . . .[8]

Dawn on Wednesday, 22 January 1879, broke with a heavy mist hanging over the
Hlazakazi Hill. As it lifted, Dartnell's command could see the thin lines of
Chelmsford's men marching out on the road from Isandlwana to join them. Yet the
Zulus, who had been so obvious the night before, had disappeared. Chelmsford was

frustrated; the encounter confirmed his preconceived ideas that the Zulus would not dare face the British in the open. In an attempt to discover where they had gone, he organized a sweep through the hills, but while both the NNC and the Volunteers encountered small isolated groups of warriors, there was no sign of the main *impi*. Realizing that his battle would not take place after all, Chelmsford sent a message back to Pulleine ordering him to strike the camp and advance it to join Chelmsford. To this he received an enigmatic reply which suggested that fighting was going on in the vicinity of the camp. At first, neither Chelmsford nor any of the men under his command took this news seriously, but:

> [a]t this juncture one of our mounted natives came galloping down from the opposite ridge, whence the camp could be seen, and reported to a Staff-officer that an attack was being made on the camp, as he had seen heavy firing and heard the big guns. On this being reported to Lord Chelmsford he at once galloped up to the crest of the hill, accompanied by his Staff, and on arrival every field-glass was levelled at the camp. The sun was shining brightly on the white tents, which were plainly visible, but all seemed quiet. No signs of firing, or of an engagement could be seen, and although bodies of men moving about could be distinguished, yet they were not unnaturally supposed to be our own troops. The time was now 1.45 p.m. and not the faintest idea of disaster had occurred to us. It was believed that an attack on the camp had been made and repulsed. . . .[9]

Nevertheless, disturbing reports of enemy action near Isandlwana continued to reach Chelmsford's troops throughout the afternoon, and at last the general decided to return with his staff to the camp to investigate. He was within a few miles of Isandlwana when, as Norris-Newman relates, he met a solitary rider coming in the other direction:

> A mounted man was then seen approaching, and was recognised as Commandant Lonsdale. He brought the dreadful news that having chased a Zulu on horseback, he got separated from his men, and had ridden quietly back to camp, but on arrival there, within about three hundred yards of it (at about 2 p.m.), he had found large bodies of the enemy surrounding it and fighting with our men. He had just time to discover his mistake, turn, and fly for his life, when several bullets were fired at him, and many Zulus started in chase. Owing fortunately, to the stoutness and admirable pluck of his well-known little pony, 'Dot', he was lucky enough to get back to his regiment, which was also marching home in false security and utter ignorance, like the rest of us had been, as to the frightful catastrophe which was occurring not five miles off. It is true that big guns had been heard during the morning, and also the rattle of musketry, but we all thought it was only a small skirmish near the camp. . . .[10]

This was news so shocking that Chelmsford at first refused to believe it. His command was still spread over several miles of country behind him, and it was some hours before they could be reassembled. By the time they set off back on the road to Isandlwana, rumours of a Zulu attack on the camp were rife, and an air of foreboding hung over the command:

> This everyone felt, and our anxiety was again increased this time by sending a small body of mounted men forward to get as close to the camp as they could, who, when they returned, reported that everything was in the hands of the enemy, and that nearly all firing had ceased. This news was hardly believed, and we still hoped that it might not be true, or at any rate, only partially true, and that our men had only fallen back on Rorke's Drift through the superiority of numbers on the part of the enemy. . . .
>
> Upon nearing to within a mile, which brought us close under the rise where the camp was placed, we could see by the shadows against the horizon from the top of the neck of land, where our road ran back to the Bashee Valley, and so on to the drift, that the enemy had dragged a large number of wagons, &c., and placed a sort of barrier against our only road back; and from behind this we could hear the hoarse cries of the enemy, and the clatter of their sticks and assegies against their shields. A halt was made, and four rounds of shrapnel poured into the barricade by the four guns, when another advance was made. In the meantime Major Black had orders to advance ahead and take, at all risks, the kopje on the left of the ridge, which, when done, would enable those holding it to pour in a destructive fire on those on the ridge, and also guard our flank. As the gallant Major moved off in the dark on this errand of almost certain death, I heard him shout out, 'No firing, boys, give them the cold steel,' and well I believe they would have done it. Another short advance, and then the shrapnel dose was repeated, after which we heard no noise whatever. A little further on we began to tumble over dead bodies lying in every direction, and in some places where there was a ditch or any kind of shelter, men were found lying thick, as though they had fought till every cartridge was gone, and had then been surrounded and assegaid. Within a few hundred yards of the top of the ridge, with the grotesque and large shadow of Insandhlwana reared up in front of us, and showing clearly against the sky in the evening light, we heard a ringing British cheer ascend from hundreds of throats, and then knew that Major Black and his men of the 1–24th had got up the kopje without resistance, and that the enemy had retired. . . .[11]

Chelmsford was now in a difficult position. The darkness hid the ruins of the camp, but it was clear that the garrison had been defeated; towards Natal, a glow of fire hung over the border post at Rorke's Drift. He could only guess at the whereabouts of the enemy, and his men were exhausted and hungry. Any further move towards Rorke's Drift could expose them to the risk of attack, and instead Chelmsford ordered them to snatch what rest they could. It was, perhaps, an inevitable decision, but it condemned his men to spend a terrible night amid the horrors of the fresh battlefield:

> Oh! how dreadful to all were those fearful hours which followed when all of us had to wait with what patience we could for daybreak, knowing that we were

James Lloyd's evocative photograph of the Isandlwana battlefield, taken in June 1879, and showing one of the burial details breakfasting on the site. Wagons and debris from the battle are still strewn across the nek in the foreground. (Ian Knight)

standing and lying among the bodies of our own comrades, though how many we little knew then. Many and deep were the sobs which came from the breasts of those who, may be, never sobbed before, at discovering, even in the dim morning light, the bodies of dear friends brutally massacred, stripped of all clothing, disembowelled, and in some cases with their heads cut off. How that night passed, I fancy few of us knew. . . .

At about an hour before daylight I arose, for I had been lying down close to the General and his staff, and went and had a quiet look around me to see for myself the state of affairs, and recognise any bodies that I could. I did this with a strong feeling of duty upon me, as otherwise I could not have got through it. I have seen many battle-fields in Europe and elsewhere, and although on some I have seen thousands lying where I then saw tens, I do not think I ever saw such a sickening sight in all my life. Mixed with the debris of our commissariat wagons, the contents of which, such as flour, sugar, tea, biscuits, mealies, oats, &c., &c., were all scattered about in pure wantonness on the ground; there were also dead horses shot in every position, oxen mutilated, and mules stabbed, while lying thick upon the ground in clumps were bodies of white men with only their boots and shirts on, or perhaps an old pair of trousers or part of their coats with just enough showing to recognise to which branch they belonged. In many cases they lay with sixty to seventy rounds of empty cartridges alongside of them, showing that they had only died after doing their duty. . . .[12]

At dawn the next morning Chelmsford marched his command away from the carnage, back down the road to Rorke's Drift, which they had marched up only a few days before. There were more surprises in store for them along the way:

. . . [as] we got down into the Bashee valley again, we saw in the distance away to our left a returning Zulu impi, numbering some thousands; and, judging from the burning kraals which we saw bordering the river on our side, we judged that they were part of the attacking force which had left the camp and attacked at Rorke's Drift, and after having made a small raid throughout the border, were now returning home. The sight hurried us a little – and although we got onto the hill and the river overlooking the drift, with our late camping ground on the other side, our anxieties were not allayed, because we saw buildings still in flames at Rorke's house. Before getting quite down to the river, I had a good look through my glass, and thought I distinguished figures on the walls or roof of the large building, one of which seemed to be waving a flag. I called the attention of the General to it, and Col. Russell, myself, and some of his mounted infantry crossed the river and galloped up to the house full of speed. Our surprise and delight may be easily imagined when we heard a good English cheer greet us, and upon getting close up saw that the place was surrounded by a barricade of mealies in sacks, with the bodies of numerous Zulus lying around. We quickly dismounted, and when inside learnt, to our great relief, that the little garrison had received warning in time from fugitives from our late camp, and were able to prepare themselves so that they successfully withstood and repulsed, with severe loss to the enemy, a large body of over 4000 kafirs. . . .[13]

Yet if Chelmsford's column was relieved to find that Rorke's Drift had held firm, there was bitter disappointment, too, to find that only a handful of men seemed to have escaped from Isandlwana. Indeed, it was some days before a rough calculation of the losses could be attempted; of the 1,700 men in the camp when the battle began, some 1,300 had been killed, including both Durnford and Pulleine. Most of the survivors were black auxiliary troops who simply scattered to their homes, and only about sixty whites had escaped, most of whom were Colonials. None of the officers of the 24th survived to tell the tale, and the disaster was all the more shocking because it remained incomprehensible. Lord Chelmsford's official despatch, written on 27 January but not published in Britain until the beginning of March, gave a concise outline of the opening stages of the battle, but admitted with stark honesty that he was at a loss to explain what had gone wrong:

On reaching Rorke's Drift I, for the first time, heard some particulars of the attack upon the Isandula camp, and am thus able to furnish the following narrative, the absolute accuracy of which, however, I cannot vouch for:–

Shortly before the arrival of Lieutenant-Colonel Durnford in the camp with his 450 natives information had reached Lieutenant-Colonel Pulleine from the left pickets that a number of Zulus had been seen on that flank. On receiving this information Lieutenant-Colonel Durnford asked Lieutenant-Colonel Pulleine to give him two companies of British infantry, in order that he might move up the heights on the left and attack them. Lieutenant-Colonel Pulleine at once stated that his orders were to defend the camp, and that, without a positive order, he would not allow the companies to leave. Lieutenant-Colonel Durnford took his 450 natives up the heights, and went, so far as I can learn, about five miles from camp, when he found himself in front of a very large army of Zulus. He at once sent back word to Lieutenant-Colonel Pulleine, and with his mounted Basutos retired slowly before the Zulus, who advanced to attack him. The mounted Basutos, I hear from many quarters, behaved remarkably well, and delayed the advance of the enemy for a considerable time. Their ammunition, however, began to grow short, and they were at last obliged to retire quickly on the camp. Being unable to find a fresh supply of ammunition, it appears they disbanded themselves and made the best of their way to the Buffalo [Mzinyathi], where they swam the river and recrossed into Natal, assisting, however, as far as they could, many of our fugitives from the camp to escape. As regards the proceedings of the six companies of British infantry, two guns, and two rocket tubes, the garrison of the camp, I can obtain but little information. . . .[14]

Norris-Newman, desperate to file his report, left Rorke's Drift on the evening of the 23rd, riding hard for Pietermaritzburg. Even then, he found that the news had preceded him, spread by survivors or panic-stricken settlers from the borders. Indeed, Lord Chelmsford himself did not stop long at Rorke's Drift; he paused only to make what remained of his command secure in the ruins of the post there, then rode to Pietermaritzburg to face the political consequences. The British war effort was effectively paralysed, and the shock waves reverberated across southern Africa. The Natal newspapers published the first accounts of Colonial survivors within a few days of the disaster, but while rich in personal detail – particularly of the fugitives' harrowing flight – few were able to explain the central mystery: how a modern European force, well-armed with artillery and breech-loading rifles, had been so comprehensively beaten by an enemy whose principal weapon remained the spear. A court of inquiry was convened at Helpmekaar to provide Chelmsford with just those answers, but the limited evidence from the survivors made it impossible to draw any definite conclusions. The senior surviving regular officer was Captain Edward Essex of the 75th, who was Glyn's transport officer. A private letter written by Essex a few days after the battle, and published in *The Times* in London in March, provided a tantalizing glimpse of the last moments of the command, and a vivid impression of the Zulu attack:

. . . About noon a sergeant came to my tent and told me that firing was to be heard behind the hill where the company of the 1st Battalion 24th had been sent. I had my glasses over my shoulder and thought I might as well take my revolver; but did not trouble to put on my sword, as I thought nothing of the matter and expected to be back in half an hour to complete my letters. I got on my horse and galloped up the hill, passing a company of the 24th on its way to the front and took a message from the officer to the other on the hill. On arriving at the top I saw the company in extended order firing on a long line of Zulus about 800 yards distant. I had been living with the 1st Battalion 24th and knew all their officers very well, and the men knew me. I therefore acted as a company officer, directing the men what to fire at and not to waste their ammunition. The Zulus returned our fire, but it was very wild, and nearly every shot fell short or went over our heads. Their line was about 1,000 yards in extent, but arranged like a horn – that is, very thin and extended on their right, but gradually thickening towards ours.

They did not advance but moved steadily towards our left, each man running from rock to rock, for the ground here was covered in large boulders, with the evident intention of outflanking us. The company of the 24th which I had passed en route took up its position on our left on its arrival and entered into action, as also a body of our natives on the right. I did not notice the latter much, save that they blazed away at an absurd rate. The movement of the Zulus towards our left still continued, and their line, which was now assuming a circular form, appeared to be constantly fed from their left and was increasing in thickness in that direction. They skirmished beautifully, and I saw that very few, considering we had now about 3000 opposed to us, were hit.

About 12.30 the Adjutant of the 1st Battalion 24th arrived on the hill with an order for the line to retire, slowly firing, as another large force had appeared in our rear. I assisted him in calling in the line and went with the two companies down the hill. Arrived at the foot, our natives took position on the right of the 24th, then came Durnford's Basutos. The enemy's left had hitherto been concealed by the hill, but the attack now became developed, and I could see their troops formed a dense black semi-circle, threatening us on both flanks. Their line was constantly fed from the rear of its centre, which seemed to be inexhaustible. Affairs now looked rather serious as our little body appeared altogether insignificant compared with the enormous masses opposed to us. The 24th men, however, were as cheery as possible, making remarks to one another about their shooting, and the enemy opposed to them made little progress; but they were now within 500 yards of our line. The two companies which had been moved from the hill were now getting short of ammunition, so I went to the camp to bring up a fresh supply. I got such men as were not engaged, bandsmen, cooks, &c., to assist me, and sent them up to the line under charge of an officer, and I followed with more ammunition in a mule cart. In loading the latter I helped the Quartermaster of the 2nd Battalion 24th to place the boxes in the cart, and while doing so the poor fellow was shot dead. The enemy's fire was now increasing and I could hear the whiz of bullets all over the place. In passing over the ground between the camp and the 24th, now decreased to about 200 yards, as the retirement had been slowly continued, I noticed that our natives were running away by twos and threes. I looked round and was horrified to see that the enemy had nearly surrounded us and was beginning to fire from the rear, coming up in that direction at a tremendous pace. I galloped off to the centre of the line where our natives were to point this out to Colonel Durnford, and see what could be done. He had, I think, already observed the state of affairs, and was looking very serious. He asked me if I could bring some men to keep the enemy in check in our rear; but hardly had he said this than those natives who had not already stolen off turned round and rushed past us followed by thousands of Zulus, assegais in hand. The right of the 24th was thus turned, and the men became unsteady. A few fixed bayonets, and I heard the officers calling on their men to keep together and be steady. It was, however, no use. In a few seconds the whole field was a rabble and the Zulus were among us. We were driven up through the camp towards the road by which we had arrived, men falling right and left. The road immediately in rear of our camp led across a sort of neck between two hills. By the time we arrived here the retreat had become a stampede, horses, mules, oxen, waggons, all being carried in the same direction.

The worst was yet to come. On gaining the neck, we found the circle our enemy had drawn round us was nearly complete, the only space not yet occupied by them being a rugged and deep water-course to the left of the road. A rush was made to gain this before the enemy, and I gave myself up for lost. I had, thank God, a very good horse and a very sure-footed one, but I saw many poor fellows roll over, their horses tumbling over the rocky ground. It was now a race for dear life. The Zulus kept up with us on both sides, being able to run down the steep rocky ground quite as fast as a horse could travel. I passed our two guns, but one of the officers has since told me they were lost half a minute later. There was no regular road, but we followed our own Caffres, who we felt sure would know some path leading to the river. It was an awful ride of ten miles, and I cannot describe the terrible scenes I witnessed further than to say that the Zulus take no prisoners, but employ the assegai in every case. At last the river was reached at a point about five miles below Rorke's Drift. There was no ford and many plunged in only to be carried away by the strong stream. I chose what seemed to be the best place for crossing, though there was not much time for deliberation, and luckily passed over in safety, my horse swimming with me in the saddle. . . .[15]

The extent to which Lord Chelmsford had been out-generalled only became clear when the first reports began to trickle through from Zulu sources. Chelmsford had, indeed, guessed correctly that a Zulu *impi* was in the vicinity of Isandlwana on the 21st, but the elements Dartnell had encountered that evening were merely local groups making their way to join the main army, which had already moved across Chelmsford's front. When the general set out on the morning of the 22nd, a force of between 20,000 and 25,000 warriors was already bivouacked in a valley about five miles beyond the iNyoni hills to the north of Isandlwana. Chelmsford had effectively been outflanked, and although the Zulus had not intended to attack the camp on the 22nd, their foragers had been spotted by Pulleine's scouts. When Durnford had arrived in the camp later that morning, he had determined to sweep the hills, and some of his men had blundered straight into the concealed *impi*. An account by an anonymous 'Zulu deserter' described the spontaneous attack which then developed:

On the 21st, keeping away to the eastward, we occupied a valley running north and south under the spurs of the Nqutu Hill, which concealed the Sandhlwana Hill, distant from us by about four miles, and nearly due west of our encampment. We had been well fed during the whole march, our scouts driving in herds of cattle and goats, and on this evening we lit our camp fires as usual. Our scouts also reported to us that they had seen the videttes of the English force at sunset, on some hills west-south-west of us.

Our order of encampment on the 21st January was as follows:– On the extreme right were the Nodwengu, Nokenke [uNokhenke] and Umcityo [uMcijo]; the centre was formed by the Nkobamakosi and Mbonambi; and the left of the Undi corps and the Udhloko [uDloko] regiments. On the morning of the 22nd January there was no intention whatever of making an attack, on acount of a superstition regarding the state of the moon, and we were sitting resting, when firing was heard to our right (the narrator was in the Nokenke regiment), which we at first imagined was the Nkobamakosi [iNgobamakhosi] engaged, and we armed and ran forward in the direction of the sound. We were, however, soon told it was the white troops fighting with Matyana's [Matshana] people some ten miles away to our left front, and returned to our original position. Just after we had sat down again a small herd of cattle came past our line from our right, being driven by some of our scouts, and just [when] they were opposite the Umcityu regiment a body of mounted men appeared on the hill to the west, galloping up, evidently trying to cut them off. When several hundred yards off they saw the Umcityu [and] dismounting . . . fired one volley at them and then retired. The Umcityu at once jumped up and charged, an example which was taken up by the Nokenke and Nodwengu on their right, and the Nkobamakosi and Mbonambi on their left, while the Undi corps and the Udhloko formed a circle (as is customary in Zulu warfare) and remained where they were. With the latter were the two commanding officers, Mavumingwani [Mavumengwana] and Tyingwayo [Ntshingwayo], and several of the king's brothers, and after a short pause they bore away to the north-west, and keeping on the northern side of Sandhlwana, performed a turning movement on the right, without any opposition from the whites, who, from the nature of the ground, could not see them. Thus the original Zulu left became the extreme right, while their right became the centre, and the centre the left. The two regiments which formed the latter, the Nkobamakosi and Mbonambi, made a turning movement along the front of the camp, towards the English right; but became engaged long before they could accomplish it, and a battalion of the Nkobamakosi was repulsed, and had to retire until reinforced by the other battalion, while the Mbonambi suffered very severely from the artillery fire. Meanwhile the centre, consisting of the Umcityu on the left and the Nokenke and Nodwengu higher up to the right, under the hill, were making a direct attack on the left of the camp. The Umcityu suffered very severely both from artillery and musketry fire; the Nokenke from musketry alone, whilst the Nodwengu lost least. When we at last carried the camp our regiments became mixed up; a portion pursued the fugitives down the Buffalo, and the remainder plundered the camp, while the Undi and Udhloko regiments made the best of their way to Rorke's Drift to plunder the post there, in which they failed, and lost very heavily, after fighting all the afternoon and night. We stripped the dead in the camp of all their clothes, and plundered everything we could find, many of the men getting drunk, and then towards sunset we moved back towards our halting ground of the night before. . . .[16]

In the aftermath of the disaster, the stand at Rorke's Drift achieved an immense symbolic significance for the British. It was widely believed that it had saved Natal from invasion – although Zulu sources suggest that this was never intended – but, more importantly, it demonstrated that British soldiers could still hold their ground, even against overwhelming odds. Although the battle was of no great strategic importance, it restored something of the prestige that had been so badly tarnished earlier in the day, and it allowed the British to snatch a vestige of victory from what was, in reality, a very serious reverse. The garrison at Rorke's Drift had consisted of little more than 130 men, mostly of B Company, 2/24th, under the command of Lieutenant Gonville Bromhead. The post held a small medical and commissariat detachment, and the senior officer was a Royal Engineer, Lieutenant John Chard, who had been supervising repairs on the pont, where Norris-Newman had seen the column cross into Zululand just eleven days before. When survivors from Isandlwana brought the first news of the disaster, the garrison made a makeshift

Rorke's Drift, from the foot of Shiyane Hill, towards the end of the war. In the centre of the complex stands the old storehouse; the ruins of the hospital have been pulled down, and the post surrounded by a loop-holed wall. (Ian Knight)

barricade round the post using the sacks of mealies and biscuit-boxes which had been stockpiled ready to send forward to the main column. The defences had scarcely been completed when, at about 4.30 p.m., the Zulus arrived. One of the earliest accounts of the action, by an anonymous eye-witness, appeared in the *Times of Natal* on 5 February:

> Soon after luncheon I took my binocular glasses and went up a very big hill, and then I heard firing in earnest, and saw crowds of kafirs around the distant camp, and coming towards us. I thought they were our native allies, and the more so because I saw some knots of horsemen in uniform galloping in the same direction. I saw several minor battles, the natives driving everything before them. When they got to the foot of the hill, I found I could scarcely realise the fact, that they were Zulus. Down the hill I went, to warn the little garrison, and found them hastily constructing a barricade of sacks of grain round the house (used as a hospital) and the store-house close by, but within twenty minutes the enemy appeared round the hill, and opened fire upon us. While half the men returned the fire, the rest went on dragging about large boxes of biscuits, and forming a barrier across our oblong enclosure, dividing it in half, in case of losing any position. There were about ninety-five able-bodied men, and 35 in hospital, a doctor and a parson. It was four in the afternoon. In about twenty minutes they were crowding in on our left, within 200 yards, and then they made a rush, came on in a dense mass, and swarmed over the parapet. Driven from this end, our men took up their position behind the biscuit boxes and mowed them down; but they got behind shelter from the barricade that we had lost, and our men began to fall. Between 7 and 8 p.m. the brutes set the hospital on fire; and by the light of the burning pile, our defenders kept up the deadly fire, but had to use great care, as our supply of ammunition was getting low. Then the house burned out, and on past midnight they rushed upon us with their hideous yells, and fired from caves and rocks upon the hills above our position. The firing was kept up all night, desultory at times, and then rapid again; and every minute we expected some rush to storm our position. But daylight dawned at last, and at about 5.15 a.m. the last shots were fired, and our enemies were gone. We do not know how many wounded or dead were carried off the field, but we found about 200 dead bodies. Our own loss was 17 killed and 12 wounded. The determined and successful resistance which, by God's help, we were able to make seems to have surprised them; and, although we have been on the alert day and night since (and reinforcements of 500 men have arrived), no fresh attempt has been made by them; but, terrible to relate, the column on that day met with fatal disaster, and it was a mighty wave of victorious barbarity which was checked by our little band.[17]

In due course the stand at Rorke's Drift would be recognized by the award of no less than eleven Victoria Crosses, a record for a single action. Nevertheless, the fact remained that by the end of January 1879 the main British thrust into Zululand had been repulsed, while Pearson's column had been effectively isolated at Eshowe. Only Colonel Wood's column on the Transvaal border was capable of remaining on the offensive.

NOTES

1. Norris-Newman, *In Zululand With the British*, p. 20.
2. *Natal Mercury*, Zulu War Supplement, January 1879: report 'By our own Special War Correspondent' – Norris-Newman – dated 'Intalala River, by Usirajo's Kraal, Monday, Jan. 13, 1879'.
3. Ibid.
4. Ibid.: report 'From the *Times* War Correspondent', dated 'Pietermaritzburg, Jan. 26th, 1879', and initialled C.L. N-N.
5. Norris-Newman, *In Zululand With the British*, p. 49.
6. *Natal Mercury*, see note 4.
7. Ibid.
8. Ibid.
9. Norris-Newman, *In Zululand With the British*, p. 58.
10. *Natal Mercury*, see note 4.
11. Ibid.
12. Ibid.
13. Ibid.
14. Lord Chelmsford's despatch dated Pietermaritzburg, 27 January, reported in the *Illustrated London News*, 8 March 1879.
15. Private letter by Captain Edward Essex, printed in *The Times*, 12 April 1879.
16. *Natal Mercury*, Zulu War Supplement, February 1879: report of a Zulu deserter supplied 'to our Special War Correspondent'.
17. Private letter published in the *Times of Natal*, 5 February 1879.

Panic

The Isandlwana disaster dislocated Chelmsford's strategy and forced him onto the defensive. To many colonists, Natal now seemed thrown wide open to Zulu invasion. In the general panic they flocked to the government and private laagers, and some even trekked out of Natal to the safety of the Orange Free State. At Pietermaritzburg and Durban there was a hasty improvisation of civil defence, while elsewhere in Natal, even in the southern districts (the length of the colony away from Zululand), there were hurried preparations against a possible onslaught.

In Pietermaritzburg, the capital, dismay and grief greeted word of Isandlwana, to be succeeded by alarm. The authorities issued detailed instructions for defence, and preparations were very soon in hand. The *Natal Witness* on 28 January carried all the details:

> Never in the history of this Colony has there been a period during which so much intense anxiety, excitement, and alarm has been exhibited as during the last few days. . . . By this time nearly everyone in the Colony must have learnt of the terrible tidings that have come to us from over the Tugela, where our own brave Volunteers and the Imperial Troops recently went forth to assert, and it was thought triumphantly to maintain, British supremacy and British honour. . . . Early on Saturday morning [25 January] the excitement commenced. The news in up to that time had had the effect of arousing everyone, and people, in their eagerness to obtain news, devoured the most exaggerated statements with a mixture of avidity and regret. Scarcely any business was transacted; the principal streets were full of groups, discussing the aspects and prospects of the situation. No official report was issued until the afternoon, by which time the excitement had intensified. When the despatch . . . was sent down and posted at the Colonial Office, it only left the minds of people more eager and unsatisfied than ever. Fears began to be expressed that there was something the Government or the authorities desired to keep in reserve, and it was not until His Excellency the High Commissioner personally assured the crowd at the Colonial Office that it was all the news to hand were they satisfied. But not till the evening, however, did the excitement reach its climax, when the list of the missing was published. It was a memorable evening; one that will be remembered for many a long year – not alone by the widow, the fatherless, and those bereft, but by all of us who know what the news meant. The details were brought down from head-quarters by the special correspondent of the *Standard*,

who made his last stage from Greytown in the post-cart, arriving here a little after five o'clock. In a few hours the official list of missing Volunteers and Mounted Police was posted, and the *Times* also published a list of the military missing. The demand for extras was something enormous; up to midnight, and even early next morning, the newspaper offices were besieged for news. Later in the evening telegrams came saying that excitement had been caused at Durban, at Capetown, and at Kimberley, by the news, and also the somewhat assuring news that all available troops would be sent here from the adjoining colony. It can better be imagined than described what effect the news of our losses created: it is unnecessary to attempt it. The City Guard turned out and the Government buildings, where a large quantity of ammunition and some rifles had been stored, was [sic] guarded by a small detachment of the Maritzburg Rifles under Captain Matterson. On Sunday affairs began to assume a slightly different aspect. On the previous day the Government had commenced preparation for the formation of a Block or Laager. This caused an impression that they knew more than had been revealed to the public and the feeling was strengthened by the publication of the memorandum below which had been delivered at all the houses in the City:–

A Few Hints to the Inhabitants of the City, as to what they should do in the possible contingency of being required to go into Laager.

These sites [of buildings designated for defence] have been chosen by Military Officers, as combining a central situation, ample space and covering, and capability for defence each building being supported and flanked by others, and a covert way of communication being all that it is needed to be constructed.

The signal for going into laager will be three guns, fired in quick succession from the Fort. NOTE. – To prevent confusion, all other gun signals from the Fort will cease for the present, except the 8 o'clock gun.

If only three guns are fired they will be meant to convey to the people that from two to three hours will be allowed them for coming into laager, but if a fourth is fired it will mean that they must come in with all possible speed.

It cannot be too strongly impressed upon the inhabitants that excitement and flurry should be avoided and suppressed by all possible means, and this will best be done by looking all contingencies in the face and by making beforehand such simple preparations as may at any moment be needed.

These preparations should include a sufficiency of food (cooked, if possible) to last the family for at least a week. A small supply of linen, two pails (one for water, the other for night-soil), a small broom and a scrubbing-brush, a supply of Condy's fluid or some other disinfectant; a mattress or two, according to the size of the family, and sufficient bedding. A small cooking pot and a few plates and drinking utensils, knives, forks, &c. As all these

Fort Napier, overlooking Pietermaritzburg, the capital of colonial Natal. (Killie Campbell Africana Library)

articles, except the bedding, will go into a small compass, they should be packed every evening ready for instant use. A long strap or cord should be provided for the mattress when rolled up.

All people on going into laager thereby agree to obey the reasonable orders of the Colonial Commandant for the City, or of any person he may depute to represent him in any part of the laager. It will be necessary to enforce the utmost cleanliness and many irksome domestic duties to which they have hitherto been unaccustomed will fall on the inhabitants, but they must make up their minds beforehand to this as being inseparable from the situation; a display of cheerfulness under the novel and trying circumstances will serve much to lighten their difficulties.

C.B.H. Mitchell, Lt.-Col.,
Colonial Commandant,
Pietermaritzburg Borough.

On Sunday morning, however, the preparations for defence commenced and that day will be remembered for a long time. The anxiety of the previous day increased to alarm amongst the more timid, especially the women and children. . . . A small mounted patrol had been raised the day before, and they were continually on the move; wagons with ammunition and stores rattled through the streets; carpenters were noisily at work barricading the windows and open spaces; wells were being sunk in the grounds, and there was generally an aspect directly the reverse of the usual Sabbath calm observable in this City. The Maritzburg Rifles turned out as a fatigue party, and assisted by numerous and willing hands, worked very hard indeed. A large number of convicts were sent down, and with the Chinese carpenters and some other coloured Government labourers, got through a lot of work. All the time people were as anxious as ever for news, and in their eagerness to obtain it, listened to the most unlikely stories. A few people were afraid, a good many were anxious, while the remainder looked upon these precautions with amusement, as being either unnecessary altogether or ill-timed. Special references were made at many of the churches in the prayers and sermons, and what with the continual interchange of opinion and the possibilities and probabilities of the situation, the public pulse beat very high indeed. . . . In the meantime, the defence operations proceeded briskly. . . . During the afternoon and evening a report was spread that the General was returning, and this had a tendency to promote uneasiness. The report was disbelieved by many people, but proved to have foundation in fact, for His Excellency and staff reached Maritzburg during the evening after we believe, a very long ride. Lord Chelmsford . . . came to report and reorganize, and will return in a few days. He reported everything perfectly quiet behind him, and this went far to calm the troubled mind of the public. The preparations, notwithstanding, continued all night. The Rifles were ordered on duty, and the City Guard turned out enthusiastically. Yesterday morning the excitement manifestly subsided and gave way to a feeling of keen interest not unmixed with anxiety in the minds of many.[1]

In Greytown, between Pietermaritzburg and the border (and therefore in more realistic danger of a Zulu raid), the *Natal Witness* correspondent described how the inhabitants actually took to their laager in the early hours of 3 February:

Here we are, safe and sound so far. At midnight a messenger arrived . . . reporting that the Zulus were crossing the Tugela in force. . . . Notice of the threatened inroad was quietly given at every house in the village, and it was satisfactory to find how calmly the state of affairs was taken. No bells rung and no guns fired, but the lanterns flitting about in the darkness showed the warning party busy at work up and down the street. Too much credit cannot be given to the women and children, for, without fuss and bother, they were soon all collected within the Laager walls. Increased confidence was given by our finding the troops, under Major Twentyman, stationed at their various posts so quickly. . . .

No enemy having arrived, we gradually returned to our homes, to make more careful selection of articles for a prolonged stay in the Laager, where we shall most probably have to sleep for several nights now. Wagons were quickly ranged in rows, beds and bedding taken down, and the thousand-and-one arrangements necessary made as speedily as possible, for we don't know when we may see the *impi* appear on the top of our hill. . . .[2]

When, despite widespread apprehensions, a Zulu invasion did not materialize, the flurries of alarm among the settler community soon began to subside, especially since defensive arrangements were increasingly put on a better – if not ideal – footing. The situation as reported during the second week of February in Verulam, eighteen miles north of Durban, was typical:

We are glad to be able to say that the excitement here seems to be gradually subsiding, and many of the outsiders have returned to their homes. The completion of our laager, about which every one seems anxious, is being but slowly proceeded with, and no doubt great blame attaches to some one for the dilatory way in which this work has been carried on for the last two months, still when complete we believe it will be a fine place of defence. We understand that through the kindness of a Durban friend a 4-pounder cannon has been lent for the time to the Defence Committee, of which the guard will no doubt make good use should occasion arise, as they have secured a supply of gunpowder and loopers for that purpose. A feeling of great dissatisfaction is abroad on account of the small supply of guns and ammunition in the magazine. The guns number only a little over a hundred, and should the necessity arise, there can be no doubt that 300 to 400 men, able to use a rifle, would take refuge in the laager. We believe that a guard patrols the village every night, and with the exception of a few croakers, the call of the Commandant for this purpose has been readily responded to. We are told that at a recent meeting of the guard one of its members withdrew his name from the list, in consequence of the disinclination of the officers of the guard to place a sentry over his henroost; his loss has been borne with equanimity.[3]

Regular troops continued to hold major border depots like Rorke's Drift and Fort Pearson, but the Natal Native Contingent also garrisoned various post in the border region. Just south of the Umsinga Magistracy, twenty-five miles down the road from

The civilian laager at Verulam, in Natal's coastal sector. (Ian Knight)

Rorke's Drift, the 2nd Battalion of the 1st Regiment, NNC (originally part of No. 2 Column) took up position on 24 January 1878 on a rocky knoll. There, as the *Natal Witness* war correspondent reported on 7 February, they built a fort named after their commander, Major Harcourt Bengough:

> Since I last wrote, things have been more or less in *statu quo*, which, I need hardly tell you, we are rather pleased at, as it has given us time to strengthen our position. In my last, I have told you we have taken up our position on the top of a small kopje, round which we built a wall breast high, but owing to a good many of our men having deserted, we have since built a Redoubt with two flanking bastions in the centre; this is composed of a plump wall some six feet high, and between three and four feet thick, where we will retire in case of need. I am sorry to say that sickness is beginning to show itself in our camp, and both officers and men are down with dysentery. . . .[4]

The situation was more volatile on the north-western frontier. On the night of 10–11 February Manyonyoba kaMaqondo sallied out from his caves along the steep banks of the Ntombe River to join a war party from Hlobane Mountain, led by Mbilini kaMswati and the abaQulusi *induna* Tola kaDilikana. The objective of the combined force of about 1,500 Zulu was the Christianized Africans (*amakholwa*) and farmworkers of the Ntombe Valley who had close connections with the settlers sheltering in the Luneburg Laager. The indignant *Natal Mercury* correspondent described the ensuing 'massacre':

> I have just time to inform you that a pretty large Zulu force has come across the Pongola and commenced their atrocious barbarities this morning. Three 'brave' Zulu warriors passed by the fort and laager of Luneburg at a very safe distance, because they would have had to encounter 'men'. The savage butchers pounced in thousands down upon single huts and houses of our friendly natives, and executed deeds of cruelty shocking to relate. They murdered old men, about 50 women, and as many helpless little boys and girls. In one place they drew seven little children deliberately into the flames of burning huts, and in another place they showed their bravery and courage by inflicting 35 assegai wounds upon the body of a young woman, about 20 years old. This happened between the hours of three and five a.m. to-day [11 February] and at a distance of from four to seven miles from the laager.
>   The first report was received at the laager, from one who had escaped the frightful massacre, at about four o'clock. Patrols were immediately sent out, and they succeeded in coming up with a lot of about 400 enemies, whom they attacked; killed about 20 and put the rest to flight, recapturing a good deal of stock; but the greater part had already escaped across the Tombe River; and the patrol had strict orders not to go beyond that river. The garrison of Luneburg is but small, and cannot afford to engage in any action beyond the region of the district. Oh! 'A Kingdom for a Horse!' How dreadfully annoying to see the enemy within clinching distance, and yet being unable to clinch him for want of horses! Footmen are excellent behind walls and ditches; but in the open an

European 'voetganger' is simply inferior to the 'noble savage': the assegai in the hand of the Zulu is quite as efficacious as the breech-loader in the hand of the European, because the Zulu makes up by agility and quickness of movement for the difference in the weapons.[5]

The garrison at Luneburg might have been inadequate and insufficiently mounted for offensive operations, but the real danger of Zulu attacks justified its presence and any hardships that had to be endured. It was otherwise for the Natal Mounted Volunteers posted to Fort Pine. Not a Zulu came in sight, and the gross inefficiencies of the Commissariat and Transport Department ensured that they had to endure appalling conditions in the overcrowded fort. Inevitably, as the scandalized *Natal Colonist* correspondent in Newcastle recounted on 12 February, they became quite demoralized:

> Sad accounts come to us of the disgraceful way in which our Volunteers have been treated by the Commissariat and other authorities at Helpmakaar. Soon after the disaster [at Isandlwana] the Newcastle Mounted Rifles and Buffalo Border Guard were ordered away at an hour's notice to garrison Fort Pine, which was about twenty miles off. Tents and provisions were to follow same day. The poor fellows went off in good faith, but for *fourteen days* no supplies of any kind for man nor beast, nor any shelter, was provided! Enduring constant rain, sleeping on the wet ground, starved and dispirited, they waited, begging stray crusts from the Boers in the laager. . . . No wonder sickness broke out. . . . When at length some supplies came, they were accompanied by the astounding and cruel instructions that after ten days the Volunteers must provide for themselves. . . . [T]here are no stores or traders, and the order is simply a piece of impertinent folly.
> . . . The few people left in Newcastle . . . at once put their hands in their pockets . . . and are sending a few supplies; but it is rough, after all our losses by this Imperial and aggressive war to have to feel that our brave defenders are dependent on charity.
> The laager at Fort Pine is an open square, with walls about fourteen feet high, with loop holes. It is entirely filled with Boer wagons and tents; in fact it is a job to get through it from one end to the other, and with such a lot of people, including children of all ages, and every family slaughtering their own meat, etc., you can imagine what a place it is. My informant states that unless sanitary precautions are speedily taken, fever in its worst form will ensue.
> No wonder the Volunteers repent their too ready aid to the Military in crossing the border, and talk of demanding their disbandment, and at all events, will prefer the guard tent to crossing the border again.[6]

If Fort Pine on the border was in no danger from Zulu attack, Durban was even less so. Nevertheless, the townspeople were gripped by panic and clamoured for the town to be entirely encircled by fortifications. Such a scheme was both unnecessary and impracticable, and Major J.W. Huskisson, the Colonial Commandant of Durban Sub-District, held fast to his plan to fortify only certain key buildings. Several vocal

Durbanites did not give up the struggle for bastions and ditches easily, as this report
of a meeting held on 22 February makes plain:

> The Defence Meeting held yesterday at the Rink, under the presidency of the
> Mayor, resulted in the reassertion by an overwhelming majority of the plan of
> defence by trench and barricade as previously demanded. The intensity of the
> interest prevailing on the subject may be conjectured when I tell you that
> between 300 and 400 burgesses found time to attend. . . . [A]fter some little
> skirmishing, Mr. John Millar moved, and Mr. Cato seconded:–

> > This meeting again records the emphatic opinion of the Burgesses that the
> > only sure defence for the security of life and property is by bank and ditch, or
> > other barrier, outside the Town, and that the Government be requested by the
> > Town Council to construct the necessary redoubts, upon sound principles,
> > leaving the Burgesses to connect them with a bank and ditch at the expense of
> > the borough.

> . . . [A]s Government agree to undertake only such works as the Commandant
> deems necessary – we are under martial law already, it would seem! – we can
> guess the result. Meanwhile we are asked by Government to trust our lives and
> property to the protection of a man whose schemes of defence are likely to be
> abandoned, one after the other, as impracticable and inadequate. . . .
> There is really nothing locally transpiring beyond these defence questions,
> which certainly call forth a great deal of argument and feeling. . . .[7]

The invasion scare at its most extreme: the barricade built across the Point at Durban, in the
aftermath of Isandlwana. (Killie Campbell Africana Library).

By contrast, in Estcourt in Colonial Defensive District No. II, the defenders were going sensibly about their business and in considerable contempt (as the *Natal Colonist* correspondent made plain) of the reported doings in Durban:

> We have . . . a very large laager here, containing a blockhouse [Fort Durnford], stables and outbuildings, the whole connected with walls of dry rubble, from eight to nine feet high, all loopholed, as are the buildings. . . . We don't anticipate any attack here, but we are quietly getting ready without any of the excitement and scare which seems to have converted your Durban folks to a set of raving lunatics. . . . Do people really think Ketshwayo is such an arrant fool that he would send any large body of his men all the way to Maritzburg and Durban – with three hostile columns in his own country, and another on the border? Depend upon it, so long as these forces remain where they are, in advance, no Zulu will cross Tugela, except perhaps a few small marauding parties who will never venture beyond a few miles from the river. . . . I consider that all danger from the Zulus to this colony is over for the present, and will continue so, unless we have another fatal blunder, like that of Isandhlwana.[8]

Meanwhile, along the southern Natal border, wrote the *Natal Witness* correspondent on 20 February, there were only the faintest echoes of the war in Zululand. So much for the deep-seated settler fears of a general black uprising being engineered by Cetshwayo and given encouragement by the Zulu victory at Isandlwana:

> Everything very quiet around us and on our southern border. There was a Kafir crossed the river to-day with some cattle which he had bought in Pondoland. He left there on Monday, and had been trading for two months all through the Pondo Country. He says he never saw any Zulus there, and that the Pondos are quiet, and do not even talk about the Zulus. They do not even know about the fighting in Zululand. At any rate, he says he heard nothing about it, and seemed quite surprised when I asked him whether the Pondos were all contented and quiet. . . .[9]

NOTES

1. *Natal Witness*, 28 January 1879.
2. *Natal Witness*, 4 February 1879: Greytown correspondent, Greytown Laager, 3 February 1879.
3. *Natal Mercury*, 12 February 1879: Verulam occasional correspondent.
4. *Natal Witness*, 13 February 1879: war correspondent, Fort Bengough, Umsinga Division, 7 February 1879.
5. *Natal Mercury*, 21 February 1879: Luneburg correspondent, 11 February 1879.
6. *Natal Colonist*, 20 February 1879: Newcastle correspondent, 12 February 1879.
7. *Natal Witness*, 25 February 1879: Durban correspondent, 22 February 1879.
8. *Natal Colonist*, 6 March 1879: Estcourt correspondent.
9. *Natal Witness*, 15 March 1879: *Colonist* correspondent, Southern Border, 20 February 1879.

Recovery

Despite the fears of Natal's settler population, King Cetshwayo's army did not cross the border in February 1879. The reasons for this were partly political, and partly pragmatic. The king, in consultation with his *ibandla*, the council of important men who, together, constituted the government of the kingdom, had decided to wage a purely defensive war. The Zulu kingdom had regarded the British as allies since the first British adventurers had arrived in Natal in King Shaka's time, but circumstances had changed with bewildering speed since the annexation of the Transvaal, and the king felt that he had been unjustly attacked. He had resolved to fight in defence of Zulu territory, but he was reluctant to carry the war into Natal for fear that it would lose him the moral high ground in any subsequent negotiations, and provoke even greater British retribution. Indeed, when the great *impi* had set out in the middle of January to confront Chelmsford's column, the king had given strict instructions that it should not cross the border into Natal; some of the young *amabutho*, who had chased the British survivors right down to the Mzinyathi, had been eager to cross, but had been recalled by their *izinduna* (commanders), who reminded them sternly of the king's orders. The Zulu attack on Rorke's Drift had therefore been carried out in defiance of the king's wishes, and was in fact little more than a border raid, undertaken by *amabutho* who had been held in reserve at Isandlwana, and who had been frustrated by missing out on the action. They had been led by one of the king's junior brothers, Prince Dabulamanzi kaMpande, an aggressive commander who had relied on his prestige and relationship with the king to see him through the consequences of the action. As it was, Dabulamanzi left oNdini under a cloud of royal disapproval when the king discovered the disastrous results of the battle.

There were other more telling reasons, too, why the Zulu army did not take to the field in the aftermath of Isandlwana. The Natal press was almost entirely reliant on rumour and the unreliable reports of captured Zulus for any impression of the situation across the border, but the *Natal Mercury* was surprisingly near the mark when it reported:

> Nothing reaches us as to fresh Zulu movements, but reports continue to come in with regard to the condition of the Zulus, who are described as utterly disheartened by their losses. We may state, on reliable authority, that a Zulu prisoner has informed Sir Theophilus Shepstone that there is nothing but lamentation throughout Zululand, and that several Zulu regiments at once disbanded on returning to the king's kraal, and refused to fight any more. Of

course all these reports must be received with due caution, but taken in
connection with the evident Zulu inaction, they seem to gain probability.[1]

While there was undoubtedly an element of wishful thinking in such reports, it was
nonetheless true that the Zulu army had been almost as paralysed by Isandlwana as
the British. Over 1,000 men had been killed outright in the battle, and as many more
were so badly wounded that their friends and kinsmen carried them to their homes,
only to watch them die from the appalling injuries inflicted by shell-fire, rockets and
heavy-calibre bullets. An unknown number – many hundreds – suffered wounds
from which they would recover only with time. The army was exhausted by the
victory, and after the great post-combat cleansing rituals had been performed at
oNdini, the men simply went home to rest. King Cetshwayo knew that they were in
no fit state to fight, even had he wanted them to, but as the weeks ticked by and the
Zulu army licked its wounds, the British, steadily reinforced from home, grew
stronger, and the king's one chance of seizing the initiative by going on to the
offensive passed. By the end of February, the moment was lost, and with it any real
Zulu hope of winning the war.

When Lord Chelmsford had first ridden back to Pietermaritzburg and passed on
the terrible news of Isandlwana to the home government, he had included a modest
request for reinforcements to replace his losses in the field. If the British government
had been reluctant to undertake armed confrontation with the Zulus, however, it was
not prepared to see Britain's reputation dragged through the mud. Regiments on
garrison duty in the UK were placed on alert for active service, and altogether seven
infantry battalions, two regiments of regular cavalry (the 17th Lancers and King's
Dragoon Guards), and four artillery batteries – including one armed with Gatling
guns – were sent post haste to South Africa. If Chelmsford had begun the war with
insufficient numbers, he would in due course receive an embarrassment of riches.
There was, however, a price to pay, for Chelmsford's original army had consisted
largely of seasoned veterans of the Cape frontier wars, who were used to Africa and
Africans; many of the reinforcements had been hastily brought up to strength by raw
recruits, who had scarcely completed their training, were unaccustomed to the
extreme weather of the Zululand summer, and were prey to the horror stories which
circulated in Natal in the aftermath of Isandlwana, with inevitable consequences to
their collective morale. Nevertheless, the spectacle of fresh troops arriving at Durban
provided a welcome tonic to the over-stretched nerves of the settlers, as the *Natal
Mercury* reported when the first infantry battalion, the 91st (Princess Louise's
Argyllshire) Highlanders, arrived in fine style on 17 March:

A large number of patriotic Scotsmen assembled on the wharf to see the men
land. The first lot came ashore soon after seven o'clock. The total number was
180, and amongst them were the pioneers. The troops were drawn up in line,
and were soon on the march to town, the pipers, who, of course, wore Highland
costume, playing some lively airs upon their bagpipes. . . . As they marched up
the Point road they were welcomed by the residents, who rushed to their doors,
and in many cases, heartily cheered the new arrivals. The scene was a most
interesting one, the troops being followed by a large crowd of townspeople both

on foot and on horseback. . . . The 91st will probably leave for the Lower Tugela on Wednesday.[2]

Throughout the second half of March the reinforcements streamed into Durban, allowing Chelmsford to take stock of the situation. His first priority was the relief of Pearson's column which had been bottled up at Eshowe since the first news of Isandlwana at the end of January. Both the 91st Highlanders and the 3/60th Rifles, six companies of which arrived at Durban on 20 March, were moved up to the Lower Thukela, where Chelmsford was assembling a relief column. Nevertheless, it took time to make the necessary preparations, especially in the cautious climate that prevailed after Isandlwana, and it was not until the very end of the month that Chelmsford was ready to make his move. The Zulus had established a loose cordon around Eshowe long before, cutting Pearson's communications with the Thukela, and his men had effectively been under siege for more than two months. On 28 January, Pearson had reduced his command in the hope of making his supplies last longer, sending Barrow's mounted men and the NNC back to the Thukela, but although their fortifications were sufficient to dissuade the Zulus from attempting an outright attack, life for the remaining garrison had nonetheless become both dangerous and uncomfortable in the cramped and insanitary camp. The grim realities of Pearson's position at Eshowe are evident despite the cheery tone of a report written by one of his officers, and published in the *Natal Mercury*:

We were roused at half-past five, sharp, and at eight o'clock, sharp, lights were out. For one month we existed very comfortably on full rations, but at the end of that time we were put on short rations, made up as follows: – One and a quarter lbs. trek oxen beef, 6 ozs. meal, 1¾ ozs. sugar, third of an ounce of coffee, one-sixth of an ounce of tea, one-ninth of an ounce of pepper, and a quarter of an ounce of salt. Life of course was very monotonous. The bands of the two regiments played on alternate afternoons and every morning they were to be heard practising outside the entrenchment. The most pleasant part of the day was just after six o'clock when we used to be enlivened in the cool of the evening by the fife and drum band, playing the retreat. The water with which we were supplied was indeed excellent, and the bathing places, I need not say, was [sic] very extensively patronised. The grazing was not nearly sufficient for the cattle, and from the first they must have suffered very much from want of nourishment. You will have heard of the fate of the 1100 head of oxen and the span of donkeys which we sent away from the camp in expectation of their reaching the Lower Tugela. They left us in charge of 19 kafirs; but at the Inyezane they were attacked by a large body of kafirs. The natives in charge of the cattle decamped, and reached the fort in safety, and the enemy got possession of the whole of the cattle, which they drove off. The donkeys were all killed, with the exception of one, and this sagacious animal surprised everybody in camp by returning soon after the kafirs had come back. . . . The sickness in the fort was indeed very distressing. On one occasion, on visiting the hospital, I saw no less than 19 out of the 300 men of the 99th on their backs there. Nearly all these were young men, fresh from England, unaccustomed to a hot climate, and whose experience in matters of warfare had not extended beyond the autumn manoeuvres in their own country. The hospital on this occasion was filled with invalids, and to provide the necessary accommodation several tents had to be pitched outside. These were also filled. . . . We buried altogether 28 men at Etshowe, and one could not help being struck with the simplicity of the graves. The good comrades of the deceased soldiers had done their best to give the last resting places of the poor fellows as becoming an appearance as possible. Small wooden boards took the place of headstones. . . . The first two or three funerals were conducted in accordance with military custom; but sad to say they came so often that it was decided by the Colonel to stop volley firing, and to carry out only the obsequies which are observed in connection with the funerals of civilians. Large quantities of water accumulated in many of the graves long before the bodies, wrapped in flannel, were lowered. The body of one poor fellow, named Lewis, was observed to float before the earth was thrown down. . . .

Private Kent, of the 99th Regiment, [was] sent out on vidette duty in a certain direction. Five armed kafirs suddenly ran out of the bush and attacked Kent. [Two men with him] witnessed the attack, but instead of going to their comrade's assistance they hurried back to the fort to report the occurrence. They were told they should have stood by him and both were made prisoners. A company of the 99th regiment was immediately sent out after Kent, who was found lying dead with seventeen assegai wounds on his body. . . .

Carsons, one of the 99th regiment who volunteered into the mounted infantry, had a narrow escape one day. He was out on vidette duty, and when by himself fifteen kafirs rushed out of the bush and tried to catch hold of the bridle of the horse he was riding. He had the presence of mind to put spurs to his horse and galloped off. As he rode away the kafirs fired on him, and he received five shots, one in the muscle of his arm, two in his thigh, and one in his shoulder blade. Fortunately he had his rifle slung across his shoulder, and the manner in which the weapon was marked by bullets showed it had been the means of saving his life. He galloped into the fort as coolly as possible. . . .[3]

To keep up his men's morale, and in an attempt to seize the initiative, Pearson organized occasional forays against local Zulu settlements. The most daring of these took place on 1 March, and was directed against eSiqwakeni, an *ikhanda* believed to be under the control of Prince Dabulamanzi. The results of this expedition were somewhat mixed, as the same officer recalled:

A force consisting of two companies of the Buffs, a half company of the 99th regiment, the Naval Brigade, the whole of the Engineers, the whole company of the Pioneers, and the Artillery with one seven-pounder, started at a quarter past two one morning . . . with orders to burn Dabulamanzi's kraal. The kraal was understood to be situated about seven miles from the fort. As soon as we got within a mile of the Insquagane, where there were a number of kraals, a kafir rushed out of his hut and spread the alarm that the soldiers were coming. By the time we got down to the stream, all the kafirs had disappeared. The mounted men were sent down to burn the kraals, and they were very soon reduced to ashes. As soon as this had been done, a company of the Engineers, and the gun boys of the Pioneers were sent on to burn Dabulamanzi's kraal, which was situated about a mile a-head. Immense numbers of kafirs were seen on the hills. Colonel Pearson, who was in command, ordered the retreat. Dabulamanzi was distinguished plainly, riding on horseback, and as soon as he saw us advancing, he had ridden over towards the top of a very high hill. As we retreated, the kafirs followed us in bodies. On the way back we burnt three more kraals, and this was done whilst we were being fired upon, but none of the shots hurt us. . . .[4]

Despite such incidents, the truth was that throughout February and March Pearson was effectively neutralized, and the only force in a position to continue offensive operations was Wood's No. 4 Column in the north. Wood had moved his camp to a secure base on Khambula Ridge in the aftermath of Isandlwana, and his cavalry, under the command of Lieutenant-Colonel Redvers Buller, whose energy and courage were legendary, constantly harried the homesteads of Mbilini's followers and the abaQulusi. In the middle of March Wood also brought off the greatest diplomatic coup of the war, when he persuaded an important member of the royal house to abandon his support for the king, and to defect to the British.

Prince Hamu kaNzibe, the Ngenetsheni chief and King Cetshwayo's half-brother, had long had his eyes on the Zulu crown. He had opposed the war with Britain, and had early made known to the invaders his preparedness to collaborate. Early in

Prince Hamu kaNzibe, photographed by James Lloyd. Hamu was the most senior member of the Zulu royal house to defect to the British while hostilities were still in progress. (Ian Knight)

March he finally defected, dealing Zulu morale a heavy blow. Cetshwayo attempted to prevent his escape to Utrecht. The British, after negotiation with the Swazi among whom he had taken refuge, had to send out a patrol to bring him safely in. Once secure in Wood's camp at Khambula, Hamu freely discussed the king's plans with the *Natal Mercury* correspondent while trying at the same time to minimize his own role in the defence of the kingdom:

> Our sixth day of rain closed on Monday morning [10 March]; the camp was in such a state of mud that a move became necessary, so it was moved yesterday to the upper side of the fort, where a separate laager was formed for the oxen under the guns of the camp. Oham [Hamu], with about 150 followers had arrived in camp the night previous, with an escort of 30 of the F.L. Horse, accompanied by the General's interpreter and guide, and this morning 179 more of Oham's people arrived in camp, all armed with guns, assegais, and rifles; some of the latter belong to the 24th, 80th and volunteers, who served with the ill-fated No. 3 column. . . . Oham has conditionally surrendered himself and placed his people under the command of Colonel Wood. In explanation of his conduct for not coming in direct, he says that on the first day appointed he was *en route*, but was interrupted by Umnyamana's people [the Buthelezi], and that it would have been very difficult and risky to attempt to force his way here with the families and cattle of his tribe, as they would have had the force at the Zlobane [Hlobane Mountain] to have encountered; that 2000 of his men are still near their homes, concealed in the caves and forests, therefore he stole out by crossing the Pongolo, below the Zlobane, and on reaching the Swazi border sent a message to Captain McLeod [MacLeod], requesting assistance. . . . Captain McLeod, with two white men, went to meet Oham and bring him to Luneberg, where he was met by the escort and [Colonel Wood's] travelling cart. Oham says that he only sent a few men to join Cetywayo's army, and seven were killed at Isandhlwana, and that the survivors brought back seven guns and three horses as their share of the plunder, which he wishes to restore, and that the Zulu army lost 4040 men. There was still another battalion who has not given in an account of their losses. He does not know what plans Cetywayo has formed since he (Oham) left the King's kraal, further than that Cetywayo is endeavouring to re-organise another strong army, but that he has great difficulty in collecting men enough. It is Colonel Wood's belief that the defection of Oham has influenced Cetywayo in trying to make terms with the General. Colonel Wood's operations have also greatly embarrassed Cetywayo. Oham's warriors will assist in the attack on the Zlobane, and when this obstruction is removed, the rest of their tribe will come on and join this column. The cold wet rains did not prevent our volunteers and Boers from sending out patrols to scour the country. . . .[5]

Further south along the border, British and settler morale was steadily improving. The special war correspondent of the *Times of Natal*, Norris-Newman, made the journey from Greytown to Fort Bengough, garrisoned by the 2nd Battalion NNC, and communicated his finely detailed impressions on 10 March:

Many a change has come o'er the spirit of this road since I came down it last, just after the disaster at Isandhlwana. Even from Maritzburg itself the change is apparent, and when once past Greytown one might as well be in Zululand for all the chance of meeting with company or traffic on the road. Some time ago, in consequence of the scare then prevalent as to the probability of a Zulu inroad, all the drivers and foreloopers of the wagons en route for Rorke's Drift at that time deserted *en masse*, and caused endless trouble, confusion, and expense to the Government in order to straighten things again. To prevent such an event recurring, this road is now closed as far as Government is concerned, and all the wagons, &c., proceed up the main road to Ladysmith, and from thence come through Dundee to Helpmakaar and Rorke's Drift. This state of things, of course, has had necessarily a great effect upon this border road, and it is now simply used by officers and men on leave coming and returning from town. I came the whole way into Greytown without passing a single wagon, and did not even pass any horsemen or foot passengers. The farms all seem deserted – at any rate of their female inhabitants – and the laager at the Umvoti, although now empty, bears traces of recent occupation. . . . On my arrival at Greytown, where I found everything perfectly quiet, I at once proceeded to the laager, and there found a change for the better in the shape of an earthwork, which has been constructed in front of one end of the laager (that facing the north), and surrounded by a deep ditch, thorn and wire entanglements, and in fact all the necessary adjuncts for receiving and treating the wily Zulu with that care and attention which is his due. This earthwork has been constructed entirely by the men of the three companies of the 4th King's Own at present quartered there, and reflects great credit on them, as also on the officer who superintended the erection of the same. The laager itself has been improved by adding another series of sand bags to the height of its original wall. They are also loopholed, and thus give additional opportunity for treating any enemy to a warm and gratuitous reception. During the time not devoted to military duties, the officers of the regiment have gone in for conviviality with the many inhabitants of this pleasant little town; and what with picnics, tea, fights, &c., &c., not only manage to while away the time, but have also succeeded in creating a most favourable impression on the Greytownites of both sexes. . . . We all left Greytown early on Saturday, and after a short stay at Burrups, which is still deserted by its owner and fair ones, reached Mooi River that evening. The roads were in a dreadful state, and the river was simply impassable, owing to the heavy rains, so we crossed in the pont.

Early next morning we started again, and reached Fort Bengough that evening. . . . The kafirs live in one of the end divisions, and the officers in the other, although many of them have nice huts of grass, &c., built on the flat below for the purpose of messing and living in during the day. This must materially assist in keeping the camp healthy. The officers are a very jolly lot of men, and seemed thoroughly inured to the work, while the natives under them are certainly favourable specimens of the race. At the time of the great scare at Helpmakaar two companies deserted, and it speaks well for the officers that these men are now returning of their own accord, in twos and threes, so that in

'Dinner time at Fort Bengough': members of the 2nd Battalion NNC in the fort commanding the plain below Helpmekaar. (Ian Knight)

another week the battalion will have its full complement of 1,000 men again. There are at present 880. Patrols from this force are constantly sent down to the Tugela River, ten miles off, and in many cases have crossed over. Only the other day a small skirmish took place over the river, between some of the enemy and some officers, who managed to shoot a few of them. The great anxiety among the officers of this Battalion seems to be with reference to their future movements, as none of them care to be left behind doing border guard duty, when next we re-enter Zululand. . . .[6]

The British might be beginning to prepare for a renewed offensive against Zululand, but the unburied dead at Isandlwana continued to haunt them. On 14 March a patrol under Major W. Black left Rorke's Drift to reconnoitre the stricken field. A *Natal Witness* correspondent recounted the harrowing experience:

Before us lay the camping ground thickly strewn in many places with the remains of those who fell. Wagons were standing in every direction many of them having been moved a considerable distance from their original positions – some of them stood as they were left when the oxen were outspanned, with the trek-tow and yokes laid out ready to inspan – others again had their dessel-booms broken, but had the motive power been there the greater number of them could have been brought away then and there. All had been emptied of their contents, which were lying thick on the ground. Tinned fish, meat, jam, milk, etc., was there in abundance, but the tins in many cases had been pierced with assegais; letters, papers, and photos, were mixed up with brushes and boots of every description. Saddle bags and saddlery of all sorts were lying about, generally cut pretty well to pieces. Scarcely a square foot of tent canvas was to be seen, and only one waterproof roof wagon cover was left. The stench from the carcasses of horses, mules, oxen, and the remains of the poor fellows who fell was fearful. In most cases we were able to distinguish what branch of the service the latter had belonged to from the uniforms, but they were long past other recognition. I may here state that the birds of prey do not appear to have been at their horrid work inside the actual Camp, but there were undeniable traces of them outside and along the way the fugitives took. After a good look, and having first posted videttes, the whole party dispersed through the Camp, many of us to look for our own property which had been left behind, and others to do the same for their comrades. One of the first things picked up was the sling for the colours of the 24th, but no trace of the missing colours was to be found. Many of us recovered letters and photos, very little the worse for their six weeks' exposure. Some of the regimental books were found, together with a considerable amount of money in cheques, the property of one of the officers. After a considerable time spent in this way we fell in for a ride round previous to our departure. During this ride, we found at some distance from the Camp one of the Royal Artillery gun-carriages, but no trace of the guns was to be seen. As we were quitting the Camp a few shots were fired at us by Zulus on the hill beyond the Camp, but the bullets did not reach to where we were. On leaving, a *détour* was made to the left along the path the fugitives took. Here many more bodies were lying, and the other Royal Artillery gun-carriage, with the horses and harness a little in advance, was discovered, though again no trace of the gun. Our return journey was effected in the same uninterrupted way as the advance, until we were emerging from the Bashee Valley, when six or eight shots were fired at us from the Heights. No damage, however, was done, though we heard two or three bullets whiz over our heads. We arrived back at Camp about 3 p.m., and I must say that some of those who remained in Camp looked considerably relieved and equally pleased to see us again safe and sound.[7]

Only a few days before Black's reconnaissance, disaster once again struck the British who failed to take adequate precautions against a surprise attack. At dawn on 12 March Mbilini and at least 800 of his men fell on the inadequately laagered camp of Captain D. Moriarty and 106 men of the 80th Regiment (Staffordshire Volunteers). Moriarty had been bringing up supplies to Luneburg from Derby when the rain-swollen Ntombe River had forced him to halt at Myer's Drift with 35 men of his force under Lieutenant H.H. Harward already across. Moriarty, 60 men, a civil surgeon, 2 white wagon conductors and 15 black drivers were killed, while the survivors conducted a fighting withdrawal to Luneburg, eventually supported by the men of the garrison under Captain L. Tucker. Mbilini's men, whose losses are unknown, withdrew with all the cattle and most of the ammunition and supplies that had been in the wagons. The *Natal Witness*'s Luneburg correspondent reported on the event three days later, and transmitted the harrowing account of a survivor:

No further details worthy of mention regarding the attack on the wagon laager at the Intombe river have come to light. A small party of mounted men belonging to the 80th Regiment were sent out on the 13th, early in the morning, to scour the country round the scene of the misfortune, and to endeavour to discover any of those missing. They did not return to camp until late at night, having thoroughly searched both banks of the river for several miles, in addition to the mealie fields and long grass; but I regret to state the search was futile. There is a possibility yet that some of the missing have found their way to Derby.

The more the affair is analysed, the more certain it becomes that but for the cool and intrepid behaviour of the thirty-five men on this side of the Intombe, not one single man from the laager could have escaped. These men, after keeping up a continual fire for some time, when they saw their comrades mixed with masses of Zulus, fighting for their lives in the river, and also the rush of 300 or more Zulus some way further up the river to cut them off from Luneburg, then saw that all resistance was at an end. They therefore retired steadily, firing at the Zulus who pursued them with fearful yells and shouts. These men covered the retreat of their twelve comrades who had escaped from the Derby side of the river, who had lost their arms and ammunition while crossing the river, which was ten feet deep.

At Meyer's Mission Station, about half a mile from the Intombe, the men made a stand for some short time, but seeing the Zulus crossing the river in hundreds, and fearing they would be completely surrounded, they very wisely continued their retreat. The Zulus were now on both sides of the enclosed land belonging to the Mission Station, the Luneburg road as it were cutting the Mission Station in two, buildings being on each side of the road. This *ruse* on the part of the enemy allowed the soldiers a few moments start up the road, and as the Zulus came again into the veldt, they (the Zulus) received a volley right and left which checked their advance. The retreat of the soldiers was continued, followed by the enemy, skirmishing, who occasionally closed, evidently with the intention of making a rush, but a volley from the small party of soldiers soon scattered them.

Arriving at the Spruit below Mr. Rabie's farm, more Zulus were seen coming down a hill on the right, plainly with the intention of cutting off our men's retreat. The men, who were now very much exhausted, and were compelled to halt, while halting had several volleys fired at them. They allowed the Zulus to approach within two hundred yards and then fired volley after volley, the Zulus retiring to the hills. The soldiers then continued their retreat to Luneburg almost unmolested, occasional shots being fired at them at long ranges by the enemy.

I was sleeping, as usual fully accoutred; some time during the night I heard a shot, and turned out with all the others to their proper posts. This appeared to be only a false alarm, and then men were dismissed to lie down again. About an hour afterwards I heard another shot, and immediately someone shouted 'Guard turn out.' In a moment I was outside my tent, and then saw the laager completely surrounded, except on the river side, with Zulus, who jumped on the wagons and were immediately afterwards in the laager mixed up with the cattle. All this time, as far as I could see, our men were fighting for their lives, hand to hand with the enemy, who appeared to be there in thousands. Finding all was up, I attempted to get to the river, (although I cannot swim), and, in doing so, had to struggle through cattle and Zulus. Just as I got to the river bank I was wounded in the head with an assegai. It is impossible to describe what I saw. I waded up to my neck in the river, I then threw my rifle away, and stepping in further, was carried down the stream; my feet touched the ground, and being quite under water, thinking I was drowning, I undid my belt; on coming to the surface I found myself close to the opposite bank. I managed to get hold of some grass and pulled myself up to the top of the bank, having swallowed a lot of water, and being exhausted I remained on my hands and knees. A Zulu came at me and attempted to stab me with an assegai, which I caught hold of, the blade cutting me between the finger and thumb; we struggled, and the assegai broke, the blade being left in my hand, with it I stabbed the Zulu, and then fell over the bank into the river where I lay covered with the long grass, my body being covered with water. Presently I heard a voice from the other bank shouting out in very good English 'come out Jack they're all gone.' I was coming out, but seeing a man with a shield I thought all was not right. Soon after this I could hear them going away, and about twenty minutes after they had all gone I heard horsemen approach, and recognising Major Tucker's voice I came out of my concealment.

Mr Archibald, conductor, who was in the wagon laager at the time of attack, states that the men fought bravely, and that the coolness and intrepidity of the men on this (Luneburg) side of the river, was the means of himself as well as many others being saved. . . . Since writing the above, the bodies of Colour-Sergeant Frederick, Private Eli Hawkes, and Private Hy. Smith, have been discovered by a party of the 80th sent out this day [15 March]. The bodies were found in the river, close to the disaster, and were there buried. Privates Tucker, Lodge, and Furness, have also been found in the river. Mr. Whittington, George Campbell, and the driver, were buried at the Intombi [sic]. Thirty-five of the 80th Regiment were buried where they fell at the Intombe [sic] River. Captain Moriarty's body and that of Surgeon Cobbin were brought in and interred in the burial ground at Luneburg.

About three miles from the Intombe River – on the return of the 150 men of the 80th – the bodies of four men of the 80th Regiment were found. These were brought in, and buried in one grave in the burial ground, by torch-light, the scene being very impressive. Major Tucker read the burial service.[8]

Mbilini's successful attack showed that the British had not yet achieved full ascendancy in the Pongola region, despite Wood's widely flung and successful mounted raids. Further south along the border, below the sector where troops were beginning to concentrate for a new offensive, more black levies were raised to reinforce what was in reality the considerably less threatened line near the confluence of the Mzinyathi and Thukela rivers. One of these units was the Weenen Contingent, which was drawn from men of the former 3rd Regiment NNC which had been disbanded after Isandlwana. The Weenen County correspondent of the *Natal Colonist* reflected on their calibre:

On Tuesday, the 8th April, a body of natives were mustered at Estcourt for the purpose of being armed and equipped preparatory to marching to the Umsinga, where they are to form part of a considerable native force collected there for the purpose of guarding the border. . . . [T]he greater part of them have already seen service, having formed part of Lonsdale's Native Contingent, which was attached to Colonel Glyn's column, and many were at the fatal field of Isandhlwana. . . . The men were equipped with blankets, each tribe being supplied with a different colour, and muzzle-loading Enfields were issued to them to the extent of 25 per cent. of their number. . . . The men all went off for the Umsinga in high spirits . . . but they complained bitterly of the way in which they have been previously handled, being placed under officers who knew nothing of their language, drilled from morning to night, and then sent off in small parties to face overwhelming masses of the enemy. The Government has now very wisely consented to let them fight in their own fashion, and under European leaders who know something of their language. . . .

If our natives were only called out tribally, massed in considerable bodies, and allowed to fight in their own fashion, I have no doubt they would give a good account of any body of Zulus of equal numbers they might come across, if only backed up by the presence of mounted European troops, regulars or volunteers.[9]

Strengthening the forces along the border also served Chelmsford's plans for the relief of the beleaguered Eshowe garrison. He intended that while the relief column advanced through Zululand, the troops on the frontier should create a diversion by demonstrating and raiding wherever they could across the Mzinyathi and Thukela. This policy of 'active defence' opened the way for Zulu retaliation, and was consequently opposed by the colonial authorities. The military prevailed, nevertheless, and on 2 and 3 April Major A.C. Twentyman, Commander of the Imperial Forces in District VIII, ordered two minor raids at Middle Drift. A larger one was planned for 14 April. In his report, the *Times of Natal*'s occasional correspondent at Greytown reflected the prevailing negative colonial sentiment concerning cross-border raiding:

A few days ago there was a raid made into the Zulu country from the Middle Drift, near Krantzkop, when a few fowls were captured and two or three kraals destroyed. I am not informed as to whether any shots were exchanged.

Another raid is to be made this morning under command of Captain Cherry, who takes with him about 300 of the Native Contingent and several volunteers from Pot Spruit.

In the first raid they did not proceed far inland, but to-day they propose to proceed to a considerable distance, returning at sun-set with the booty, of course. Now, one can imagine that the first raid should be an unmolested and successful one – a few fowls. But will this second one be so? Had the Zulus their own choice, it strikes me that this is exactly the kind of warfare they would like – the destruction of small raiding parties by the usual surprises and the pressure of overwhelming numbers. . . .

If a couple of thousand men were to cross the adventure would assume a
different aspect; but even then it is no mean question as to whether this would
not result in denuding this side of the border of that protection which is so
manifestly exposed to attacks from the Zulu side. I hope I may be mistaken in
these views, and that if such a raid is to be made, we shall have no one to charge
with a foolhardy madness.[10]

The Imperial troops concentrating for Chelmsford's planned renewed advance were
still far away from any actual hostilities. Camp bazaars, as Dr Glanville described for
the *Graphic*'s readers, became a commonplace:

While the troops . . . were at a standstill waiting for reinforcements, the market
became a familiar sight. Every morning troops of Kaffir women came into the
camps from the neighbouring kraals, bringing with them milk, maas (milk
curded in a calabash), sugar cake, pumpkins, melons, and other vegetables. The
business is conducted in a most orderly manner, the salewomen occupying the
centre of an enclosure, while the buyers take their places outside. The
merchandise is then disposed of according to a fixed tariff laid down by order.[11]

This peaceful introduction to southern Africa was not to last, however; for them, too,
the storm was to break anew.

NOTES

1. *Natal Mercury*, Zulu War Supplement, February 1879, quoting the *Natal Witness*
   of 11 February.
2. *Natal Mercury*, Zulu War Supplement, March 1879: report dated 18 March.
3. *Natal Mercury*, Zulu War Supplement, April 1879: report from 'an officer who
   was with the garrison', published on 19 April.
4. Ibid.
5. *Natal Mercury*, 22 March 1879: Kambula Camp correspondent, 12 March 1879.
6. *Times of Natal*, 12 March 1878: special war correspondent, Fort Bengough,
   10 March 1879.
7. *Natal Witness*, 20 March 1879: correspondent, 15 March 1879.
8. *Natal Witness*, 27 March 1879: Luneburg correspondent: account of a survivor,
   15 March 1879.
9. *Natal Colonist*, 17 April 1879: Weenen County correspondent.
10. *Times of Natal*, 16 April 1879: Greytown occasional correspondent, 14 April
    1879.
11. *Graphic*, 26 April 1879: report by Dr Glanville.

Turning Point

By the end of March 1879 it was clear to both sides that the Anglo-Zulu War was about to enter a new active phase. Lord Chelmsford's army was already heavily reinforced, and Zulu spies noted that a column was assembling on the slopes of Fort Pearson, at the Lower Thukela Drift, evidently with the intention of marching to the relief of Eshowe. The British readiness to renew the conflict was also evident in the increasingly aggressive behaviour of the border garrisons. If King Cetshwayo had failed to follow up the advantages afforded him by the victory of Isandlwana, however, he was not prepared to allow the British to undertake new offensives unchallenged. For the best part of six weeks his warriors had been at their homesteads, recovering from the effects of Isandlwana, but towards the end of the month the king called them up to oNdini once more, and they responded enthusiastically, buoyed up by the belief that they were more than a match for the British redcoats so long as they could catch them in the open. Nevertheless, the king's strategic dilemma remained much the same as it had been in January. If it was clear that a British column was poised to enter Zululand from the south, the king was also under pressure from Mbilini and the abaQulusi chiefs in the north, who had been suffering from Wood's constant raiding. Once again, it seemed that the British threat would come simultaneously from two directions, and the king and his councillors were forced to divide their troops to meet it. One small army was sent to reinforce the warriors who were already investing Eshowe, while the greater part was sent north, to try to neutralize Wood's column.

The British, with their inadequate intelligence services, knew little of the Zulu intentions. Chelmsford's plan was to relieve Eshowe and extricate Pearson's forces, while waiting for the full complement of reinforcements then on the high seas to arrive. Despite King Cetshwayo's diplomatic overtures, neither Frere or Chelmsford ever contemplated a political compromise; it had always been their intention to overthrow the Zulu kingdom by force if necessary, and after Isandlwana they became, if anything, more determined in their resolve. Nevertheless, the easy confidence with which the British began the war gave way in the aftermath of Isandlwana and Ntombe to an extreme caution. Chelmsford fully expected to be attacked en route to Eshowe, and there would be no more indefensible camps and widely scattered firing lines; from now on every camp would be laagered in the Boer style – the wagons run together in a square – and protected by a rampart and trench, and the troops would fight shoulder to shouder. By 25 March the relief column was assembled, and Chelmsford himself rode to the front to take command, but the advance was delayed by the continuing bad weather, and it took several days to ferry the reinforcements across to Fort Tenedos on the Zulu bank. In the meantime, Chelmsford requested the border garrisons and Wood's column to make what diversions they could to try to distract the Zulus.

Wood had, in any case, been contemplating further action since the attack on the 80th convoy at Ntombe on the 12th. Buller's horsemen had scoured the Ntombe Valley in the immediate aftermath of the attack, but had found it largely deserted, and it was apparent that Mbilini had abandoned his stronghold there and retired to his other homestead on the slopes of the Hlobane Mountain to the south. Hlobane, one of a chain of interconnected flat-topped mountain plateaux, was only about twenty miles from Wood's camp at Khambula, and had long been at the heart of the Zulu defence of the northern border. The mountain was about three miles long, with a gently undulating summit cut off by cliffs all round, which were broken by rugged paths in only a handful of places. It was a stronghold of the abaQulusi people, who did not live on the mountain itself, but drove their cattle up to the summit in times of trouble, and blocked off the paths with stone walls. Wood had already fought a number of skirmishes in the region; on each occasion the Zulus had rallied on Hlobane, and Wood had lacked the strength to drive them off. Chelmsford's request to create a diversion therefore seemed a happy coincidence, and Wood therefore resolved to make a demonstration against Hlobane, although he later admitted that he had not been optimistic about the enterprise from the start. His plan was to assault the mountain at either end, using his mounted troops and black auxiliaries, and hopefully catching the abaQulusi in a pincer movement along the summit. In the event, his instincts proved correct: the attack on Hlobane was a disaster. An anonymous participant in the battle gave a remarkably clear account of the confusing and horrifying running fight to the *Natal Mercury*:

> On the 27th [March], a force consisting of detachments of the Frontier Light Horse, Raaf's [sic] Corps, Weatherley's Rangers, Baker's Horse, and the Burgher Force, under their respective Commandants, started from the camp. This force consisted of about 400 horsemen, and the Native Contingent, under Major Leet, 1–13th regt., and Lieut. Williams, 58th regiment. We left camp at 8 a.m., another column consisting of mounted infantry, Kaffrarian Mounted Rifles, under Comdt. Schermbrucker, Wood's mounted irregulars; Colonel Wood and his staff were to leave later; the whole to attack the west point of the mountain, so as to create a diversion.
>
> Colonel Buller's column halted at 12 noon, near the old camp of the 23rd February, on the south side of the Zinguin Neck. Colonel Weatherley, with his corps, arrived half an hour later. At 3 p.m. [we] saddled up, leaving the Rangers as we supposed, also saddling up to follow. As the columns passed the south side of the Zlobane [Hlobane] two shots were fired with an elephant gun from the mountain, and three fires were lit on a shelf of rock near the summit. We passed on out of range of fire, diverging towards the Kukuze valley to mislead the enemy, and halted six miles distant just at sun down, lit fires and cooked coffee and green mealies; but just as the moon set we saddled up and rode in a north-easterly direction. This march was performed in silence, a precaution necessary, as several spies had been seen near our camp before dark.

Commandant Uys acted as guide. At about 10 p.m. we halted in a valley, tying the horses together with their reins in a line, each man lying down in front of his horse, which stood saddled and bridled.

At 1 a.m. a heavy thunderstorm came on, raining very heavily for four hours. At 4 a.m. we silently saddled up and rode on towards the east side of the mountain, which we reached at daybreak. I forgot to include Major Tremlett and the artillery men with rocket tube in the force of the column. As we approached the pass, Commandant Uys, Colonel Buller, Majors Leet and Tremlett taking the lead, the Zulus did not open fire, but allowed us to approach within 500 yards of the top before they did so, then they commenced with volleys from some hundreds of guns. It was a cross fire, but it only killed Lieut. Williams and one horse. Several horses were severely wounded, and a few men slightly, and the mountain was gained; but some severe fighting continued for about another hour, the brunt of it falling on the Light Horse, killing two officers and two troopers. After silencing the fire from the Zulus, who had done this damage, Colonel Buller and Commandant Raaf rode to the westward end of the mountain, where the track divides it. The Zulus had fortified the pass with stone walls, from which they were annoying our rear, where Commandant Uys, with the Burgher force, had attacked. In the meantime, parties of Raaf's, Baker's Horse, and the Burgher Force kept up a hot fire on the Zulus under the krantzes on the north-west side of the mountain, where the Zulu troops had built huts for encampment. These operations occupied us four or five hours; and as Colonel Buller, Commandant Raaf and Commandant Uys returned from silencing the force at the pass, where the enemy only fired occasional shots, a body of Zulus made their appearance on the northern extremity of the mountain, and Colonel Buller rode off to attack them; but before he could get half way he perceived that strong bodies of Zulus were climbing every available baboon path, with the intention of cutting us off from the only two passes by which it was possible to descend. At the same time two large columns were seen approaching along the top of the mountain to the eastward, and another dense black mass of men, the main Zulu army were observed coming on from the southward. Colonel Buller passed us at a gallop, ordering us to ride hard for the pass over the kranz at the neck, the only road open. This pass may well be termed the infernal, or Devil's Pass. The descent is at an angle of ninety degrees, full of huge boulders. How a single horse got down alive is a perfect miracle, more especially when crowded in such a narrow space; but hundreds of men did tumble or roll down without knowing how they got there. Many did not attempt to try to get their horses, but abandoned everything on top, and were saved in the cruppers of those who luckily saved their horses; but the greatest disaster of the day was the loss of Mr. P.L. Uys, who was stabbed by the Zulus while returning up the hill to save one of his sons who was in danger of falling into their hands. Although Colonel Buller, Commandant Raaf, Majors Leet and Tremlett did all that they could to rally sufficient of the fugitives to cover the retreat of those descending, the loss here was seven men.

The other column suffered serious loss of valuable lives, amongst them being Captain the Hon. Ronald Campbell, Lieut. Lloyd, Mr. Chas. Potter, and

Mr. Duncombe; Calverley was also killed. . . . Captain Campbell and Lieutenant Lloyd were buried in a grave dug on the spot, under fire, by the Colonel's mounted escort. Colonel Wood's horse was shot under him, and he had a couple of narrow escapes. Besides, Colonel Weatherley's Rangers missed their road by not up-saddling when the rest of the column did, and the last that was seen of him was when surrounded by the Zulus; he was then seen slashing at his foes with a sword; and of his troop of 52 men, only one officer and seven men escaped destruction. The brave Captain Barton, of the Frontier Light Horse, who had been delegated to perform some duty on the left, is supposed to have fallen into an ambush and was cut off. . . . The loss on the day has been estimated at over one hundred and twenty belonging to the various corps, and the escape of so many is a miracle. . . .[1]

Although Hlobane had been stoutly defended by the abaQulusi and Mbilini's followers, it was the arrival of the main Zulu army which had turned it into a British rout. Wood had been aware when planning the attack of rumours that an army was on its way from oNdini, but had chosen to ignore them; in the event, the army's appearance at the height of the battle was purely coincidental, and in any case only a few elements advanced rapidly enough to join the last of the fighting. Nevertheless, it had effectively trapped Buller's men on the summit, and greatly encouraged the abaQulusi in their attacks. By the end of the day most of the British survivors were scattered across miles of country, with small parties of Zulus in pursuit, while the main Zulu *impi* moved westwards to bivouac for the night, in preparation for an attack on Khambula the next morning.

It is said that the great Napoleon once commented that what he required from his generals first and foremost was luck, and Colonel Henry Evelyn Wood was undoubtedly lucky on 29 March. His attack on Hlobane had been badly conceived, and was to prove the worst disaster of the war after Isandlwana; Wood himself had seen two of his staff, Campbell and Lloyd, killed before his eyes, and had been unnerved by it. Nevertheless, the battle had at least given him due warning of the Zulu presence near his camp, and he spent the early hours of the 29th in careful preparation. The position on Khambula ridge consisted of two wagon-laagers, protected by trenches and ramparts, and a narrow earthwork redoubt. Wood struck the tents and cleared the camp, placed his artillery in an open space between the laagers, stood his men to, and placed open ammunition boxes in close proximity. The Zulu army came into view at about midday, advancing towards the camp. King Cetshwayo had ordered them not to attack the British in defended positions – it was, he said, like attacking wild beasts in their lair – but the temptation proved too much, and as the Zulus drew near, columns swung out to surround the camp on either side in the traditional 'chest and horns' formation. The right horn, attacking from the north, was in position while the rest of the army was still manoeuvring, and Wood seized the opportunity to provoke it into launching an unsupported attack. The battle which followed would prove the most hard-fought of the war so far:

At 1.26 p.m. the first shot was fired (but the Zulus kept up a fusillade as they marched down the road from 3000 to 4000 yards away) by the Horse, which made the Zulus halt and extend into skirmishing order when the Artillery opened on them from the mountain guns at the fort and the four field pieces at the laager, throwing shell at 2500 yards with admirable precision. Our horsemen drew them on, but kept up a retreating fire until the Zulus were within rifle range of the fort and laager. The first shell was fired at 1.45 p.m., and not withstanding the heavy loss of the enemy they pressed forward to surround the laager and take up positions under cover, a dodge they have learned to perfection. While the right wing were keeping us employed on the north-east side of the laager, the left wing were hastening to attack the west and south-west side, and when these had commenced, the two wings were reinforced by the main body, who also advanced to attack the fort and cattle kraals, and before 2 p.m. we were surrounded on all sides. The most desperate attack was made on the cattle kraal; the troops defending it had to retire, and the Zulus took possession of several wagons, from which they returned fire on the laager at short range, and made an attempt to advance on the wagons; but two companies of the 90th regiment made a sortie to drive the Zulus back, and charged them with the bayonet. Here they were exposed to a heavy cross-fire, suffering severely, losing Major Hackett, and Lieut. Bright wounded (the latter since dead), while a sergeant and ten men were killed and wounded. The Zulus made a similar attempt on the south-west corner of the laager, and were driven back at the point of the bayonet by a company of the 1–13th. Both of these sorties were most gallant affairs, and many acts of heroism were performed by several of the officers and men, which no doubt will be mentioned in despatches. Many of our troops were shot in the back by the enemy in the rear while they were firing at the foe in front, for the bullets whizzed across the camp like a perfect hailstorm, killing and wounding several horses near the picket lines. An officer of Raaf's Contingent was killed in the laager, and several of the troops killed and wounded in the fort and laager.

The Zulus would not face the bayonet, and soon, after some charges from the troops, and a few wholesome discharges of canister shot from the cannon, at fifty yards range, the Zulus began to run, and the horsemen and artillery, with one gun, and our Native Contingent, started off in chase, playing fearful havoc amongst them, from 4.45 p.m. until nightfall, when the exhausted state of the horses compelled them to retire. The Zulus were also completely done up; and had there been two more hours of light, and fresh horses, few would have been left to tell the tale of their disaster. The last shot was fired at a quarter past five, but after that great numbers were killed with assegais, the men economising their ammunition.

Prisoners captured say that nine regiments were sent to attack this column. They were 23,000 when they left Ondine, and several others joined on the road, and the lowest estimate would be 25,000 in all. They also say that the day the King sent them away he also sent five regiments to reinforce his army on the coast, and attack Colonel Pearson's column. The loss the army sustained that attacked this camp on the 29th instant cannot be estimated at less than 3000 killed; 1500 lay about the vicinity of the camp, and great numbers have been seen in rivers and ditches at a distance. Over 600 stand of arms have been brought in, and a great number have been kept as trophies by those who fought on the eventful and glorious day – a day of redemption for South Africa.

On Sunday, Monday and Tuesday, fatigue parties with wagons have been fully employed collecting and burying the slain.[2]

As this account suggests, the British pursuit was particularly ferocious. The compassion for wounded Zulus demonstrated at Nyezane had given way to a ruthless desire to avenge Isandlwana and Ntombe, and many of those engaged in the pursuit of Khambula had escaped Hlobane only the day before, and were not inclined to be merciful. Generally, the Natal press were reluctant to report this aspect of the fight, but at the beginning of May the *Natal Mercury* published a letter by a Commandant Schermbrucker which outlined the true extent of the slaughter, with the uneasy proviso that 'Schermbrucker has got a rather energetic way of expressing himself generally':

As soon as we saw them turning their backs, I got all my Kaffrarians rapidly to mount the horses already saddled, and shortly afterwards all the mounted forces in camp were ready, and we raced helter-skelter after the flying Zulus. I took the extreme right, Colonel Buller led the Centre, and Colonel Russell, with the Mounted Infantry, took the left. For fully seven miles I chased two columns of the enemy, who tried to escape over the Umvolozi [Mfolozi], but I came beforehand and pushed them off the road. They fairly ran like bucks; but I was after them like the whirlwind, and shooting incessantly into the thick column, which could not have been less than 5000 strong. They became exhausted, and shooting them down would have taken too much time; so we took the assegais from the dead men, and rushed among the living ones, stabbing them right and left, with fearful revenge for the misfortunes of the 28th inst. No quarter was given.[3]

Indeed, when news of the ruthless nature of the pursuit reached England, in the form of a gloating letter from one of Wood's soldiers, passed on by his family to a local paper, Wood himself was prompted to issue an official denial, as the *Graphic* reported towards the end of the war, under the headline 'Alleged barbarity of British troops':

The Secretary of War has sent to the Aborigines Protection Society a letter from Sir Garnet Wolseley, in which the general refers to a statement of Private John Snook, published in the North Devon Herald to the effect that on the 13th March [sic] the British troops found about 500 wounded Zulus near Kambula Camp begging for mercy, but that 'they got no chance after what they done to our comrades at Isandlwhana'. Brigadier-General Wood reports that there is not a shadow of truth in the statement. He adds:– 'I believe no Zulus have been killed by white men except in action, and, as I rewarded Wood's Irregulars for every live Zulu brought in, I had many saved'. We are glad to read this authoritative denial of the statement, and should not be sorry to hear that Private Snook had been severely punished for thus grossly slandering his comrades.[4]

In the light of other evidence, Wood's disclaimer rings a decidedly hollow note. Whatever the circumstances, the Zulu losses at Khambula were appalling, and the unpleasant duty of cleaning up the battlefield continued for several days. An anonymous correspondent to the *Natal Colonist* left an unusually graphic account of conditions at the camp in the aftermath of the battle:

> There have been so many funerals since the day of the engagement, that it has cast a gloom over every one in camp. They have nearly succeeded in burying the dead in the vicinity of the camp, but I hear there are so many bodies of the fallen Zulus lying about in the veldt at the distance of two-and-a-half miles from camp that it will take a long time to bury all of them. Now and then we get a sniff of the stench wafted towards the camp whenever the breeze blows from that direction. We had a heavy shower of rain yesterday, which was very acceptable, as it washed the brains and pools of blood that were saturating the ground down the hill and ravine, making the air smell a little sweeter.[5]

The battle of Khambula was arguably the turning point of the war. Most of the Zulus present had fought at Isandlwana, and they had attacked Wood confident of success, but after several hours' fighting they had been driven off with heavy losses. Under pressure from the pursuit, the army had disintegrated, the warriors making their way home as best they could, and refusing the urgings of their *izinduna* to keep together and report to the king. Yet, because the battle had taken place a long way from Natal's embryonic communications network, the story did not reach the press for several days, and only appeared at the same time as that of another British victory, which had actually occurred four days later, on 2 April.

On 29 March, Lord Chelmsford had finally begun his march from the Thukela to relive Eshowe. Norris-Newman, who had been observing the arrival of reinforcements at Durban, had ridden up to the Lower Thukela to join the expedition, but found that the news of Isandlwana had brought a host of distinguished British journalists out to South Africa in expectation of a good story, and that most of them had the same idea as he:

> I found that I had been preceded by Mr. Francis of the *Times*, Melton Prior, *Illustrated London News*, Fripp, the *Graphic*, Dormer, *Cape Argus*, and Mr. W. Peace, who represented the *Daily Telegraph* until the arrival of Mr. P. Robinson from Afghanistan. Other English, Colonial, and Provincial papers were also represented. Some of them, however, did not accompany us beyond the Tugela.[6]

Curiously, Melton Prior was among those who remained behind. The most celebrated 'special artist' of his day, a veteran of the Asante, Balkan and Cape Frontier campaigns, Prior had a premonition on the eve of the expedition's departure:

> I am now going to mention a subject of which I am not particularly proud. I had been through several campaigns, some of them very disagreeable ones. I had run many risks and fear had never entered my mind, but unfortunately, on my journey out on this occasion, I had a bad dream. I call it a dream, but I think it must have been a nightmare. It took place after I had arrived at Durban.
>
> Now this nightmare had such an effect on me that I have never forgotten it. I dreamed that I went out with the relieving force to rescue Colonel Pearson at Etchowe. I saw myself shot, and I saw myself buried.

Strange to say, by the next mail arriving from England I received a letter from my mother, in which she told me she had had a dream that I had gone with the relieving column to Etchowe, that I had been killed, and that she had seen my funeral, and she wound up by begging me most earnestly not to go with that column, and it is now that I am ashamed to own that this had such an effect on me that I made up my mind I would not go, and even wrote to Mr William Ingram at my office to inform him of my determination. Some weeks later I received a cablegram from him: 'Sorry you did not accompany force, no doubt saved for better things to come.'

However, I did not wish the *Illustrated* to be unrepresented in this expedition, and I succeeded in enlisting the services of Colonel Crealock, the Chief of Staff, and also engaged the services of a private individual named Porter.

Now comes the curious incident of this act of mine. When the fighting did take place, at Ginghilovo [Gingindlovu], on the road to Etchowe, my specially appointed artist was one of the first killed. . . .[7]

Chelmsford's advance was made in the face of the usual appalling weather. To reduce the transport train, Chelmsford had prohibited tents on the expedition, and the men slept beneath the wagons. The frequent nightly downpours added to their misery, and turned the tracks into muddy quagmires. Each river across the path became a major obstacle, and a good deal of every evening was taken up with the cumbersome duty of arranging the wagons in a laager – and an hour each morning in disentangling them. From the moment the column set off, the troops – most of whom were new to Africa – were tense at the expectation of a Zulu attack. Chelmsford took a route rather more to the east than Pearson's original road, then turned inland towards the Eshowe heights. His progress was all too obvious to the Zulu forces lying in the hills around Eshowe who, reinforced by a contingent from oNdini, moved out to meet him before he could effect a junction with Pearson's troops. A correspondent with the *Natal Mercury* described the progress of the campaign:

The [British] force was represented by nearly every branch of the service, and consisted of the 57th, 60th, 91st and part of the 99th regiments, whose head-quarters were at Etshowe. There were also two companies of the Buffs, whose head-quarters were also at Etshowe. Major Barrow's mounted infantry, the naval Brigade of the Shah, Boadicea, and Tenedos with two guns, two Gatlings, 84 rocket tubes, the 4th and 5th battalions of the Native Contingent, and several mounted irregular corps of natives and colonial horse, made up the whole complement of 6000. The wagon convoy numbered about 120, and was well arranged as to oxen and mules.

A start was made early on Saturday morning at daylight, and the column laagered for the night on the Inyoni River. I must not forget to mention that John Dunn with over a hundred of his best men, accompanied us throughout, and rendered the greatest service. On Sunday we moved on to the Amatikulu, and on Monday to a spot about three miles further on, the passing of the river having taken a long time and detained us, so that a longer trek was impractical. Another move was made on Tuesday, when we arrived at some high hills which border the Inyezane Valley on the south; on one of these, not half a mile from a large military kraal of the enemy [kwaGingindlovu] which had been burnt, a site was selected for our fourth entrenched laager. Up to this time no bodies of the enemy had been seen, but on this day both the mounted patrols and scouts saw a few here and there. News had been received the evening previous that a large force of the enemy was marching down along the border towards us, and an attack might be made at any time. Every arrangement was therefore made, and precautions were doubled, to be prepared at any time, either during the day or the night.

Our now famous camp at Ginginhlovo was constructed with some care, and was 130 yards square. This calculation had been made by the staff as giving plenty of room for 2000 cattle, &c., and two men to each square yard, the natives being placed in position behind them, and between the wagons and the trenches. We had a false alarm at about eight o'clock in the evening, when the men all stood to their arms for some time. After this subsided nothing of interest occurred until daylight, when our mounted natives and scouts went out to begin their usual day's work of scouring the country round about. A little before six, shots were heard down the valley towards the river, and it was seen that a lot of our men were falling back, firing steadily while so doing, and immediately after two large columns of the enemy were seen coming down the Inyezane hills, while one came round the left by the Amatikula bush, and another smaller one from the direction of the old military kraal. In ten minutes' time our laager was completely surrounded, and the attack began. The enemy came up with a rush to within three or four hundred yards of our position, being favoured in many places by the nature of the ground. They then scattered more, and advanced skirmishing, under a hot fire, to about one hundred yards of the laager, all round. Unfortunately there was plenty of long grass and bushes to shelter them, and as they lay down immediately after firing, our men were not able to dislodge them. The engagement now became general, and a heavy fusillade from both sides was kept up for an hour and a half, with slight losses on our side, and doubtful ones on the other.

The Gatlings, both 9-pounder guns and rocket tube, were all in action, and added to the men in the trenches. [S]ome good work was done by men, non-combatants, who had rifles and took up positions on the wagons, picking off kafirs whenever they showed themselves. The General and staff throughout the whole action were constantly round and round the trenches encouraging the men and telling them to fire steadily and low. Lord Chelmsford was not mounted, but his staff were. Colonel Crealock was slightly wounded in the arm, and lost a horse, and Capt. Molyneux had two horses shot under him. Lieut. Milner [Milne] had a bullet through his clothes. At about half-past seven the mounted men and those of the Native Contingent were got ready to charge and drive the enemy from their positions in the grass, and upon a cheer being given, out they went, driving the Zulus before them. In a few cases the enemy when retiring fired upon their pursuers, but as a general rule they fled as fast as they could in all directions, and after being chased four miles, large and disjointed masses of them were seen in the distance, going over the surrounding hills, to our front, left and right. A good many assembled together on some of the hills, and quietly waited to see what followed, but after receiving a few shells amongst them, they cleared out for good. Then commenced the work of scouring the surrounding ground for dead bodies, wounded men, and firearms. Until we had been at this for some time we had no idea what number we had killed; but as 473 were found in heaps within four hundred yards of the laager, we were in hopes that their losses had been pretty severe. This idea was confirmed when three hundred more bodies were also found within a centre of 1000 yards.[8]

Inside the laager, Norris-Newman was in his element. The Victorian war-correspondent made no pretence to the impartiality upon which his modern counterpart places so much emphasis, and Norris-Newman had in any case seen the bodies of friends and acquaintances lying stripped and gutted on the field of Isandlwana. He was as keen as any in Chelmsford's force to exact revenge from the Zulus, and was to play an enthusiastic part in the battle:

> During this time I and a friend of mine named Palmer, who had accompanied the expedition as conductor, with a lot of waggons, had each got a rifle, and were steadily taking pot-shots, at any native who made himself visible, from the top of the waggon, which position gave us great advantage. Palmer (who is a crack shot, having hunted large game in the interior for years) brought several to the ground. One shot in particular was a great success; about a hundred yards off, – straight in front of us, three Zulus had managed to gain the shelter of a thick bush, whose roots formed an impenetrable barrier to even our hot fire, and it was from this bush that the shot was fired which killed poor Johnson [2nd Lt. G.C.J. Johnson, 99th Regt.]. His death was, however, quickly avenged, as we both arranged to wait quietly until the Zulus fired again, and then taking good aim we fired together just as two of them had raised themselves on their knees to get fair aim. The one aimed at by Palmer sprung up high in the air, with outstretched arms, and fell backwards dead, shot clean through the forehead, as we found out afterwards. The one I aimed at was only wounded, but in a little while both he and the third Zulu were killed by some of the 99th. After the battle the three were found close together, and Palmer and I took and divided the trophies of war, including their native dress, arms, and accoutrements; and we keep them yet, as most prized and hardy won trophies.[9]

The British pursuit after Gingindlovu was, perhaps, less severe than at Khambula, but the Zulus nonetheless lost heavily, particularly as they tried to escape across the swollen Nyezane. Here they had to abandon many of their wounded, and most of these were butchered, either by the mounted men or the NNC. Even Norris-Newman was moved by the sight of their losses into an appreciation of their courage, and to investigate their dispositions:

> The crushing nature of their defeat was also evidenced by the fact that during our farther advance to Etshowi and return thence, not a single Zulu was seen, excepting those found at Dabulamanzi's kraal. No praise can be too great for the wonderful pluck displayed by these really splendid savages, in making an attack

by daylight on a laager entrenched and defended by European troops with modern weapons and war appliances. This fully confirmed the opinion I had never failed to express, that they would fight us again and again, no matter how often they were beaten, as soon as any trusted Chief could assemble some thousands of them.

From the prisoners we learnt that the King Cetywayo had sent this Impi down to attack us, under the command of Dabulamanzi and Somayo [Somopho]. It numbered 115 companies, of over 100 men in each, equal to nearly 12,000 fighting men, belonging to five of their best regiments, viz., the Uve, Tulwana, Umcityu [uMcijo], Umbonambi and Ukobamakosi [iNgobamakhosi]. Their object was to prevent the relief of Colonel Pearson, and they had marched for two days without food, until they had arrived at a spot, on the old Inyezane road, about six miles from our laager, and hidden from it by intervening hills. Arriving so late, they had been unable to send out scouts, and were, therefore, ignorant of our strength. Some difference of opinion had arisen among them as to whether the attack should be made at once that (Tuesday) evening; but Dabulamanzi favoured the plan of having food and a night's rest before attacking in the morning; and this was ultimately decided upon, partly on account of our having sent up a rocket signal at 8 p.m. of which they did not understand the meaning. The fighting men belonging to the district in our vicinity were stated to be away in the Engoa [Ngoya] Forest, farther up the coast, together with their women and children.[10]

The rest of that day, 2 April, was spent burying the dead. Chelmsford had decided to take part of his force as a flying column to relieve Eshowe on the 3rd, while the remainder guarded the old laager, which was accordingly reduced in size. The flying column set out the next morning. Eshowe was only fifteen miles away, but it would prove a gruelling march, for the day was hot, and much of the route lay up through steep hills. As they neared their goal, the 'specials' with the column were keen to scoop their rivals and be first into the beleaguered fort, Norris-Newman among them:

It was now about 4.30 p.m., and as we were nearing Etshowi, I rode off to the front to get ahead, and first into the fort, if possible; remembering that Colonel Pearson had made a new road, shortening the way, and avoiding the vicinity of the Hinza [Dlinza] Forest. Profiting by this short cut, I had the pleasure of being the first man of the Column to shake Colonel Pearson by the hand at the relief of Etshowi. Two other 'specials' – Francis, of the *Times*, and Dormer, of the *Cape Argus* – had already left us, and I saw them, racing each other for the honour of being first in, along the broad road, a mile in front. They found out their mistake, when they saw the gallant Colonel at the head of 500 men, coming down by the new road from Etshowi. They then tried to cut across the country to attain their end; but it was too late, and the last I saw of them, on that occasion, was that one was 'bogged', and the other's horse, nearly pumped out, could not be got over a very nasty spruit. Leaving Colonel Pearson to proceed and meet the General and relief column, I galloped on to the fort, where I had a most cordial welcome all round. After exchanging the news, I went out to watch the arrival of our troops, which lasted from 7.30 p.m. till midnight. Colonel Pearson speedily returned to make all necessary arrangements for the encampment of the flying column outside the fort. The scene which occurred as the troops came up, the shouts, cheers, and congratulations on all sides, would beggar description. . . .[11]

Chelmsford had decided to abandon Eshowe, and retire to a secure position close to the border before committing himself to a fresh invasion. The following morning, 4 April, Pearson's force dragged their wagons out of the barricades, where they had been emplaced for over two months, and began to retreat to the Thukela. Before he went, Chelmsford himself was keen to make one last demonstration against the Zulus. Prince Dabulamanzi's personal homestead, eZulwini, was situated only a few miles away, and had escaped Pearson's earlier raids. Early on the 4th Chelmsford set off with a small column to destroy it. Despite the speed of the advance, the Zulus had already abandoned the homestead by the time the British arrived, and Chelmsford's men put it to the torch. A group of Zulus stood watching from a nearby hill-top, and Dabulamanzi was recognized among them; the two sides exchanged a desultory fire, but the range was too great to hit anything. Chelmsford's force returned to Eshowe, and by nightfall the post was deserted. Once the British were safely out of range, the Zulus came down and set fire to the buildings.

The Eshowe expedition had been almost a complete success, but on the return march it was marred by a tragedy which suggested that the troops had not yet overcome their nervousness of the Zulu:

> The General bivouacked on Friday evening near Etshowe Fort, and left early the next day passing Colonel Pearson's column on the road, but just after turning off to the left, so as to reach our laager at Ginginhlovu by a short cut over the Myanzane [Nyezane], lower down. His column was not able to reach the laager the same day, and had again to bivouac out, this time in a very bad place. At about 3.30 on Sunday morning, a picket of the 60th Rifles thought they saw some figures moving about in the dim light, and fired at them. Some of Dunn's scouts who were in front rushed back immediately, and unfortunately the men of the 60th behind the trenches, thinking that their picket was attacked by the enemy, fired into the midst of them, killing one man and wounding five of their own men; also two of Dunn's scouts and six others were wounded. This affair cast a gloom over all, which was not dispelled when the colour-sergeant who had charge of the party was courtmartialled, and sentenced to five years' penal servitude. After this unfortunate contretemps, the General moved his force back to a new position nearer the Amatikulu than our old laager, which was by this time becoming unfit to live in or near. . . .[12]

In many ways the Eshowe expedition marked the true end of the first British invasion of Zululand. Chelmsford had recovered from the shock of Isandlwana, but had effectively been driven from the country: the only British troops inside Zululand were the camp near Gingindlovu and Wood's base at Khambula, both near the border. The Zulus had largely repulsed the British, yet in doing so had suffered body blows which were so serious that they profoundly affected their ability to prolong the resistance. Throughout April and May, while Chelmsford's reinforcements arrived at Durban and marched up to the front, the Zulus recovered at their homesteads from the battles of Khambula and Gingindlovu, twin defeats endured at either end of the country within days of each other. There was a lull in the active pursuit of the war, but even as it lasted, the balance of power shifted significantly in favour of the British.

In the absence of more dramatic news, the colonial press contented themselves with reporting troop movements, speculating on the state of the Zulu kingdom, and in telling a bizarre postscript to the battle of Khambula. The *Times of Natal*'s correspondent with Wood's column sent 'Gossip from Kambula' on 16 April, which included details of the extraordinary – if not entirely credible – adventures of Trooper Ernest Grandier of the Border Horse, who was captured by the Zulus at Hlobane, and would prove the only British prisoner-of-war of the entire campaign:

> I was over at Utrecht on Saturday [12 April] and interviewed Oham, in company with Mr. Nunn, and that fugitive scion of Zulu royalty expressed the opinion that after the repulse here, the Zulus had mostly returned to their kraals, and it would take some time to organise another attack. He was further of opinion that there would not be more than one more big fight; that that would most likely be in the open, when the columns were on the move, and that if the Zulus were then defeated, the war would practically be over. He did not think Cetywayo, however, was likely to surrender; he was too 'proud' for that, and that he would end by becoming a fugitive, unless his own people solved the difficulty by making an end of him.
>
> Colonel Wood, I am sorry to say, is not well; he has been suffering from that common camp complaint diarrhoea, but I have no doubt the skilful treatment he is receiving will soon set matters to rights. Though he would have been better in bed, he yesterday appeared at a general parade in his great coat, to read to the troops a letter of thanks he had just received from Lord Chelmsford, for the successful repulse of the Zulu attack on the camp. . . . Colonel Wood then addressing the force, said he had refrained from thanking them on his own account, on the occasion of receiving a letter of congratulation from Sir Bartle Frere, immediately after the repulse of the Zulus, because of military matters he always waited for the approbation of his military superiors as the highest reward he could receive. He now, however, desired to thank them for what they had done, including Colonel Buller, and all the mounted men, for the operations of the 28th [the repulse on Hlobane]. It was true those operations had not been crowned with success, but that was not owing to any fault of those engaged, unless, it was his fault for not having been able to foresee what could not be foreseen. . . .
>
> We had quite a sensation here this afternoon by the arrival in camp of Mr. Rudolph, landdrost of Utrecht, who had been out scouting on the Zunguin Nek, with five men, where he encountered a party of forty Zulus, killing four and wounding five, and reported that the spoor of a large impi led towards the King's kraal at Ulundi. He brought in with him a poor fellow named Grandier, a Frenchman, who belonged to Weatherley's Troop of Border Horse, and who was made prisoner by the Zulus when so many of his comrades fell. His story, which

The making of an unlikely hero: *The Pictorial World* depicted Ernest Grandier's escape from the Zulus as the triumph of civilization over barbarism. (Rai England Collection)

was told by him in the first instance, to Colonel Wood and his staff, Captain Maude taking official notes, was as follows:– He was one of the very few who succeeded in charging through the mass of Zulus by whom they were beset in front and rear. He had got on to fairly good ground, and had set a comrade on his horse, he running by the side, when a kafir caught him by the leg, and he was immediately overpowered by numbers and made prisoner. His captors took him to Umbeline's kraal, on the south side of the Zlobane, about half-way up. He saw that chief, who asked him where Shepstone was, and who was the commander of the commando to which he belonged. He was kept prisoner that night in a kraal, and sent out the next morning to work in the mealie fields. Soon after he was taken by two or three mounted men to the middle of a big commando, all of whom threatened him with death, while the chief Manymane ordered him to be sent prisoner to Cetywayo. He stopped one day after that at the Zlobane, starting the next day for Ulundi in charge of four men riding, while he was made to walk and carry their provisions. He was quite naked, all his clothes having been taken from him. They took 4 days to make the journey, arriving in the evening, when a messenger was sent forward to announce their coming to the King. He remained all that night and next day tied in a field. On the following day at noon he was taken to Cetywayo, where a half-caste Dutchman, with long hair, translated. Cetywayo asked what the English wanted coming in that way to his country. He asked after Oham, where he was stopping, and said he would kill him and Shepstone and everyone else, as he had plenty of men to do the work. He was very particular to learn the name of the commander of the Kambula column. After replying to these questions Grandier was removed in custody to a kraal where he was threatened and beaten with very little respite, and for four days had nothing but mealies to eat. Some messengers then came and reported to Cetywayo that Umbeline and his brother had been killed in the attack on Colonel Wood's camp. On this Cetywayo ordered Grandier to be sent back to Umbeline's kafirs that they might sacrifice him to the *manes* of their deceased chief. He was sent back next day with a guard of two Zulus, only one of whom had a gun, though plentifully supplied with assegais. On the 13th about noon, they were resting, after a long tramp, and the Zulus being sleepy Grandier watched his opportunity, snatched an assegai and pinned one man to the earth, the other woke up in a fright and ran for his life. Grandier then made off in the direction of the camp, walking all night and steering a course by the stars, when this morning he was seen by Mr. Rudolph's party and brought in, so crippled in the feet that he is at present in hospital. He saw at Ulundi a Portuguese, who makes guns for Cetywayo, and on the morning of the 14th so large a force of kafirs driving cattle passed him that he was obliged to remain hid all the morning to let them pass. This confirms Mr. Rudolph's reports and those of our own cavalry who say that the Zlobane is nearly deserted. It would see from this that the Zulu are concentrating at Ulundi. Grandier reports that the Zulu are saying they are only afraid of Wood's column. They have a good number of Martini's, but he did not see any ammunition, and the two guns captured at Isandhlwana were at the King's kraal, but both were spiked.[13]

NOTES

1. *Natal Mercury*, Zulu War Supplement, April 1879: account 'From our own Correspondent', dated 'Kambula Camp, April 1st, 1879'.
2. Ibid.
3. Ibid.: account credited to the *E.P. Herald*, dated 2 May.
4. *Graphic*, 6 September 1879.
5. *Natal Colonist*, 11 April 1879: correspondent 'with Col. Wood's Column, Camp Kambula, 31st March, 1879'.
6. Norris-Newman, *In Zululand With the British*, p. 130.
7. Melton Prior, *Campaigns of a War Correspondent* (London, 1912), pp. 90–1.
8. *Natal Mercury*, Zulu War Supplement, April 1879: report 'From our own Correspondent', dated 11 April.
9. Norris-Newman, *In Zululand With the British*, p. 139.
10. Ibid.
11. Ibid.
12. *Natal Mercury*: report of 11 April (see note 8).
13. *Natal Witness*, 26 April 1879: *Times of Natal* correspondent with General Wood's column, 16 April 1879.

The Second Invasion

With the arrival of his full complement of reinforcements, Chelmsford was able to put into effect his plan for a new invasion of Zululand. Strategically, it was largely the old plan modified: a new column, basically consisting of Pearson's original column and the Eshowe relief expedition combined, would advance up the coast. This was styled the 1st Division, and was placed under the command of a new arrival, Major-General H.H. Crealock. Crealock's instructions were to destroy two large *amakhanda* (military homesteads) which had hitherto remained unscathed, and to establish a line of fortified supply depots running towards the coast, where it was hoped to establish a landing stage at a point on the open beach known as Port Durnford. A new column, the 2nd Division, was assembled at Dundee, north of Rorke's Drift, and commanded by another newcomer, Major-General E. Newdigate, although Chelmsford intended to accompany this division in person. A cavalry brigade, consisting of the newly arrived 17th Lancers and 1st (King's) Dragoon Guards, was attached to the 2nd Division, under the command of Major-General F. Marshall. The 2nd Division was to cross the Mzinyathi at Landman's Drift, then follow a line of advance which took it across the Ncome into Zululand at Koppie Alleen, skirting north of Isandlwana before striking the planned route of the old Centre Column. There was still a garrison at Rorke's Drift, but Chelmsford was reluctant to follow the ill-omened road of January, if only to spare his fresh troops the sight of the battlefield, where the dead still lay unburied. Wood's column was now re-designated the Flying Column, and was to advance from Khambula to affect a junction with the 2nd Division. Although the two columns would thereafter maintain separate command and administrative functions, they would advance in tandem, as one single striking arm. All three columns were stronger than their original counterparts: the 1st Division included a total of 7,500 men and 13 guns, while the 2nd Division and Flying Column combined consisted of over 8,000 men, 16 field guns and 2 Gatlings.

The 1st Division was ready to begin its advance by the third week of April. The exaggerated fear of the Zulus had to some extent been displaced by the victories at Khambula and Gingindlovu, at least on the coast, where there were few signs of enemy activity. Nonetheless, Crealock's advance was painfully slow, hampered by a shortage of transport equipment, and the need to build fortified supply depots every few miles along the road. Furthermore, the concentration of humanity, continuing rain, and presence of scores of dead oxen – which collapsed from exhaustion along the road, and were simply dragged aside and left to rot – combined to produce a high incidence of disease which further eroded the column's efficiency. Nevertheless, Crealock's progress was initially better than that of the 2nd Division, which was not ready to cross the border until the end of May. This delay was partly due to the time it took to assemble the column at such a remote location – especially since the regular cavalry horses, brought out from Britain, took several weeks to acclimatize to local grasses – and partly because Chelmsford had one further duty to perform before he began.

Pressure had been mounting in both Natal and Britain for Chelmsford to bury the dead at Isandlwana. Several patrols had visited the site since January, and their reports of the mouldering dead lying out amid the overgrown wreckage of the camp had weighed heavily on Colonial society and the military alike. Chelmsford had postponed a formal expedition to bury the dead, partly to allow the worst aspects of the process of putrefaction to pass, and partly out of fear of the Zulus. With a new column assembling, however, there was another consideration: the dozens of wagons still lying on the field, which would be needed for the fresh advance. On 21 May the cavalry brigade finally set out from Rorke's Drift to retrieve the wagons, and cover over some of the dead; at Colonel Glyn's request, those who could be identified as belonging to the 24th were to be left until their comrades within the regiment were able to bury them. Most of the 'specials', including Melton Prior, Norris-Newman and Archibald Forbes, had travelled north to join the 2nd Division, in expectation of witnessing the decisive fighting to come, and a number of them were curious enough to join the expedition. While Melton Prior made sketches of the scene, and Norris-Newman wandered around the ruined camp site, searching out his own belongings and the bodies of his friends, Archibald Forbes composed a haunting account of the visit, which is arguably one of the finest pieces of journalism produced by the war:

On the lower neck were clearly visible up against the skyline the abandoned waggons of the destroyed columns. No Zulus were seen. Flanking parties covered the hills on each side of the track, along which the head of the column pressed at a trot, with small detachments of Natal Carbineers in front of the Dragoon Guards. Now we were down in the last dip, had crossed the rocky bed of the little stream. Already tokens of the combat and bootless flight were apparent. The line of retreat towards Fugitives' Drift along which, through a chink in the Zulu environment, our unfortunate comrades who thus far survived tried to escape, lay athwart a rocky slope to our right front, with a precipitous ravine at its base. In this ravine dead men lay thick, mere bones, with toughened discoloured skin like leather covering them, and clinging tight to them, the flesh all wasted away. Some were almost wholly dismembered, heaps of yellow clammy bones. I forebear to describe the faces, with their blackened features and beards bleached by rain and sun. Every man had been disembowelled. Some were scalped, and others subject to yet ghastlier mutilations. The clothes had lasted better than the poor bodies they covered, and helped to keep the skeletons together. All the way up the slope I traced by the ghastly token of dead men, the fitful line of flight. Most of the men hereabouts were infantry of the 24th. It was like a long string with knots in it, the string formed of single corpses, the knots of clusters of dead, where (as it seemed) little groups might have gathered to make a hopeless, gallant stand and die. I came on a gully with a gun limber jammed on its edge, and the horses, their hides scored with assegai stabs, hanging in their harness down the steep face of a ravine. A little further on was a broken and battered ambulance waggon, with its team of mules mouldering in their harness, and around lay the corpses of soldiers, poor helpless wretches, dragged out of an intercepted vehicle, and done to death without a chance for life.

Still following the trail of bodies through the long grass and among stones, I approached the crest. Here the slaughtered ones lay very thick, so that the string became a broad belt. Many hereabouts wore the uniform of the Natal Police. On the bare ground, on the crest itself, among the waggons, the dead were less thick, but on the slope beyond, on which from the crest we looked down, the scene was the saddest, and more full of weird desolation then any I had yet gazed upon. There was none of the stark, blood-curdling horror of a recent battlefield. A strange dead calm reigned in this solitude of nature. Grain had grown luxuriantly around the waggons, sprouting from the seed that had dropped from the loads, falling in soil fertilised by the life-blood of gallant men. So long in most places had grown the grass, that it mercifully shrouded the dead, whom four long months tomorrow we have left unburied.

As one strayed aimlessly about, one strayed over skeletons that rattled to the touch. Here lay a corpse with a bayonet jammed into the mouth up to the socket, transfixing the head and mouth a foot into the ground. There lay a form that seemed cosily curled in calm sleep, turned almost on its face, but seven assegai stabs have pierced the back. Most, however, lay flat on the back, with the arms stretched widely out, and hands clenched. I noticed one dead man under a waggon, with his head on a saddle for a pillow, and a tarpaulin drawn down over him, as if he had gone to sleep, and died so. In a patch of long grass, near the right flank of the camp, lay Durnford's body, the long moustache still clinging to the withered skin of the face. Captain Shepstone recognised him at once, and identified him yet farther by rings on the finger and a knife with a name on it in the pocket, which relics were brought away. Durnford had died hard – a central figure in a knot of brave men who had fought it out around their chief to the bitter end. A stalwart Zulu, covered by his shield, lay at the Colonel's feet. Around him, almost in a ring, lay about a dozen men, half being Natal Carbineers, riddled by assegai stabs. . . .

Close beside the camp, at the picquet line, a gully traverses the ground in front of the camp. About 400 paces beyond this was the ground of the battle before the troops broke their formation, and on both sides of this gully the dead lie very thickly. In one place nearly fifty of the 24th lie almost touching, as if they had fallen in a rallying square. The line of the straggling rush back to camp is clearly marked by skeletons all along the front. Durnford's body was wrapped in a tarpaulin and buried under a heap of stones. The Natal Carbineers buried their dead roughly. The gunners did the same by theirs. Efforts were made, at least, to conceal all the bodies of the men who had not belonged to the 24th. These were left untouched by special orders. . . .

Wandering about the desolate camp, amid the sour odour of stale death, was sickening. I chanced on many sad relics – letters from home, photographs, journals, blood-stained books, packs of cards, Lord Chelmsford's copying book, containing an impression of his correspondence with the Horse Guards, was found in one of his portmanteaus, and identified, in a kraal two miles off. Colonel Harness was busily engaged in collecting his own belongings. Colonel Glyn found a letter from himself to Lieutenant Melvill, dated the day before the fight. The ground was thickly strewn with brushes, toilet bags, pickle bottles, and unbroken tins of preserved meats and milk. Forges and bellows remained standing ready for the recommencement of work. The waggons had in every case been emptied, and the contents rifled. Bran lay spilt in heaps. Scarcely any arms were found, and no ammunition. There were a few stray bayonets and assegais, rusted with blood. No firearms.

All this time teams of horses were being hitched somehow to the soundest of the waggons, till about forty fit to travel had been collected on the crest. . . .[1]

While the military prepared to renew their contest with the Zulus, the defence of the border was left largely to Colonial troops and black auxiliaries. Chelmsford's new plan made no provision for strong Imperial garrisons on the border, since it was felt the Zulus no longer had the capacity to mount a serious strike into Natal. Nonetheless what remained of the war was characterized by occasional raids and skirmishes on the borders. By the end of April, many Colonial Volunteers, parcelled out in remote posts along the borders, began to feel decidedly forgotten and disgruntled, as the *Natal Mercury* correspondent with the Alexandra Mounted Rifles at Potspruit, a camp between Greytown and the Middle Drift, complained:

It is just a fortnight since we arrived on this bleak and barren spot, and though not encamped on our old camping ground, we are very near to it.

Potspruit was, on our former visit [in December 1878], wet and disagreeable; now, it is just as bad, being cold and miserable – in fact, for the last day or so, the weather has been so cold, and the wind so keen and piercing, that we have to be constantly on the move, otherwise we should fall to pieces, as our bones rattle against each other, and our teeth nearly fall out of our jaws, through excessive fits of shivering.

We have all come to the conclusion that our kind and fatherly government has evidently not the slightest care or value for the volunteers, or it would not treat us as it has done. During times of peace and quietness, the volunteers were patted on the back, and encouraged by all kinds of toasts and nice speeches. . . . What is it in reality now? Simply that the volunteers are bound hand and foot; they see that any man except a volunteer has the chance of receiving from 15s. to 30s. per day in any of the various border guards, or by being interpreter, instead of 6s. per day. . . . Any one, not a volunteer, has the opportunity of leaving his business or estate properly cared for during his absence; whereas a volunteer called out at twelve hours' notice, has no such chance. . . .

Volunteers owning farms or estates are not only bound to accept their 6s. a day and no more, but have had their kafir labourers, who were left behind to do the best they could in the absence of their masters, deliberately taken from them, not once only but twice, by Government agents, in the guise of kafir chiefs, to fill up the ranks of deserters in the so-called Border Guard. Again, all volunteers were obliged to leave behind them, at Etshowe, all their kits, and have since had to buy others. . . . The volunteers have heard also that their stores and goods at Etshowe were sold at exceedingly high prices for the benefit of the troops there; but they have not heard whether that money will be refunded to them. . . . We think you will allow that this neglect and disregard of our interests will not encourage others to join, but that it will cause every present man in the corps of Natal to bitterly rue the day when he became a volunteer.[2]

Chelmsford hoped to supply the 1st Division massing at Fort Pearson by sea once it had advanced into Zululand. In the third week of April HMS *Forester* sailed up the coast to investigate the potential of Point Durnford as a landing-place:

. . . The Tugela mouth was reached the morning after the *Forester* left here [Durban], and the work of taking soundings was immediately commenced, slow progress being made towards Point Durnford. No Zulus in large numbers were seen until the morning of the 24th. The *Forester* on that day lay off Point Durnford, and two boats manned with sounding parties were sent close in and proceeded with their work for some time without any signs of interference. All being apparently quiet and safe at dinner time, the boats being then close in, the anchors were dropped, and the men commenced to partake of their meal. Suddenly a volley of musketry was heard, and at the same time shots came close up to the boats. A large body of Zulus was then observed on the beach, and a second volley was fired. The fire was returned by the men in the boats, and the lifting of the anchors was the work of a minute only. The boats made towards the *Forester*, continuing their fire as they got into deep water. None of the shots had touched the boats, but they had had a very narrow shave. The Zulus were seen retreating to the bush, which was at once shelled by the *Forester*, and no doubt a number of the enemy were killed. Of course there was no means of ascertaining the extent of the Zulu losses. They had forty head of cattle with them when they first fired, and of this number thirty-six were seen lying dead after they had retreated. . . .[3]

Even before the 1st Division's advance was fully under way by mid-June, it was clear that the allegiance of the coastal chiefs to Cetshwayo was beginning seriously to waver. On 21 April Prince Makwendu kaMpande gave himself up to British advance parties. The special correspondent of the *Natal Witness* interviewed him:

. . . I had an opportunity of seeing the famous chief Makwendu, half brother of the Zulu King, who, with a large party of his men and women, had surrendered to this column a few days previously. This was a peace [sic] of good luck quite unexpected. I found the chief closely guarded (ready to be handed over to the

Prince Makwendu kaMpande, photographed with his attendants and British officers shortly after his surrender on 21 April. (Ian Knight)

party that had come on convoy duty) to be transferred to Fort Pearson on the Tugela. In appearance he bears a striking resemblance to many of those photos of the Zulu King, I have seen. He is a well-built fellow, as indeed are all the Zulus, with a large open face. He was sitting in the centre of his men, some thirty, a smile playing round the corners of his mouth at the curiosity centred in him by the soldiers. He looks a thoroughly good natured fellow, quite at home, but to the physiogomist there was an expression about the lower jaws as well as in the sometimes compressed lips, which told plainly that Makwendu was a chief of determination, and one into whose hands it would not be safe to fall when his temper was ruffled. His right eye has got a peculiar turn in it, which, to a great extent, mars what would otherwise be a good-looking face. His story is: that it was the intention of the whole of his tribe to give themselves up, as they are heartily tired of this war; and with a discernment which is highly laudable are able to see that against the English they have not the remotest prospect of upholding the position they have assumed; but that Cetywayo, becoming aware of their intention, cut off the remainder of his tribe. This is his story, and so far as I can judge it is worthy of credence. Zulus continue to arrive daily in this camp, and are forthwith sent to Fort Pearson. Their accounts of the social condition of Zululand at the present moment are that the army is disorganized, and that all Zulu soldiers would readily lay down their arms were it not for the terror which is inherent in them of their King.[4]

The impending dissolution of the Zulu kingdom under the renewed hammer-blows of the British presented problems for its neighbours. As more and more Zulus and their livestock began to take refuge in Swaziland, King Mbandzeni, who was balanced uneasily between the Zulu and the British, was presented with an unwelcome dilemma. An occasional correspondent for the *Natal Mercury* explained his predicament:

> The Swazi border, north of the Pongolo, at the present time, is in a very unsatisfactory state, and will inevitably lead on to great trouble. The Swazi nation, in numerical strength, is far beneath that of the Zulu . . . and from past experience of their power, live in dread of them. While it is certain the Swazi wish to be regarded as friendly to the white faces, he is naturally deterred from declaring openly for them. . . . His motto is self-defence – hence watching events. To this no one can take exception. He is not at war with the Zulu nation. In addition to their close national proximity, the nations have family ties, having married each other's daughters to an extent known to none but themselves. Hence their sympathies are blended with each other. . . . Umbandine [Mbandzeni] has always said, 'My impi is ready, sleeping with assegai in hand and shield for bed, but will take no action until shots are fired across his frontier.['] War is now raging in Zululand, of this the king is duly apprised. He heard of the disasters at Isandhlwana, Intombi, and Hlobane, more through a Zulu than an English medium, and it has had of course a most deterrent and disheartening effect, Cetywayo's messengers always representing their arms victorious and the English forces defeated – nay destroyed. For months past the Zulus have been sending their cattle and helpless and enfeebled people to their friends or relations, until at this moment there are thousands of cattle and hordes of people in Swaziland, against which the young king remonstrates, but is powerless to prevent it. He is afraid to oppose the Zulus . . . [but] knows one day he may be . . . held responsible for giving refuge to the Queen's enemies – thus perplexed he knows not what to do. . . .[5]

Thoroughly alarmed at the renewed British offensive and at the disaffection of his leading chiefs, Cetshwayo sent out two experienced and trusted emissaries, Mfunzi and Nkisimana, to attempt to treat with Chelmsford. They had no success. On 8 June they crossed the Mooi River at Keate's Drift on their way to Pietermaritzburg under flag of truce provided by H.F. Fynn, the resident magistrate at Rorke's Drift. A *Natal Mercury* correspondent with the Durban Mounted Rifles posted at Keate's Drift sarcastically described them as 'model messengers of peace'. He contemptuously continued:

> . . . 'Messengers' they were to all appearances. They bore a white flag on high, and carried also a magisterial document from Mr. Henry Fynn, Umsinga, addressed to the Secretary for Native Affairs. These men, who stated they were merely acting in a preliminary capacity, were neither chiefs nor indunas. They wore regulation blankets, which they said had been given to them by Macanda (Mr. Fannin). Both were old ring kafirs; one of them was an out-and-out

villainous-looking little beast, with a head like an ape; while the other, who had apparently been in contact with white people before, was not half such a thorough savage.

These men were escorted by three of Fynn's police. They had two youths with them as bearers. According to their own words, their business was to 'prepare a place' for the King's indunas to come and speak in.[6]

In late May, in order to draw Zulu forces who might fall on the right flank of the 2nd Division when it advanced, Chelmsford ordered all the border forces to raid Zululand once more. One of the required raids was mounted by Major Twentyman on 20 May at Middle Drift. A Natal Volunteer, who was a member of the raiding party, 'favoured' the *Natal Colonist* with a detailed account of the operations and their likely consequences:

We started from Potspruit Camp (new ground) after breakfast, on Monday May 19th, with orders to proceed to Fort Cherry for further instructions. We met Mr Fannin there, who took us on to Kranskop, all in the meantime wondering at the meaning of so much mystery. At Kranskop we were told Major Twentyman purposed making a raid into Zululand, and that he wanted some volunteers to cross over with him, the others remaining behind to guard the drift in case of a retreat. We then proceeded down the steep sides of the Tugela Valley leading our horses the greater part of the way, over boulders and under thorns. . . . It was dark before our camping ground for the night was reached about a mile from the drift, in a sheltered valley with any amount of beastly thorns and knobby stones. We were ordered to off-saddle, tie our horses up, and turn ourselves in with as little noise as possible, and glad we were to do so, for all were well tired. Shortly afterwards Captain Cherry's Natal Native Contingent joined us, also a company of Pioneers and about 100 of Walker's mounted men [Ixopo Native Contingent]. By morning star we moved down to the river, arriving there shortly before daybreak, where there was a short delay waiting for Commandant Wheelwright's men [Border Guards] who also had orders to form a drift guard. Just as the sun rose, an advance into the river was made by about thirty volunteers under Sergeant Duckham, of the Natal Hussars, Major Twentyman crossing with them. When the party got to the island in the middle of the drift, there was some difficulty in tracing the ford across to Zululand. Whilst this was being seen about, a volley was fired by about a dozen Zulus. Immediately after firing they shouted the war cry 'Usutu,' and disappeared over the brow of the hill. Major Twentyman's horse was wounded, and another bullet whizzed close past his face. Fortunately, the shooting generally was wide. The same may be said of the Natal Native Contingent, who fired about one hundred shots in return, mostly in the air. Our army of invasion, mustering 1,000 men, now followed the Mounted Volunteers, who had found the missing ford. The party then advanced three or four miles into Zululand, burning kraals and a large quantity of mealies and corn. They also captured sixteen goats and two chickens; the dozen Zulus already mentioned, firing as they advanced and we returning fire, but without effect upon either side. A well-ordered retreat enabled the invading army to safely return to Natal without losing the sixteen goats and two chickens, the result of this raid.

In the meantime, Commander Crabb, at a drift higher up the river, was not idle. He also had orders to 'raid' the Zulus, and crossed the river accordingly; but after advancing some distance into the enemy's country, he was met by about four hundred Zulus, who speedily taught him he was a trespasser, and drove him and his followers [Border Guard levies] back into Natal, fortunately without any loss of life. The Zulus encamped at the river bank that evening, and called over that they would return the visit next morning, and burn a few kraals. Our force had got to a nice camping ground, and were preparing for a good night's rest, when a messenger from Crabb aroused us with this news. Vedettes were at once posted, and Major Twentyman proceeded to the river to ascertain further particulars. Shortly after he had left a second messenger came and stated that an impi had crossed the drift, we had just left, and was burning huts and capturing cattle. A pretty fix we were in, an impi on each side of us! Fires were put out, guards doubled, horses saddled, the men lying down close to them. It was a sharp cold night, and we were pretty well starved before morning.

At seven a.m. (Wednesday) [21 May], to our great relief, a messenger arrived with news that Crabb's impi had not crossed and with orders for a general return to camp. . . . When near a mission station [eMakhabeleni] deep in the valley, some of Wheelwright's men passed. They told us the enemy had burned some huts during the night, and were hiding now on the opposite side of the river. . . . After consulting it was resolved to send three volunteers up to the camp to tell the officer there what detained us, whilst the remainder stayed to bring up the missionary [Revd H. Blomeier] his wife and children. Seven of us went to the station and soon came back; four troopers, each with a child on the front of his saddle, two others walking, they having given up their horses to the old gentleman and lady. . . . Next morning Wheelwright's men brought in a Zulu scout. He was very chatty, and amongst other items of news, said Ketshwayo intended keeping clear of the big columns, but would sweep through the whole of the Tugela Valley; this is the certain result of these foolish raids. They can do no good, but will probably cost many innocent lives, even if the impis are not tempted further into the colony. . . . On the same day, Captain Walker crossed at a drift still further up the river, and captured 150 head of cattle, only seeing one old Zulu, who was herding them. They lost no time in beating a speedy retreat far into Natal with their booty. . . .

The question naturally arises, who is to pay for the damage that the Zulus will inevitably commit in retaliation for these outrages. The Contingents and Volunteers who are *ordered* to commit them are stationed miles away from the Border, and afford no protection to the unfortunate residents along the river side, yet are rewarded with the cattle, goats, and fowls stolen. Who can wonder if, after this, our Natal Kafirs waver in their loyalty?[7]

The 1st Division began its laborious advance in earnest during late May. The *Illustrated London News'* correspondent with the column filed a detailed account on 3 June of the division's activities, his own adventures and Zulu peace feelers:

Build-up for the second invasion: an ammunition train and supplies at the Lower Thukela Drift, May 1879. (Killie Campbell Africana Library)

The main road from Fort Pearson to Fort Crealock is perfectly free from the enemy. Fort Crealock lies thirteen miles from Lower Tugela, and overlooks the banks of the Amatikulu. A short ride from there takes you to the battle-field of Gingihlovo. This lies to the left of the main road going in the direction of Fort Chelmsford. . . . Luckily, an officer of the 91st Highlanders was going for a ride in the afternoon, and we started on our expedition to the battle-field. Of course we kept our eyes open as we jogged along, especially as only the week before this same officer was stalked by two Zulus, who glided like panthers through the long grass. . . . Just as we came to the road which turns off from the main track we overtook two of the Native Horse, and they volunteered to accompany us.

A sharp canter of ten minutes brought us to the Laager, which is still covered with debris. A great many Zulu shields are scattered about the field; any heap which gives the slightest covering is a sure find. The tombstones of Lieutenant Johnstone and some men of the 99th, and that of Colonel Northey, which lies close to them, were rapidly sketched. These were in a good state of preservation; the wooden fencing around Colonel Northey's tomb has a rustic aspect, and the gravestone looks solemn and impressive, standing alone in the centre of this dreary plain. No dead bodies were to be seen, but I was told that they were lying in the surrounding bush. Luckily, no Zulus made their appearance; they swarm in the hills opposite. . . .

On our return to Fort Crealock we heard the alarm sounded. My friend leaped off his horse and rushed into the fort. In less than five minutes all the four faces of the fort were lined with men, two deep. The Native Contingent seemed perfectly happy, thus protected, squatting in the centre of the fort. A perfect stillness reigned during fifteen minutes. It had a peculiar effect to see so many men, with not a whisper to be heard among them. The setting of the sun heightened the picture still more. When the tattoo was sounded, a sudden transformation took place. What had seemed statues, were now animated with life and motion. The natives, as they marched to their own huts, uttered unearthly sounds.

A neighbouring hill, a mile and quarter distant, on which a vidette is stationed, is connected with the fort by a telephone. It is the first time that instrument has been used in warfare. It is of the greatest service, as voices are easily recognised by the sound. The telegraph has been laid between Fort Pearson and Fort Crealock, and the posts for it have been fixed nearly up to Fort Chelmsford.

The movement of the 1st Division will be a slow one; the first steps will be to cover the landing-point at Port Durnford, and to built a pontoon bridge across the Umhlatosi [Mhlathuze] river. These will of necessity be slow operations, but it is well to take such steps that another disaster may practically be impossible. This 'haphazard' war is a slow and tedious one, disliked both by officers and men. The general desire is for a successful termination of it this year. . . .

There are eight hundred men *hors de combat* from the 1st Division. This is a big number, out of a total force of less than six thousand. If the present rate of sickness continues there will be no field officers left at the disposal of the General. Brigadier Clark is now laid up with fever. Yellow jaundice has lately appeared among the troops. A great deal of the sickness may be ascribed to the effluvia which arises from the carcases of oxen in different stages of decomposition. These lie on the road where the troopers have to escort the convoys, and at every hundred yards this horrible atmosphere has to be breathed. If detachments of mounted men could have been told off to drag the carcases a reasonable distance from the road, this would have greatly lessened the evil.

The rain which has been long expected has at last come down. The grass, lately burnt up, will now soon change its arid aspect. Already green shoots are appearing. The three-days' rain did not flood the rivers to any extent; at present they are easily fordable on horseback. The huts at Fort Pearson, for the reception of the sick, are being rapidly run up. Four are already completed; they are built of reeds, and will be whitewashed inside. These huts will be a great boon to the sick; they have the advantage of being more comfortable and healthy than canvas tents. While the Engineers were cutting reeds from a lonely swamp, Mr. Dickens, the proprietor, came up and said that he would send in a claim against the British Government for damage. . . . But he totally ignores that, if it were not for our troops, the Zulus would cross the river and burn his house, taking with them his cattle and all his moveable property. . . .

Two months' provisions have now been accumulated at Fort Chelmsford, and a movement in advance will take place at the beginning of next week. The inaction has caused great complaints among the men, but the transport difficulty alone stops the onward march of the British soldier.

Fort Chelmsford, one of a chain of impressive supply depots built in Zululand by the 1st Division. (Ian Knight)

> The two Zulu emissaries, who made their appearance at Fort Chelmsford, did not come direct from Cetewayo, but only with his sanction. The chiefs had brought pressure upon the King to allow them to make overtures for peace. . . .[8]

While the war was carried to the Zulu with renewed vigour, everyday life in Natal continued to be disrupted as defences were maintained and strengthened and the Volunteers and black levies remained in the field. What this meant to a frontier community is made apparent by the report sent in early June from the *Natal Witness* correspondent in Greytown:

> . . . On the arrival of a detachment of the 94th Regiment, under command of Captain G. Froom, the 4th King's Own were ordered to the front. The fort [Fort Moore] was then found to be much too large for the reduced garrison, it could not be properly manned, something also was said about 'dead angles,' or parts which were not enfiladed from the laager. To remedy this a new fort was decided upon, much smaller, and shaped like an inverted V. This work has been carried out more leisurely than the previous one and is a most formidable and artistic entrenchment; by its peculiar formation both ditches are completely enfiladed, the centre of the gorge being opposite the gateway; a couple of wagons drawn across the road at the end of each parapet completing the circle of defence in case of need. The ditches are eight feet deep, ten feet wide at top,

Defending the settler community: the military camp at Greytown, protected by wire entanglements and broken bottles (foreground). (Ian Knight)

one and a half at bottom; eastern parapet four feet high, western parapet six feet high to suit the lay of the land; outside of all, a lot of wire entanglement and fencing protect the fort against a sudden rush. Certainly Fort Froom may be considered a valuable addition to the strength of Greytown.

. . . But about these hut taxes the Magistrate has gone to collect; a very proper thing that taxes should be collected even in these disturbed times, but how can taxes be paid if the Government do not pay the natives in their employ. Most of the Contingent and Levy Natives have been paid each month regularly, but others who reside in the Tugela valley, and who have the real watching to do, have not been paid a penny wages for the six months' service they have already given, and now they are called upon to pay taxes. . . .

Our volunteers are feeling the protracted war very seriously. To many of them their long absence from business is simply ruinous, and they very naturally blame the General and Sir Henry Bulwer for keeping them in the field so long without relief. . . .

We are having frosty nights; grass fires may be expected now for the country is drying up fast, notwithstanding the late welcome rains.[9]

That continuing settler apprehensions were not always idle was confirmed in the report the *Natal Mercury* correspondent sent in from Luneburg on 16 June. Wood's force, renamed the Flying Column, had advanced to join the 2nd Division, leaving the vicinity of Luneburg open to repeated Zulu raids. These raids were not sufficiently intensive to threaten Wood's rear, but they made life very uncomfortable for the Luneburg settlers and their African dependents:

> . . . A large Zulu army, calculated at from 6000 to 7000, is in occupation of the country between the Intombi and Assegai River. Raids have been made upon the friendly natives, numbers of them killed, and thousands of cattle and sheep swept away; whilst on the other hand the Boers occupy their farm-houses, and carry on ploughing without fear or hindrance, in the very midst of a Zulu army. Great vigilance is absolutely necessary. . . . An attack upon the fort or laager of Luneberg is out of the question; the Zulus would never attempt it. We have now, besides the 4th regiment, under Major Blake, also the whole of Schermbrucker's Horse here, and they would be quite sufficient to hold both fort and laagers against any number of Zulus. With a view of clearing the road we have taken down the graveyard enclosure, behind which a number of the enemy might have found shelter, just opposite the laager. . . .
>
> The weather has turned miserably wet and cold; quite contrary to the usual experience in this country, we had a terrific thunderstorm the night before last. Lightning and thunder raged for fully two hours, and the rain poured down most copiously. It is now dangerous to cross the spruit at the bottom of the laager. The enemy occupies the hills opposite, and numbers of Manyonyoba's kafirs are daily parading before our eyes. Unfortunately our mounted force is paralysed by the miserable state of the horses. . . .[10]

Nor was the middle border immune from Zulu incursions. On 25 June the retaliatory raid long feared by critics of Chelmsford's vaunted 'active defence' took place. It was far more extensive and successful than any of the transborder raids mounted earlier by the British in Defensive District No. VII. As a consequence, the British border forces were thrown entirely on to the defensive, where they remained until Chelmsford's victory at Ulundi transformed the situation. A 'thoroughly trustworthy informant' provided the *Natal Mercury* with 'authentic particulars of this lamentable occurrence':

> Mr. Household [Houshold], in charge of the Border Guard at Impino [the Mpisi Drift], hearing the firing, obtained assistance from the border guard in Victoria County, and arrived on the scene in time to intercept one party of Zulus, several of whom were killed and wounded as they recrossed the river. He recaptured a small herd of cattle that they were driving off. Mr. Crabb, at Middle Drift had a narrow escape; being surrounded by the Zulus, he had to conceal himself for a short time. The damage and loss of life in this raid has not yet been accurately ascertained, but the following is approximately correct:– 74 kraals burnt, about 500 head of cattle and about an equal number of goats captured; 9 men, 15 women, and 3 children killed; about 40 women and children carried off captive, the latter mostly related to Zulus; two women wounded. The loss of the enemy was nine or ten killed, and many wounded.

The raid was conducted in the true savage Zulu manner, neither age nor sex was spared. Among the killed was an infant, several helpless old women, two of whom, and a rich man, were burnt alive in huts. They were guided by the natives who left Natal for Zululand last November; the raid was made by order of Cetywayo. Some of the party who were desirous of climbing Tugela heights were recalled, and reminded of the King's orders to raid the Tugela valley only. At the raid made by the Zulus on the 25th, they crossed the Tugela at daybreak under cover of a dense fog which hung over the valley till about nine o'clock. One party, about 500 strong, crossed at the hot springs, were discovered before emerging from the river by the border police, who fired on them. They replied by a volley, and then rushed on the police, killing one of them with assegais. This firing gave the alarm, and the border guard at Middle Drift hastened up the river, when they were surprised to hear further firing in the direction of Krantzkop. The Zulus had passed on in that direction, burning kraals as they went. They turned close under Bishop Schroeder's [Schreuder's] residence [kwaNtunjambili], burning four kraals on his land, and hurried back to Middle Drift, destroying everything on their way. They recrossed the river about eleven o'clock. The police and border guard attacked them at several points, and recaptured nearly all the cattle they had taken. Out of 24 kraals burnt by this party, the Zulus only carried off the cattle of five.

The second party of Zulus, about 500 strong, crossed lower down, a few miles below Middle Drift, and swept the Mamhulu [Mambula] valley. The mist lay thicker in this part, and the natives were more completely surprised than in the other. About 50 kraals were burnt, and the greater part of the cattle captured.

The natives behaved well, and had they been better shots and been all armed with guns, the Zulus would have been driven back. The raiders are the border Zulu tribes, whom it is to be hoped will now be cleared out. A great fallacy has prevailed with reference to these men; it has been said they contemplated coming into Natal, whereas the truth is, they have been seeking permission from Cetywayo to raid the Tugela Valley ever since the river became passable. It is to be hoped that the column which was to have entered here under the late Colonel Durnford will now be reformed and sent in at Middle Drift. If immediate steps are not taken to put this border in a better state of affairs, more raids will be made by the same men who have carried out this one so successfully.[11]

The stunning Zulu raid at Middle Drift unsettled the whole Thukela border. The war was still the dominant factor in people's lives, and was made all the more vivid, as a *Natal Mercury* correspondent reported from Verulam on 30 June, by the passage of sick or wounded soldiers from the front:

. . . Nearly all interests are at present absorbed in, or sacrificed to the military operations at present being carried on; and the great proportion of the residents, not only here, but elsewhere, throughout the colony are suffering severely if not directly, at least indirectly, unless they happen to be themselves engaged in the military service. Although our colony is not, and it is to be hoped will never be, the immediate theatre of hostilities, still the minds of the inhabitants are unsettled, and business of all kinds is more or less disturbed and interrupted. From the news recently received from the border, a feeling of considerable anxiety prevails, in case the Zulus should attempt a raid in any large numbers; and the impunity with which the last raid at the middle drift seems to have been made, might be expected to induce them to try the same thing on a large scale. I am informed that there are at present only about 150 regulars at Fort Pearson, so that the protection of the Zulu border is for the most part left in the hands of the volunteers and native contingent. The volunteers have, of course, already proved themselves to be the most efficient force yet engaged in the war, but we must not lose sight of the fact that their number is comparatively small.

Still large numbers of sick and wounded soldiers are continually passing. On Friday afternoon [27 June] over 100 arrived, and proceeded to Saccharine on Saturday forenoon. Some of them were so helpless that they had to be carried on stretchers from the hospital tents to the ambulance wagons, and were evidently in a very low condition. Again, yesterday [29 June] a number came in, and I believe there are still about 200 awaiting removal from the front. The Army Medical Corps have now established a regular station at Verulam, and have pitched several comfortable hospital tents close to the railway terminus. The rails are now laid all the way to the Verulam Railway Station, so that I suppose very shortly the military station at Saccharine will be done away with, and the sick and wounded be transported all the way from Verulam to Durban by rail.

During the whole of last week the weather has been dry, the roads are once more dusty and unpleasant, and the rivers almost devoid of water. . . .[12]

Despairing of Chelmsford bringing the war in Zululand to a speedy conclusion, the British government decided to supersede him with the dynamic and reforming General Sir Garnet Wolseley. Chelmsford learned as early as 16 June of Wolseley's appointment over him, though he did not receive formal notice until 9 July. Knowledge that Wolseley was on his way spurred him to bring the war to a decisive conclusion before his arrival should rob him of the credit. For his part, Wolseley was determined to rush to the front and attempted to land at Port Durnford on 3 July to circumvent the lengthy journey overland. The *Natal Witness* correspondent described how he was foiled by the rough surf:

At seven o'clock this morning a large number of officers and men from the camp assembled along the shore to witness the expected landing of Sir Garnet Wolseley and staff from the *Shah*, which is riding at anchor about a mile off. The surf was very high, higher indeed than it had been for a few days past, and it was thought by many that no attempt would be made; but, notwithstanding the weather, Sir Garnet, with his staff, was seen to push off from the great black hull of the war ship, in a lighter, which, as we looked from the beach, seemed to roll fearfully, and apparently shipped a deal of water. After half-an-hour's struggle with the tempestuous waves, and there being not the slightest chance of the boat reaching the shore, it was considered necessary by the naval authorities to advise Sir Garnet to return to the ship, which they did, by means of a flag denoting 'danger,' being hoisted. Soon after this the boat's course was altered, and she again made for the war ship, which was reached about half-past nine, the sea still being very high. The whole party several times narrowly escaped being immersed in the ocean. Until the sea has abated its fury it will be impossible to land any more supplies from the transports in the offing. Our present stock of provisions is obtained from Fort Chelmsford. . . .[13]

NOTES

1. Archibald Forbes in the *Daily News*, 21 May 1879.
2. *Natal Mercury*, 28 April 1879: Potspruit correspondent, April 1879.
3. *Natal Witness*, 1 May 1879.
4. *Natal Witness*, 3 May 1879: special correspondent, Ginginhlovu, 27 April 1879.
5. *Natal Mercury*, 16 May 1879: occasional correspondent, 1 May 1879.
6. *Natal Mercury*, 13 June 1879: correspondent with the Durban Mounted Rifles, Keate's Drift, 9 June 1879.
7. *Natal Colonist*, 31 May 1879: correspondent.
8. *Illustrated London News*, 26 July 1879: Lower Tugela correspondent, 3 June 1879.
9. *Natal Witness*, 14 June 1879: Greytown correspondent.
10. *Natal Mercury*, 28 June 1879: Luneberg [sic] correspondent, 16 June 1879.
11. *Natal Mercury*, 2 July 1879: trustworthy informant.
12. *Natal Mercury*, 3 July 1879: Verulam correspondent, 30 June 1879.
13. *Natal Witness*, 15 July 1879: Port Durnford correspondent, 3 July 1879.

Retribution

On the morning of 1 June 1879, Melton Prior of the *Illustrated London News* had a chance encounter on the outskirts of the camp of the 2nd Division at Telezeni, in Zululand:

> It so happened that I was outside my tent that morning, when I saw the Prince Imperial on horseback coming from the laager, and as he passed me he said, 'Goodbye, Mr Prior'.
>
> 'Goodbye, sir. I hope you will have a jolly morning,' I replied, as he rode away to join Lieutenant Carey and his escort, which consisted of six white men of Bettington's Horse, six Basutos, and a loyal Zulu guide. The object of this expedition was to survey and make a sketch of the next proposed camping ground.
>
> Having seen him disappear in the distance, I returned to my tent to work, but a few hours afterwards I realised that I wanted a good piece of background for

The military earthwork at Utrecht, built by the men of the 80th Regiment in December 1877, and the Depot of the Flying Column. (Killie Campbell Africana Library)

Prince Louis Napoleon, the exiled Prince
Imperial of France; killed in a skirmish on
1 June 1879. (Ian Knight)

the sketch I was engaged on, and, ordering my horse, I started to ride in search
of the correct position. I had not gone very far when I saw General Wood and
Colonel Buller riding together, and in the extreme distance I saw a man
galloping madly towards them. I was not near enough to hear exactly what took
place, but it turned out to be Lieutenant Carey returning from the deplorable
disaster which had occurred in the village of Itiotiozi [Tshotshozi].

I heard afterwards that as he approached he was stopped by the General and
asked, 'Where are you coming from?' He was so exhausted, confused, and
nervous that he could scarcely speak, but at last he said that they had been
attacked by the Zulus when resting in the village and had to bolt.

He was immediately asked, 'Where is the Prince Imperial?', and holding
down his head, with some hesitation he replied he did not know. . . .[1]

By rights, Prince Louis Jean Joseph Napoleon Bonaparte had little enough business
to be in Zululand. The son of the Emperor Napoleon III – who was a nephew of the
great Napoleon – Louis spent his boyhood amid the splendour and military pomp of
the Second Empire, but when French *élan* collapsed in the face of steely Prussian
efficiency in the Franco-Prussian War of 1870/1, the royal family had fled to Britain
and exile. Queen Victoria had set aside the nation's traditional hostility towards the
Bonapartes, and had taken the family under her wing, but the emperor died in 1873,
leaving Louis as the legitimate heir to the dreams and aspirations of the Imperial
party in France. But, in the aftermath of war, the French government had passed to
the Republicans, and Louis was condemned to sit on the political sidelines. Deeply

imbued with the military ethos of his family, Louis had trained in the professional skills of a British officer, but there was no possibility of a Bonaparte being given a commission in the British army, and he seemed destined to lead the empty life of the prince in exile, awaiting the call to reclaim his brithright which would probably never come.

To Louis, at least, the news of Isandlwana came as a godsend. The despatch of troops to South Africa to reinforce Chelmsford offered him both the opportunity for adventure, and to repay something of his debt to his host nation, while at the same time affording minimal personal and political risk; France was, after all, a colonial power itself, and could scarcely afford to be high-minded in defence of African rights. Louis persuaded his reluctant mother to appeal directly to Queen Victoria, who in turn secured the consent of the Duke of Cambridge – the Commander-in-Chief – to allow Louis to travel to Zululand in a private capacity. He was given no official rank or appointment, and was nothing more than an observer, although Cambridge requested that Chelmsford should take him onto his staff as an ADC. 'He is a fine young fellow', wrote Cambridge privately to Chelmsford, 'full of spirit and pluck, and, having many old cadet friends in the Artillery, he will doubtless find no difficulty in getting on, and if you can help him in any other way, pray do so. My only anxiety on his account would be that he is too plucky and go-ahead.'[2] Louis sailed for Africa towards the end of February, and the *Graphic* described his departure in a mood which summed up the English public's attitude towards the exiles: a mixture of romantic melancholy, suspicion, and disdain for the political and military volatility of a traditional rival:

> As our French neighbours are at present in possession of a Reupublic, which shows greater promise of durability than either of its predecessors, it is, perhaps, more courteous to call the son of the late Emperor of the French by this title [i.e. Prince Louis Napoleon] than to style him 'The Prince Imperial', a phrase that implies that theirs is an empire in posse. Since that disastrous year when he received his ill-omened 'baptism of fire' at Saarbruck, this enterprising young gentleman has seen no real fighting. But he has received a careful education at the Royal Military Academy, Woolwich, and hence it has been thought advisable by himself and his friends that he should gain some lessons in war, albeit a war conducted against a savage leader. . . . The Prince and his mother, who accompanied him, were warmly cheered both at Waterloo and the Southampton terminus on Thursday, the 27th ult. [February]. The ex-Empress walked on board the 'Danube' leaning on her son's arm. She was dressed in partial mourning, and looked anxious and careworn. In her hand she carried a bunch of violets. As she stepped on the deck two young ladies each tendered her a bouquet, but as her hands were already full, the Prince, who was in private clothes, received them on her behalf, and raising his hat in recognition of the cheers which went up on all sides, said, in the best English 'Thanks, very much. Indeed, I am very grateful to you for your kind reception.'[3]

The prince's arrival in Durban on 1 April went largely unnoticed by the Colonial press, overshadowed as it was by the dramatic news of the victories at Khambula and

Gingindlovu. For Chelmsford the prince's presence was clearly something of an embarrassment at a time when he was preoccupied with planning a new invasion of Zululand, but he admitted that he liked Louis well enough, and found him a place on his staff. When Chelmsford rode up to see how the assembly of the 2nd Division was progressing at the end of the month, Louis was unable to accompany him, however, being sick with fever. By the time the prince reached the front, patrols were regularly scouring the triangle of land between the confluence of the Mzinyathi and Ncome rivers, searching for a viable track from Landman's Drift westwards towards Telezeni, where the planned junction with the Flying Column was to take place. Louis, eager to see some action at last, attached himself to these patrols whenever he could, although his superiors did not appreciate his enthusiasm. An extensively published letter, written from the Flying Column on 16 May, suggests why:

> I returned this afternoon from a three days' patrol, in which little was done, little was seen, and many were disappointed. The force numbered about sixty of the Frontier Light Horse, under Captain D'Arcy and Lieutenant Blaine; forty of the Basutos, under Captain Cockerell and Lieutenants Henderson and Raw, and about eighty of Baker's Horse, the whole being under the direct command of Colonel Buller. This active commander was accompanied by the Prince Imperial, Lord W. Beresford, A.D.C. (who has already made himself familiar with the country), and Mr Drummond. We first went to Conference Hill, where the tents of the 94th are now pitched; and a more uninteresting, bare, and stony spot to pitch tents on could not be discovered elsewhere outside the Kalahara. . . . From Conference Hill we went afterwards to a farmer's house about five miles off, and here we bivouacked while our horses fed contentedly in the mealie-fields. At dawn the next morning the troops took a slightly southerly course, crossing the Blood River and passing onto a hill from which one could see Rorke's Drift some four miles distant. The country from Conference Hill is open, and a good road might easily be made between the two camps. We off-saddled at a kraal where the Zulus had been overnight – in fact, a few of their number had been there that morning, but did not wait for us. I saw them making off up to Sihayo's Hill, just opposite, and they did not stop until they reached the top, when they took instant proceedings to call a gathering of the clan. The town-crier, on a grey horse, gave due notice to all the citizens living in kraals; and very soon we beheld, from our halting place below, a respectable assembly of blackskins on the ridge above. The man on the grey horse acted as general as well as town-crier, and divided his forces judiciously. He posted his infantry on the left and the cavalry on the right of the pass. The infantry, I should say, numbered fifty, while the horsemen could only muster eight. Opposed to this army was Colonel Buller's Irregular Horse. Some of the young hands thought a bloody conflict was about to be fought out on the hill-side; the older hands calculated that the Zulus would disappear as soon as we moved upwards. The older hands were right. When Lieutenant Raw, who had been sent on ahead with six of his Basutos, reached the summit, he found himself in undisputed occupation of the field. After galloping about from point to point, the Prince espied a Zulu on a distant kopje, and made after him. Off went Lieutenant Raw

and the six Basutos after the impatient Prince, and on came Baker's Horse in the wake of the Basutos. The kopje was reached in time for them to see a few scared Zulus making off across country, far down on the plains below. In the hopes that one bullet out of fifty might find a billet in a black man's body, Baker's Horse opened fire upon the flying specks beneath: There were no casualties. . . . Baker's Troop and the Frontier Light Horse went away down the north-west slope of the mountain, and burnt the kraals there, while Colonel Buller, with the Basutos, descended on the south-east slope, coming out on a kraal where the Zulus had recently been engaged in shelling mealies. When the horses had had their fill, these were destroyed, and we proceeded to another kraal, where we were joined by the other mounted men. After this we proceeded homewards. The wind blew cold, most bitterly so; and for those who had no blankets there was no sleep that night. The Prince was among the forlorn and coverless ones, and he wandered up and down discontentedly. Next day nothing occurred. We breakfasted, we dined; we saw no Zulus, killed nothing; met with no accidents, and got into camp as quiet as you like.[4]

The 2nd Division began its move from Landman's Drift to Koppie Alleen on the Ncome towards the end of May. To curb the prince's over-exuberance he was attached to the staff of Lieutenant-Colonel Richard Harrison, the 2nd Division's Quartermaster-General. As such, he was chiefly employed in scouting out and sketching future camp sites for the column, a responsibility which kept him closer to the main column and away from the far-ranging reconnaissance patrols. On 31 June the column crossed the Ncome into Zululand once more, and began the advance to Telezeni. By now, Wood's Flying Column had already advanced from its base further north, and the two forces were only a few miles apart. The prince, eager to be in enemy territory, rode out with a small patrol to sketch the site of the proposed camp for the night of 1 June, through countryside which had been repeatedly swept by British patrols, and which had been proclaimed free of the enemy. What happened next is best described by Lieutenant Jahleel Carey of the 98th regiment, the senior officer present, in a statement which he gave in his defence at the subsequent court of inquiry:

Having learned that his Imperial Highness would proceed on June 1 to reconnoitre the country in advance of the column and choose a site for the camp the following day, I suggested that, as I had already ridden over the same ground, I should accompany him. My request was granted; but at the same time, Colonel Harrison, Acting Quartermaster-General, stated that I was not in any way to interfere with the Prince, as he wished him to have the entire credit for choosing the camp. Shortly before starting, I found that no escort was prepared, and applied to the Brigade-Major of Cavalry. I received the necessary orders, and at 9.15 six men of Bettington's Horse paraded before head-quarters. With these and a friendly Zulu, provided by the Hon. Mr Drummond, we started. Six Basutos of Captain Shepstone's Corps were also under orders to proceed with us, and before crossing the Blood [Ncome] river I sent to him to ask for them. The messenger returned to say that they would meet us, on the ridge between the Incenzi and Itelezi [Telezeni] Hills. I again sent the man with orders to bring the escort back with him. On our right and left flanks I saw large bodies of Basutos scouting. Arrived upon the ridge, we dismounted, wishing to fix the position of some hills with our compasses. Colonel Harrison then rode up and told us that General Marshall's cavalry was coming up. When he had left I suggested to the Prince to wait for the remainder of the escort. 'Oh no; we are quite strong enough'. At a mile and a half we ascended a commanding and rocky range of hills beyond the Ityotozy [Tshotshozi] River. I proposed that we should here off-saddle, but the Prince said that he preferred to off-saddle near the river. We remained for half an hour sketching and surveying the country with our telescopes. Seeing no one, we descended to a kraal in the valley below and off-saddled. No precautions were taken, as no Zulus were expected to be in the neighbourhood. The Prince was tired, and lay down beside a hut. The men made coffee, and I reconnoitred with my telescope. At 3.35 I suggested saddling up. His Imperial Highness said, 'Wait another ten minutes'; but in five minutes gave me the necessary order. I repeated it, and then went to fetch my horse from the mealie fields. I had saddled and mounted on the home side of the kraal when I heard his Imperial Highness give the order, 'Prepare to mount'. I looked round and saw his foot in the stirrup. At the same time I said 'Mount', and as the men vaulted into their saddles I saw the black faces of Zulus about twenty yards off, rushing towards us through the mealie fields. I thought that all were mounted, and, knowing that the men's carbines were unloaded, I judged it better to clear the long grass before making a stand. Knowing from experience the bad shooting of the Zulus, I did not expect that anyone was injured. I therefore shouted as we neared the donga, 'We must form up on the other side. See to the retreat of everyone.' On looking back I saw one party following us, while another on our left was attempting to cut off our retreat across the ridge. Meanwhile we were under a heavy fire, and after we had crossed the donga a man said to me, 'I fear the Prince is killed, Sir.' I paused, looked back, and seeing the Prince's horse galloping on the other side of the donga, asked if it was any use returning. The Zulus had already passed over the ground where he must have fallen, and he pointed out the men creeping round our left. I paused for our men to come up, and then galloped to find a drift over the Tombocto [Tombokala] River.[5]

The survivors fled helter-skelter back towards the 2nd Division camp, but were met by Wood and Buller, scouting ahead of the Flying Column. The news passed rapidly around both columns like a thunder-clap; it was by then late in the afternoon, and it was not possible to send out a search party. Soon after dawn the next morning, however, a strong mounted force set out from the 2nd Division camp to search for the prince's body. Melton Prior recalled how the 'specials' were keen to be first on the scene:

They were the French correspondent of the Paris *Figaro*, Archibald Forbes of the *Daily News*, Francis Francis of *The Times*, Mackenzie of the *Standard*, Charles Fripp of the *Graphic*, and myself. The search party was spread out over a large area, as it was not known where we might come across the bodies of the unfortunate men. I was riding by the side of Forbes, when, a short distance on our left, we saw one of the troop holding up his rifle and calling out loud. Forbes immediately said, 'There it is, Prior. Come on, ride for it!', and a magnificent rider he was.

I followed hard on his heels and was the fourth man to arrive on the spot. . . .[6]

It was the *Figaro* correspondent, Deléage, who left perhaps the most moving account of the discovery of the prince's body:

We hastened forward, and all doubt was at an end; it was the Prince that lay before us. We could recognise, even from a distance, the small white and well-knit body, in which the grace of form did not interfere with strength and activity. The Prince was lying on his back; his arms, stiffened by death, crossed a little above the chest; the features showed no sign of pain, or any contraction whatever; the left eye was half closed; the right eye had been destroyed by an assegai stab. The chest was pierced by seventeen wounds, and according to their custom, the Zulus had cut open the stomach, but the incision was only a small one, and the viscera had been spared. Judging from the position of the body and the expression on the features, the Prince must have been killed by the first blow. . . .[7]

The corpse was lifted onto a stretcher, improvised from a blanket wrapped around lances, and carried back towards the camp, where it was met by an ambulance sent out for it. Two troopers of Bettington's Horse had been killed in the attack; their mutilated bodies were found nearby, and buried close to where the prince had fallen. When the body reached the camp, a funeral parade was called, and Louis was carried

The prince's body, draped in a Tricolour, is drawn through the British camp at Nondweni on 2 June 1879, the day after his death. Lord Chelmsford and his staff walk behind. (Ian Knight)

Saint Mary's Roman Catholic Chapel in Pietermaritzburg, photographed when the body of the Prince Imperial was lying there in state. (Ian Knight)

The prince's body is loaded on board ship at Durban, destined for burial in England. (Ian Knight)

on a gun carriage past the troops in line, with Lord Chelmsford and his staff following behind, while a Catholic priest read the service. This was to prove the first of many such services, for rather than bury the Prince in the field, it was decided to send his body to his mother in England. The *Graphic* described the grim progress through Natal to Durban, where at each stage of the journey mournful crowds of soldiers and settlers turned out to pay their respects:

> On the 3rd inst. [June] the Prince's body left for Koppie Allein, with an escort, and from thence was taken to Pietermaritzburg, where it was received with great military honours, the funeral procession coming finally to a halt before the little schoolroom of the Roman Catholic mission. There the remains were formally identified by General Clifford, M. Delaeage, the correspondent of the Figaro, and the Prince's valet, Uhlmann, and the coffin was finally sealed up, being then moved to the Chapel, where it lay in state. Next morning a solemn mass was performed, and the coffin was sent on to Durban, where it was expected on the 11th of June. Thence it would be put on board H.M.S. *Boadicea* and taken to Cape Town, where it would be transferred to H.M.S. *Orontes*, which would at once set sail for England, the late Prince's remains being under the command of Col. Pemberton, of the 60th Rifles.[8]

The death of the prince provoked an extraordinary degree of press interest, far more than had done the slaughter at Isandlwana. Melton Prior had realized the importance of the event, and prided himself on scooping his rivals with his sketches of the scene:

> I went to General Newdigate and told him that I wanted to work all night, and asked permission to have a light in my tent. I assured him that I would cover it round with a blanket and that it should not be seen outside in the smallest degree. He informed me that it was against the rules of the camp, but under the circumstances, and on this special occasion, he would grant me permission, and an order was written so that the sentry near my tent should not interfere with me.
>
> Once alone I lighted my lamp and sat down and pitched into work, and by five o'clock in the morning I had made nine sketches in connection with the Prince Imperial's untimely end.
>
> My best horse was saddled, and my man, with my sketches in the regulation red envelope of the office, was only waiting for daylight to start and gallop to Landman's Drift to save the post, which he succeeded in doing, and my sketches were the only ones that appeared in London in connection with that sad event.[9]

Prior was, perhaps, flattering himself, for the *Illustrated London News* published its supplementary issue devoted to the prince on 16 July, while Charles Fripp's sketches of the recovery of the body were published in the *Graphic* only ten days later. Every stage of the prince's last pathetic journey was described and illustrated. The *Orontes* anchored at Spithead on 10 July, and the body was landed from the Thames at Woolwich, where it was formerly identified. Louis was finally buried in a state funeral, attended by Queen Victoria herself, at the family mausoleum at Chislehurst,

PUMPING PUBLIC OPINION.—THE COLD WATER CURE.

John Bull :—" YOU'D BETTER TAKE IT QUIETLY, MY MEN; YOU GOT YOURSELVES INTO HOT WATER AND REQUIRE COOLING."

John Bull pours the cold water of 'common sense and fair play' on bickering army officers in the aftermath of the Carey court-martial, in this cartoon from the satirical magazine *Fun*. (Ian Knight) in Kent, on 12 July. The funeral did little to dampen the press interest, however, which transferred instead to the unfortunate Lieutenant Carey. Carey's spirited defence had not been enough to save him from a charge of misbehaviour before the enemy, and he was sent back to England to be cashiered. He arrived to find himself the subject of intense public debate, and portrayed in many quarters as a scapegoat for the failings of his superiors. In the event, the queen refused to confirm his sentence, and he was allowed to return to his regiment. Norris-Newman displayed an uncharacteristic sense of proportion when he wrote that:

> The death of the Prince Imperial, considered per se, can only be regarded as a minor episode of the campaign, especially from a military standpoint. But various causes – his rank and misfortunes, his connection with the British army, the actual incidents of the fatality, arising out of the duties of the expedition, and lastly, the subsequent proceedings of the court-martial – combine to invest it with a special pathos and interest, almost world-wide.[10]

Long before the unfortunate Louis was buried, the Zulu War had moved on. On 3 June the 2nd Division had resumed its march, and affected a junction with the Flying Column. The two columns advanced in tandem, and on the 5th encountered the first serious resistance of the second invasion. Scouts had suggested that the Zulus were massing near several homesteads belonging to Chief Sihayo along the banks of the Ntinini (Phoko) stream, at the foot of a hill named eZungeni. It was not clear whether these were merely the chief's retainers, or the advance guard of a major army, and on 5 June Buller led the irregular cavalry out to investigate. He found the Zulus in some strength:

> . . . drawn up in columns flanking the larger and three lesser kraals, as if challenging an attack, which Colonel Buller, after collecting the scouting parties determined to accept before the enemy could be reinforced; and giving the order to advance at a trot, followed the cattle tracks through the river. As we advanced, nearing the kraals, the enemy retired into the belt of thorn bush surrounding the base of the mountain, distant about 300 yards in the rear of the kraals, from which they poured a heavy fusilade on us as we advanced on the kraals. Col. Buller with his usual gallantry led the way. At the kraal we found three goods wagons and an ammunition cart, with the Government marks, showing that the four vehicles were the spoils of Isandhlwana. In one of the wagons there were 3 military saddles, some pick axes and shovels. The four kraals were successively fired, one of the burnt huts was full of military equipments. A pair of military boots were picked up outside the kraal marked with the 80th regiment, and the regimental number of one of the victims of the Intombe [Ntombe] mountain, showing that Usirayo's [Sihayo's] people were there then with Umbeline [Mbilini]. After firing a few volleys, and half an hour's independent firing, at the enemy concealed in the bush, it was perceived that their fire slackened, and the order was given to retire across the river, and form on the heights opposite, in the hope that the enemy would leave their cover and follow us into the open. Before we arrived at the position selected the

Lancers and Dragoons were seen coming over the ridge, but before we left, a party of Zulus had crept down the donga on the left of Baker's and MacDonald's Horse, and crept up in their rear through the long grass, and poured in a volley at 30 yards range, and while they were getting into the saddle they had got a second one from their wily friends, at about the same distance. The Lancers and Dragoons crossed the river after the retreat of the volunteers, but not being supported by the artillery could not dislodge the enemy, and had to retire after loosing a valuable and much esteemed young officer, Adjt. Frith, who was shot through the left arm and through the chest by a shot from the donga.

After the retreat of the Lancers the Zulus crept down the donga and river bed, and fired on a troop of the F.L. Horse who were saddling up to fall back on the ridge, and the Zulus came out of the bush and tried by creeping down the donga on the right to cut off or surprise the retiring videttes, but Captain T. Shepstone checkmated them by marching down his troop of the Natal Mounted natives, and pouring in such a fire as made the enemy retreat. After this, the Zulus did not advance beyond the burnt kraals, but stood shouting out defiance to us. . . .[11]

Although Buller had successfully proved that the Zulu position concealed no major army, it is difficult to avoid the impression that the Zulus had come out of the incident with honours more than even. The body of Lieutenant Frith was taken back and buried close to the 2nd Division camp. Coming so soon on the death of the Prince Imperial, his loss exaggerated the tension which had been mounting among the inexperienced 2nd Division troops since they had first crossed into enemy territory. The result was a spectacular scare on the night of the 6th, the worst of a number of false alarms which would characterize the march to oNdini. Melton Prior was working in his tent when:

. . . I heard a distant shot from our pickets, followed by another, and then two more. Instantly there was a commotion in our laager as everyone rushed off to the tents to obtain firearms, or came out of them ready for eventualities, and then a volley from the picket's supports was distinctly heard. At the same moment our alarm bugle sounded, and tents were struck, that is to say pulled down, and we all rushed to take up our position by the wagons. My boy gave me my helmet, greatcoat and revolver, and then down came my tent.

Suddenly some of our officers imagined they could see a black mass approaching, and gave the word to fire, and instantly a most terrific fire was going on all round the laager. For some ten minutes or so the most deafening noise of musketry was kept up; horses got loose and careered about amongst us. Our native allies appeared almost mad with fear, and the danger we ran of being shot by our men was horrible; as it was, five of our own men were wounded by our own fire.

I went up to the edge of the laager, and looking over a wagon tried to see if I could catch sight of the enemy, and as I turned round I saw any number of our native allies with their muskets pointing straight towards me.

I need scarcely say that I soon cleared out of that position. The brutes were firing all over the camp, and I could hear the bullets whiz through the air, from one point of the laager to the other. A more disgraceful scene I have never witnessed, more particularly when we realised that six rounds of canister were actually fired by the artillery, without having seen a single enemy. There was one redeeming feature in the whole affair, and that was that the pickets fell back and came into camp in Indian file, as steady as on parade, although under a terrible fire from our own square. The bugle sounded the 'Cease fire', but we kept under arms all night. . . .[12]

Despite the widespread British nervousness, the Zulus were scarcely in a position to mount an offensive against the invading columns. The heavy losses endured at Khambula and Gingindlovu had shocked the nation, and the warriors spent more than two months in their homesteads recuperating. It was not until the beginning of June that Cetshwayo felt confident enough to recall them and, although the majority responded well enough, large numbers remained in the countryside, either to defend their homes against the British columns, or out of a reluctance to face the firestorm of battle again. While the king was quite prepared to make one last stand in defence of the Zulu heartland, he had lost faith in a purely military solution, and at the same time put out tentative feelers to see if the British were prepared to negotiate. To the British, this dual approach smacked of duplicity:

Cetywayo's latest overtures of peace appear to have been as vague and unsatisfactory as their predecessors, and Lord Chelmsford is understood to have sent back the intimation that if the King desires to be thought in earnest, he must return the two field guns captured at Isandhlwana, accompanied by duly accredited and creditable ambassadors. Meanwhile hostilities will proceed. To show how little dependence can be placed upon these peaceful professions, on the part of either Cetywayo or his people, we may state a fact or two in connection with General Crealock's coast column. About the 28th of May, 100 men of Nettleton's Native Contingent, patrolled the Amatakula [amaTigulu] bush from Fort Crealock, seeing no signs of the enemy. Upon their return to camp, 10 men broke away without permission and stayed behind to gather sweet potatoes. Whilst so engaged, about 40 Zulus crept up to shot range and fired a volley, killing one of the natives. The remaining nine bolted, but rallied within a short distance, and began to fire volleys from their breechloaders, when they drove the Zulus back. . . .[13]

In fact, King Cetshwayo had long since lost any opportunity for a negotiated settlement. Frere and Chelmsford had never regarded the terms of the ultimatum as negotiable; if, in the dark days after Isandlwana, they had stuck by their original demands, there were few enough reasons why they should abandon them when the tide of war had swung so clearly in their favour. Chelmsford's demands were no less impossible in June 1879 than Frere's had been in December 1878 and, while the king tried desperately to find some common ground, Chelmsford prepared for the final confrontation which would vindicate his reputation and wipe out the stain of

Isandlwana. The combined 2nd Division and Flying Column advance was slow but inexorable; the British advance crawled past Babanango Mountain, and on to the Mthonjaneni Ridge, overlooking the beautiful emaKhosini Valley – the birthplace of the Zulu kingdom, where the ancestors of the Zulu kings lie buried – and was poised for the final descent into the White Mfolozi Valley, and oNdini itself. At each step of the way the British established forts to protect the supply convoys which toiled endlessly along the lines of communication, while the cavalry raided and destroyed the deserted Zulu homesteads which lay all around.

Nevertheless, the Natal press became increasingly impatient at the slow progress of war, especially after the Zulu raid through the Thukela Valley on 25 June. This exasperation was exaggerated by the imperfect communications with the 2nd Division: while the 1st Division's telegraph lines extended all the way to Port Durnford, the telegraph to the 2nd Division had only been laid as far as Landman's Drift, and all communication thereafter was by rider. While news arrived daily, therefore, from the coast, Chelmsford's advance seemed to have been swallowed up in a fog of silence and conjecture. The arrival of General Sir Garnet Wolseley at Durban on 28 June promised to inject some much needed vigour into the campaign, and in a sense it did; Chelmsford became increasingly concerned to bring the war to a successful conclusion before Wolseley could reach the front to replace him. The *Natal Mercury* correctly guessed that Wolseley's unsuccessful attempt to reach the front by sea at Port Durnford would give Chelmsford the opportunity he needed:

> We were sorry to learn by our last night's telegram [3 July] from Port Durnford, that Sir Garnet Wolseley had not been able to land. Should the sea have continued intractable last night, we believe that His Excellency means to return in the Shah to Durban, and will probably proceed overland to the front. No further telegraphic news reached us last night from Lord Chelmsford, but in military circles a belief that a very heavy engagement was imminent prevails. . . .[14]

On 26 June the combined cavalry from the 2nd Division and Flying Column descended from the heights between Babanango and Mthonjaneni into the emaKhosini Valley:

> All the cavalry had made a reconnaissance, in force about fourteen hundred strong; they had found two large military kraals with about four to six hundred huts in each; they were soon in flames, and by the end of the day the cavalry had burnt quite 2000 huts. The military kraals were in circles, surrounded by a high wall, and outside a wooden stockade, and outside this again a prickly-pear wall. One of Colonel Baker's troop picked up, in the ashes of a burnt kraal, two nuggets of gold, and £5 in sovereigns. The natives all retired to the bush, without any damage done on either side.[15]

The expedition, one of the most destructive of the war, held a particularly unfortunate significance for the Zulus. Unbeknown to the British, one of the *amakhanda* they had razed – esiKlebheni – had housed the *inkhata yezwe yakwaZulu*, a totem of immense spiritual importance, a coil of grass rope, bound in python skin, which incorporated substances embodying the spirits of the Zulu kings since Shaka, and of the various clans which made up the nation. The *inkatha* was said to bind the kingdom together, and its destruction foreshadowed a terrible national catastrophe.

Chelmsford established a fixed camp on the Mthonjaneni heights, and on 30 June his troops began their descent into the Mfolozi Valley, leaving much of their baggage behind them, and carrying only rations for ten days. The vanguard did not reach the river until the following day, and here Chelmsford established what was to prove his most forward base in Zululand during the war; on the other side of the river lay the Mahlabathini Plain and the complex of *amakhanda* which constituted the Zulu capital, including oNdini itself. Here the king made one final attempt to stave off disaster. Zulu envoys had braved the aggressive cavalry patrols to approach the columns twice at the end of June, bringing with them on one occasion two enormous ivory tusks, and on another the Prince Imperial's sword, taken from near his body on 1 June. Chelmsford was prepared to modify some of his immediate demands in order to bring about an armistice, but insisted that any subsequent negotiations would be based on the terms of the ultimatum. Chelmsford allowed Cetshwayo until 4 July to reply, during which time he undertook not to cross the Mfolozi – a cynical touch, since he needed several days to make his final preparations for battle.

During the first few days of July, Chelmsford amassed men and supplies at his camp on the river. Cetshwayo had called up his army, and the British troops could clearly see the *amabutho* moving between the *amakhanda* on the Mahlabathini Plain. For the reinforcements who had come out to South Africa after Isandlwana, the presence of the enemy was unnerving. During the descent into the valley the 2nd Division had panicked at the sound of Zulu chanting across the river, and had begun firing blindly into the bush, to the indignation of the nearby Flying Column. On 1 July Chelmsford himself had been convinced that an attack was imminent, and ordered the columns into laager, but no Zulu threat materialized. That night, there was a more serious scare. Most of the reporters with the column preferred to draw a veil over such incidents, but Phil Robinson of the *Telegraph* admitted that:

> A number of the Native Contingent, who were sleeping outside the shelter trenches, took alarm and rushed in over men of the 2–4th [sic; 1/24th?] regiment. Seeing these naked figures rushing past them, assegais in hand, the men were sized with a panic, imagining that it was a great Zulu surprise, and rushed in the greatest confusion in the laager. All on this side of the camp was in the direst disorder, the men quite demoralised, and refusing, until their officers actually used physical force in the shape of kicking, to return to their posts outside. . . . The conduct of the young soldiers has been admirable in respect of bearing fatigues, but their steadiness in the face of the enemy has, on more than one occasion, shown signs of shortcoming.[16]

On 2 July the king's last attempts to avoid confrontation were thwarted. He tried to send a herd of his famous milk-white royal cattle to the British as a sign of appeasement, but the warriors guarding the Mfolozi drifts – young men of the uKhandempemvu *ibutho* (age-grade regiment) – indignantly refused to let them pass. Later that day the king addressed his warriors, and told them that their continued defiance was foolhardy, and that the British were likely to win the coming fight; but the warriors would not listen to him, and clamoured to be allowed another chance to defend their homeland. At noon on the 3rd the time Chelmsford had allowed for his conditions to be met expired, and Buller immediately led the irregular cavalry across the river to scout out the Mahlabathini plain, driving Zulu snipers away from the river and searching for a place to give battle. It was a move the Zulus had anticipated, and it led to a spirited skirmish, which Archibald Forbes, the ex-cavalryman, described in typically dashing style:

> The Zulu induna, bringing up the rear of his fleeing detachment, turned on the lone man who had so outridden his followers. A big man, even for a Zulu, the ring round his head proved him a veteran. The muscles rippled on his glistening black shoulders as he compacted himself behind his huge flecked shield of cowhide, marking his distance for the thrust of the gleaming assegai held at arm's length over the great swart head of him. Bill [Lord William Beresford, ADC] steadied his horse a trifle, just as he was wont to do before the take off for a big fence; within striking distance he made him swerve a bit to the left – he had been heading straight for the Zulu, as if he meant to ride him down. The spear flashed out like the head of a cobra as it strikes; the sabre carried at 'point one' clashed with it, and seemed to curl round it; the spear-head was struck aside; the horseman delivered 'point two' with all the vigour of his arm, his

Lord William Beresford's rescue of a wounded man during the skirmish at Ulundi on 3 July not only earned him the Victoria Cross, but also made him the subject of a number of drawings by the appreciative 'specials', such as this one from *The Penny Illustrated*.
(Rai England Collection)

strong seat, and the impetus of his galloping horse; and lo! in the twinkling of
an eye, the sabre's point was through the shield, and half its length was buried
in the Zulu's broad chest. The brave induna was a dead man before he dropped;
the sword drawing out of his heart as he fell backward. His assegai stands now
in the corner of Bill's mother's drawing-room.

Beresford's Zulu was the only man slain with the 'white arm' in hand-to-hand
combat during the day, but of the fugitives whom the dead induna had
commanded, several fell under the fire of the fellows who followed that chief's
slayer. The surviving Zulus ran into the nearest military kraal, Delyango
[kwaBulawayo]. Out of it the irregulars rattled them, as well as the few Zulus
who had been garrisoning it. A detachment had been left behind – a fortunate
precaution taken by Buller – to cover the retreat by holding the kopje in the
rear; and then the force – Beresford and his scouts still leading, the main body
spread out on rather a broad front – galloped on through the long grass across
the open, bending rather leftward in the direction of the Nodwengo
[Nodwengu], the next military kraal in the direction of Ulundi [oNdini]. In front
of the horsemen there kept retiring at a pace regulated by theirs, about two
hundred Zulus, all who were then visible anywhere on the face of the plain.
These shunned Nodwengo, leaving it on their right, and heading straight for
Ulundi. The irregulars drew rein long enough for a patrol to ride into Nodwengo
and report it empty. Then the horses having got their wind, the rapid advance
recommenced. It really seemed a straight run in for Buller and Beresford as they
set their horses' heads for Ulundi and galloped on. The idea had occurred to
many in the force that Cetewayo must have abandoned his capital and
withdrawn his army into the hill country close behind Ulundi.

Those irregular horsemen had no very keen sense of discipline, and in a
gallop, a forward gallop especially, were rather prone to get out of hand.
Buller's hardest task was to restrain this impulse, and it was well that day that
he was exerting himself all he knew to curb the ardour of his fellows.
Beresford's advance-detachment, scouts as they were, were of course straggled
out rather casually over the whole front. Everything seemed prosperous. No
enemy showed anywhere save the two hundred fugitive Zulus, falling back
ahead of our fellows at the long easy run which takes the Zulu over the ground
with surprising speed and which he can keep up hour after hour without a
symptom of distress.

Their flight was a calculated snare; those fugitives were simply a wily decoy.
Suddenly from out of a deep, sharply-cut water-course crossing the plain, and
visible at two hundred yards' distance, sprang up a long line of Zulus, some two
thousand strong, confronting at once and flanking the horsemen. Simultaneously
the whole plain around them flashed up into vivid life. Hordes of Zulus had
been lying hidden in the long grass. Buller's alert eye had caught the impending
danger, and his voice had run out the command 'Retire' ere yet the bullets of the
sudden Zulu volley whistled through and over his command. Three men went
down smitten by the fire. Two were killed on the spot and never stirred; we
found their bodies next day shockingly mangled. The third man's horse slipped
up on the abrupt turn, and his rider for the moment lay stunned. But Beresford,

riding away behind his retreating party, looked back at this latter man, and saw him move up into a sitting posture.

He who would succour in such a crisis must not only be a brave man, but also a prompt man, quick to decide and as quick to act. The issue of life or death hangs at such a time on the gain or waste of a moment. The Zulus, darting out from the watercourse, were perilously close to the poor fellow; but Beresford, used on the racecourse to measuring distance with the eye, thought he might just do it, if he were smart and lucky. Galloping back to the wounded man, he dismounted, and ordered him to get on his pony. The wounded man, dazed as he was, even in his extremity was not less full of self-abnegation than the man who was risking his life in the effort to save his. He bade Beresford remount and go; why, he said in his simple manly logic – why should two men die when death was inevitable but to one?

Then it was that the quaint resourceful humour of his race supplied Beresford with the weapon that prevailed over the wounded man's unselfishness. The recording angel perhaps did not record the oath that buttressed his threatening mien when he swore with clenched fist that he would punch the wounded man's head if he did not allow himself to be saved. This droll argument prevailed. Bill partly lifted, partly hustled the man into his saddle, then scrambled up somehow in front of him, and set the good little beast going after the other horsemen. He only just did it; another moment's delay and both must have been assegaid. As it was, the swift footed Zulus chased them up the slope, and the least mistake made by the pony must have been fatal. Indeed, as Beresford was the first gratefully to admit, there was a critical moment when their escape would have been impossible, but for the cool courage of Sergeant O'Toole, who rode back to the rescue, shot down Zulu after Zulu with his revolver as they tried to close in on the helpless pair, and then aided Beresford in keeping the wounded man in the saddle until the safety of the laager was attained.[17]

Melton Prior, who had seen something of the incident from the camp on the Mfolozi, recalled a curious post-script:

Those who watched the brave little band return, declared that it was touch and go whether they would get across safely. However, they succeeded in doing so, and just as Colonel Buller was going to return to camp to report to the General the result of his reconnaissance, someone informed him that a man was left behind, and turning round and looking through his glasses he did discover someone calmly standing on the enemy's side of the river sketching.

He called out to him to come back immediately – an order to which at first no attention was paid. Buller once more called out, ordering him across, or he would have him fetched and sent as a prisoner to the rear. This energetic little man, who had been sketching, turned out to be Charlie Fripp, of the *Graphic*, who had been making notes and sketches of the background for his drawing of the retreat of the cavalry, and he was most indignant at having been ordered about by any one.

Fripp came up to us, he was fairly foaming with rage. 'The idea of being insulted and being told I should be sent to the rear as a prisoner!' Then seeing

Lord William Beresford, he rode over to him, and demanded to know who the man was who had spoken to him in that insulting manner, to which Lord William, who was still smothered in the blood of the man he had saved, replied, 'You know, Mr Fripp, quite well without my telling you.'

'I don't,' replied Fripp, 'and I desire to know who it was.' Unfortunately he spoke in such an offensive manner that Lord William said in a quiet sort of way, 'If you don't speak more politely I'll pull you off your horse and thrash you.'

This was quite enough for Fripp, who was a plucky little devil, and without more ado he jumped off his horse and squared up to Lord William, and was going for him in rare style, when, in self-defence, Beresford had to show fight. It was quite exciting for the moment that it lasted, and Fripp certainly showed that he could use his fists, but Lord William, who was a notorious bruiser and all-round sportsman, did not want to hurt him, but with a straight one from the shoulder pushed rather than knocked him down.

Fripp was so excited and in such a rage that he 'up with his foot' and kicked Lord William, whereupon it was most amusing to see the latter dance round roaring with laughter and saying, 'Oh, he's kicked me! Take him away; I'm frightened. He's kicked me!'

In another moment Archie Forbes and myself had caught hold of Fripp, who fought like a perfect little demon, and we tore his coat almost to pieces before we could get the best of him and haul him away to his tent.

It was certainly one of the most amusing incidents I remember out in those parts.[18]

That night, the troops camped near the Mfolozi could clearly hear the eerie sounds of the Zulu *amabutho* undergoing their pre-combat rituals, a sure sign that the final confrontation was expected on both sides of the river. It came the next morning; the British troops were roused at 3.45 on the morning of the 4th, formed up into columns, and marched down to the river. The Flying Column crossed the Mfolozi just before 6.30 a.m. without opposition, with the 2nd Division close behind. Screened by the irregular cavalry, they marched a mile or two out onto the plain, then halted to take up a hollow square formation. No wagons were taken except for those carrying ammunition and entrenching tools. Both columns had left numbers of men to guard their posts along the lines of communication, and five companies of the 24th regiment had been left in the camp on the Mfolozi; nevertheless, Chelmsford's combined army totalled over 4,000 white soldiers and nearly 1,000 blacks, with 12 guns and 2 hand-cranked Gatling machine-guns. Once the formation was complete, Chelmsford manoeuvred it onto a grassy rise in the middle of the Mahlabathini Plain, which Buller had selected the day before. At first the plain seemed empty, but once the square was in position Zulu *amabutho* began to rise up out of the long grass or descend from the hills for, curiously, they too had selected that same spot as an ideal place to surround the enemy. Phil Robinson of the *Telegraph* described the battle which then ensued:

Forming up in a hollow parallelogram, the 80th regiment and the Gatling battery were on the front, the 90th and part of the 94th on the left flank, the 13th and

58th on the right flank, the 2–4th [sic; 2/21st?] and remainder of the 94th forming the rear, while a battery of artillery was at each corner. . . . The advantages of the position were at once apparent. In front was a broad open country with high grass sloping down to a spruit. In rear, again the country was open, with little cover save a few bushes. On the left flank the slope was rather steeper, while on the right flank the country was fully open up to the Nodwengu Kraal, which was distant about one thousand yards. The proximity of this kraal, indeed, affording as it did the cover for the Zulus to form behind, was the only weak point in the position. It had been proposed to fire it, and some of the nearer huts had actually been set alight, but, on the suggestion of Colonel Buller, this was not proceeded with, for fear that the Zulus might take advantage of the smoke to creep close up. As soon as a halt was made, steps were taken for the burial of one of the men killed on the previous day, whose body was found lying where he was slain. While this sad task was being proceeded with, the Zulus were seen approaching in force, both from the direction of Ulundi and from the bush to the right. At half-past eight, the mounted men under Buller were thrown out on the rear, left and front, meeting the enemy and keeping them in check. Owing, however, to some mistake, the right was left uncovered by the cavalry, and the mounted Basutos, under Cochrane, were accordingly sent out on that side, with orders to draw the Zulus under fire. As the Basutos retired

'Our Death or Glory Boys': an incident from the battle of Ulundi, as depicted in *The Penny Illustrated*. An unhorsed Lancer holds off the enemy while a comrade gallops to his rescue. (Rai England Collection)

before the advancing enemy, the right face of the square came into action, commencing its fire fully five minutes before the rest of the force was engaged. At ten minutes to nine, or thereabouts, firing became general, all four sides of the square being simultaneously engaged, the Zulus, after their manner, throwing forward the horns of their army to surround the British force. Coming on steadily and in complete silence, the Zulus advanced with the same intrepidity they showed at Ginginhlovo and Kambula, and continued to advance until they reached a spot not more than seventy yards from the face of the square. The British infantry were formed in four ranks, the front rank kneeling, the rear rank reversed, facing inwards, while inside the square were all the necessary arrangements for keeping up a constant supply of ammunition. It was impossible for any force long to face the deadly storms of lead poured in among them at such short distance. A few now and then made an attempt to advance further. One man rushed up to within thirty yards of the Gatling battery, and was shot as he was turning to retire. Another body was afterwards found 28 yards from the square. But it was no use. The main body wavered and paused. The moment was a decisive one. It was not the hail from the Martini-Henry bullets alone; there was the artillery continually at work, sending shell after shell through the dark masses, breaking up every partial attempt of the Zulus to concentrate their strength for a rush. And then it became time for the Lancers to be let loose. Riding down with their lances – the English 'assegais' – levelled, the British horsemen came like a whirlwind upon the hesitating enemy, and in an instant their lines were broken through. The sabre was at work as well as the lance, and soon the Zulus, their ranks torn asunder and coherency as an army destroyed, were flying before the advancing cavalry. And still, whenever there was a chance, the artillery thundered after them, and still the dull rattle from the faces of the square told how steadily the rain of death was supplementing the sweep of the broadsword and the thrust of the lance. But the Zulu does not fly without an effort to resist. Before the Lancers had gone 300 yards Captain Edgell was shot dead, while Captain [sic: Colonel] Lowe had a narrow escape, being wounded, only slightly, as it happened, in the cheek, and Lieutenant Jenkins of the same regiment, having his jaw broken. One of the narrowest escapes was that of a Lieutenant James, of the Scots Greys, who is serving with the Lancers. He rode down two Zulus, who turned upon him. One of them threw an assegai which fortunately struck a thick leather cross-belt, penetrating it, and inflicting a slight wound. But for that belt, of which curiously enough he had often complained of being too heavy, he must have been completely transfixed. . . . Besides Captain Edgell nine men were killed, and the wounded . . . numbered about 75. . . .[19]

Inside the square, Melton Prior was busily sketching incidents from the fight to work up later into a completed picture:

The air seemed alive with the whistling of bullets and slugs and pieces of cooking-pot legs fired from elephant guns as they came banging in amongst us from all directions.

The inside of Lord Chelmsford's square during the battle of Ulundi. This was the picture
Melton Prior drew from his sketches made at the time. (Ian Knight)

Our artillery practice was very fine, but it failed to daunt the Zulus. The
rockets must have astonished them a good deal, for they did us. I saw one fired,
and watched its triumphal progress amongst the enemy, until, catching a corner
of a hut, it suddenly altered its direction, then, striking the ground, it once more
deviated from its proper course, and came straight back at us, luckily missing
our square by a quarter of a yard. My faith in rockets and tubes has considerably
weakened since that occasion.

All those who were not actually engaged in fighting were ordered to keep as
low down as possible, and I was doing so kneeling, when I discovered the Rev.
Gore, who was Principal Chaplain of the Forces, was by my side.

'It's very warm, Prior,' he said.

To which I readily agreed, as a bullet banged into one of our native allies
close to us and bowled him over. By the way, it was funny to see these men
lying flat on the ground, with their shields covering their backs.

Another bullet killed a horse behind us and made him jump at least three feet
in the air. Then all at once there appeared to be a perfect hailstorm of bullets in
our direction, and we both wriggled on our knees, until one in particular passed
between us with a nasty 'phew,' and my friend exclaimed, 'My God, Prior, that
was close.'

This sort of thing went on all the time, until I heard the Zulus were said to be
preparing to rush one of our corners.

Hastily asking one of the 2nd [sic; 1st?] Dragoon Guards to hold my horse for a moment, I ran down to where the 21st and 58th Regiments were heavily engaged with some Zulus, said to be 6,000 strong and 30 deep, who were charging, and it was then that I heard Lord Chelmsford say to the troops, 'Men, fire faster, can't you fire faster?' Now it is not my business to question the wisdom of this remark, but I cannot help contrasting it with Lord Wolseley's well-known order, 'Fire slow, fire slow!'

However, the Zulus who charged this corner did not succeed in breaking it; the terrific fire of our men made them stagger, halt, and fall back at a straggling mass, leaving a heap of dead and dying on the ground.

I have since read various statements as to how near the enemy got to our square, and it is often stated that twenty or thirty paces was the closest, but I can say that I personally went out and reached the nearest one in nine paces, so their onslaught was pretty determined. . . .

. . . While watching this exciting charge, I put my hand in my pocket for my sketch-book, when I suddenly remembered that I had left it in the holster of my saddle. I often used to carry it there, so as to have it ready at a moment's notice, which in this case was just about as stupid as a cavalryman having his sword fixed to his saddle as, if thrown and attacked by an enemy, he has naturally lost possession of his sword.

Rushing back to my horse, which was still being held by a trooper of the 2nd Dragoons, I noticed the flap of my holster was unfastened, and putting my hand inside I discovered, to my horror, it was not there. I felt again in my pockets, in my saddlebags, and my haversack, I searched on the ground; no, it was not there. The trooper said he knew nothing about it.

Now I had only been using it a short time before I ran down to the corner, so what can have become of it? The more I thought, the more horrified I seemed to become at the awful loss, and at last I stood as though petrified. My sketch-book, containing all the notes I had made in the campaign and sketches of this battle, was gone, and in sheer despair I fell on the ground and burst into tears.

General Newdigate at that moment came by, and in his most kindly way asked me what was the matter, but I was almost too miserable to be able to explain. At last I did so, and he patted me on the shoulder and told me to cheer up. At the same moment Sir William Gordon Cumming, who was by my side, said, 'Never mind, Prior, here is my sketch-book; get up and run about, and make more sketches of costume and background, and I will guarantee you will get out of your troubles.'

This kindly thought and suggestion had this effect; I took the advice given, and soon obtained enough detail for my purposes. But what of my sketch-book? I offered twenty-five pounds for it in regimental orders, but I never saw it again.[20]

The dashing charge of the 17th Lancers sealed the Zulu defeat. As they began to retire from the field, the irregular horse and NNC set out to pursue them with a vigour which equalled that at Khambula. To the embarrassment of some of the officers inside the square, all living Zulus within a radius of two or three hundred yards of the square – most of them wounded – were flushed out and killed. In one place seventy Zulus were found cut off and sheltering in a donga, and all were shot. This was an aspect of the battle upon which most correspondents preferred not to dwell. Instead, they concentrated on the triumphal rush of mounted officers into the deserted royal residence, oNdini itself. Lord William Beresford, the officer, gentleman and sportsman personified, was apparently first into the great circle of more than 1,200 huts, which the retreating Zulus had already set on fire, but the 'specials' were not far behind. Melton Prior, indeed, was in for another unnerving experience:

> I had flames on three sides of me, but I cared not. I was so delighted to be able to obtain a drawing of this savage King's residence, that I only thought of the work, and did not know that Forbes and Beresford had left me to it.
>
> I may have been some four or five minutes sketching, when I saw some black object pop up above the palisade on my left. What can it be? I thought to myself, and clambering up, I actually saw a real live Zulu, with spears and shield. Then I suddenly took in the situation: I was alone with fire on three sides of me and the Zulu running to get round the courtyards, so as, if possible, to cut off my retreat.
>
> With sketch-book in one hand and pencil in the other, I started on a run for my life. Great Scot! how I ran to try to get out of this frightful trap.
>
> As I tore through the first courtyard I saw no-one, and through the second I saw no one, but as I entered the third and turned my head I saw a Zulu turn the corner of the first courtyard, racing for me as hard as he could.
>
> My God, I thought, I am lost! The fact that I had a revolver by my side never entered my head. I simply ran for dear life, and as I emerged into the open, by everything that is holy, there was my horse still eating out of the basket.
>
> Springing on his back, and digging my spurs in, he made a wild leap forward, and as I dug my spurs more and more into him, so he went for all he was worth. I had not bothered about gathering up reins, but simply guided him by pulling his head round by the mane and ears. In his wild career he put his feet in the reins and tore them asunder, fortunately without stumbling or throwing me, for this would have meant the end of the matter. . . .
>
> . . . Safe in the laager, I was chatting with a commissariat officer when a captain who had been on picket duty outside Ulundi came in. Turning to me he said, 'You had a lucky escape this morning.' 'Yes,' I said, 'a Zulu chased me.'
>
> 'There were five,' he said, 'for I saw them, and thought that they would have you, but you were too nippy in getting on your pony. They threw several assegais at you, but luckily missed you. I was too far off to be of any use, and my troopers could not get to you in time, but by Jove, you did get away smartly!'[21]

At about 2 p.m., Chelmsford ordered his force to retire to the camp on the White Mfolozi. To the British, it seemed obvious that the Zulu kingdom had fallen. Perhaps 1,500 Zulu corpses lay on the grassy approaches to the site of the square, and the survivors had been utterly broken. All of the great *amakhanda* on the surrounding plain had been put to the torch, and oNdini itself would burn for four days, covering the battlefield with a great pall of smoke. King Cetshwayo himself had fled. The

Melton Prior, running for his life amid the burning ruins of oNdini. (Rai England Collection)

British had met the Zulus fairly, in the open, without the protection of trenches or laagers, and had scattered them. Chelmsford's honour was vindicated, and the bloody spectre of Isandlwana exorcized. For the professional 'specials' in the camp, it was the beginning of the end, for only the capture of the fugitive king promised to be newsworthy. Archibald Forbes believed implicitly in the righteousness of the British cause, but as an ex-soldier he was not uncritical of military ineptitude, and many times his despatches had contrasted the 2nd Division – and thereby Chelmsford – unfavourably with the tight professional attitude prevalent in Wood's Flying Column. Nor had Forbes been much impressed with the attitude of the white settlers in Natal, and he had made himself unpopular among them as a result; although full of admiration for the heroism and endurance of the British soldier, Forbes was moved to admire the courage of the Zulus. Charles Fripp of the *Graphic* went one step further, sensing something vaguely shameful in the spectacle of the Zulu dead lying out on the plain, who had given their all in the defence of their kingdom. Few of the part-time correspondents in the Natal press shared their qualms, however; the *Natal Mercury*'s war correspondent expressed a common opinion that the battle proved that King Cetshwayo's 'bloody organisation is, I hope, drawing towards an end'.[22]

For the 'specials', the immediate problem after the battle was over was how to get the news home in time to scoop their rivals. The nearest telegraph line was at Landman's Drift, way down the line of communication. Archibald Forbes found himself committed to one last adventure. Forbes had scribbled out a short account of the battle, and enquired of Chelmsford whether he might send it back by means of the official despatch rider. Chelmsford replied dismissively that he would not be sending his despatch until the following day, and Forbes, irritated, snapped 'Then, sir, I will start myself at once!'. To Melton Prior's delight, Forbes offered to carry his sketch of the battle too, and, although Chelmsford refused to entrust him with an official communiqué, Forbes did take a packet of telegrams from his staff. It was late evening by the time he set out, and, as he told a friend in a letter later published in the *Daily News*:

> I think on the whole I was sorry I had spoken the moment I had spoken. It was already dusk. I had been in the saddle almost without food from five o'clock in the morning. All my horses had been out, and were no longer fresh. My first stage (to our standing camp on the ridge) [Mthonjaneni] would consist of some fourteen miles through thick bush and broken ground, in close proximity to the military kraals burnt on the 28th ult. It was all but certain that broken Zulus were lurking in the bush or poking about among the embers of the kraals. A considerable movement of troops around both our flanks to our rear in the direction of our standing camp had been observed on the previous day. All these considerations flashed across me much more quickly than I can put them on paper, after I had spoken the words of self-committal; but I had not courage enough to retract them. Nor would my pride allow me to ask for an escort, which was not tendered. I volunteered to carry any communications which Lord Chelmsford might have ready, and his military secretary gave me a packet which he specified contained certain 'private telegrams', to be handed in at Landman's Drift. So I said adieu to headquarters and went to get ready to start.

Many men tried to dissuade me: my enterprise was freely characterised as 'madness' and 'd—d foolhardiness'. Evelyn Wood was the last man to urge an objection, and when that had no avail, he gave me a telegram for his wife. The night was just falling as I rode up the steep rugged track from the laager into the bush. I was riding a dark chestnut whose pluck and staying power I knew well, and I meant to test both. My great effort was to traverse as much ground as possible before it got quite dark, for I did not like the interval of pitchy darkness before the moon should rise about eight o'clock. So I sent the chestnut along at best pace. It was a gruesome ride, and I would sooner be shot at for two hours at a stretch than do it again. There was no road, only a confusion of wagon-tracks through the long grass, made by our vehicles in their advance. Everywhere the bush, in detached clumps some ten feet high, clustered thick around and among the tracks. I daren't smoke for fear the striking of a match might perchance betray me. All that there was for me was to trust to luck, see that the flap of my revolver case was open, and keep the good horse dead straight.

On we went, down into black gullies, where half a regiment might have lain hidden, through little patches of tall thorn brake, whose prickles tore my clothes and lacerated my skin, stumbling over fallen trunks, wending through long rank grass, always ears cocked, and every sense at its fullest tension. Several fires were visible through the bush foliage to right and left, doubtless the night fires of straggling bodies of Zulus. Behind me seethed the Gehenna of the blazing Ulundi and the other kraals fired that day. Their lurid blaze helped me after darkness fell, which they served to mitigate. But at length I came to a dead halt near the region where the two columns camped on their march between the ridge at Entongeneni [Mthonjaneni] and the White Umfaloosi [Mfolozi]. The multiplicity of tracks confused me. I had fairly lost my way. I could dimly see close to me the charred relics of the great Slipane [emaKheni?] kraal, and I knew I must be near a bog, into which, if I strayed, my horse at least would never emerge. There was no recourse but to halt where I was, and wait, with what patience I might, for the moon to rise. I dare say she kept her time, but I must say I thought her shockingly slow. At length the great disc shaved above the ridge, and illuminated the basin below. After a few casts, I hit off the spoor, and in ten minutes more was climbing the open grassy slope that leads to the standing camp at Entongeneni. Here the chestnut was done, and right well he had done; but Major Upcher, of the 24th, who was in command, first ordered his men a lot of rum each in honour of the good news I brought, and then furnished me with a fresh horse, and a party to guide me on the devious way. Steadily I rode all through the bitter night under the moonlight without adventure, save the occasional missing and recovery of the road. I had an escort for two stages, and then I went alone.[23]

Despite the onset of fog, shortly before dawn the next morning, Forbes reached Landman's Drift between 2 and 3 p.m. on the 5th, having ridden 110 miles in twenty hours, using six horses. To his satisfaction, Forbes heard that Chelmsford had changed his mind after he set out, and decided to send a messenger that evening after all; he had set out an hour after Forbes, with an escort, but did not arrive until

10 p.m. on the 5th. News of Forbes adventure was hailed at home, and christened 'The Ride of Death', leading his more enthusiastic admirers to suggest that he should be awarded the Victoria Cross. In Natal it received a cooler reception, and the great William Russell of *The Times* went so far as to suggest that Forbes had been drunk at the time. Even Melton Prior admitted that the ride 'was distinctly risky for the first eight or ten miles, but after that it was comparatively easy going'.[24] Certainly, the ride made a good story in an industry that assiduously encouraged the 'cult of personality' surrounding its more famous 'specials', yet it was by no means without danger. Only a few days before a lieutenant of the 21st Regiment, J.H. Scott Douglas, had left the Mthonjaneni camp with his orderly, a corporal in the 17th Lancers, to carry a message to Fort Evelyn, down the line. On the return journey they apparently lost their way in a mist, and blundered into an *impi* on its way to oNdini. Their bodies were not found until 11 July, riddled with spear wounds.

Later, Forbes was to claim that the telegrams given to him by Chelmsford's secretary were sufficiently official as to entitle him to the South Africa campaign medal. After months of wrangling he was refused by the War Office. During the course of his campaign, Forbes abandoned any attempt at impartial reporting, and published a bitter critique of Chelmsford's conduct of the campaign in the *Nineteenth Century* magazine in February 1880. It provoked a spirited defence by Chelmsford's admirers, but was to prove the first of a number of attacks which would cast a shadow over Chelmsford's later career. Perhaps disillusioned by the squabble, Forbes retired from active reporting after the Zulu War.

Within a few days of the battle – which the British, who had dithered between the alternative names for Cetshwayo's royal homestead throughout the war, finally decided to call Ulundi – the British forces broke up. From Mthonjaneni the 2nd Division moved slowly back the way it had come, while the Flying Column marched across country to establish a base at St Paul's, midway towards the 1st Division on the coast. Chelmsford had won his race with Lord Wolseley; he alone had defeated the Zulus, and now that his reputation was secure, he was content to leave whatever remained of the war to his successor. On 8 July he officially resigned his command.

NOTES

1. Prior, *Campaigns of a War Correspondent*, p. 105.
2. Private letter, Cambridge to Chelmsford, reported in the *Illustrated London News*, 16 July 1879.
3. *Graphic*, 8 March 1879.
4. *Illustrated London News*, 28 June 1879, quoting letter published in the *Natal Witness*.
5. Carey's report, published in the *Illustrated London News*, 5 July 1879.
6. Prior, *Campaigns of a War Correspondent*, p. 106.
7. *Illustrated London News*, 16 July 1879.
8. *Graphic*, 6 July 1879.
9. Prior, *Campaigns of a War Correspondent*, p. 107.

10. Norris-Newman, *In Zululand With the British*, p. 192.
11. *Natal Mercury*, Zulu War Supplement, June 1879: 12 June, report dated 'Mantzanhlopi Camp, June 6, 1879'.
12. Prior, *Campaigns of a War Correspondent*, p. 108.
13. *Natal Mercury*, Zulu War Supplement, June 1879: report dated 10 June.
14. *Natal Mercury*, Zulu War Supplement, July 1879: report of 4 July.
15. Ibid.: report 'From a Correspondent' with the Flying Column dated 20 June 1879.
16. Ibid.: report 'compiled by the *Witness* from Mr. Phil Robinson's telegrams to England', issue of 14 July.
17. Archibald Forbes, *Barracks, Bivouacs and Battles* (London, MacMillan & Co., 1891), pp. 144–5.
18. Prior, *Campaigns of a War Correspondent*, pp. 114–15.
19. *Natal Mercury*, Zulu War Supplement, July 1879: report published 14 July 'compiled by the *Witness* from Mr. Phil. Robinson's telegrams to England'.
20. Prior, *Campaigns of a War Correspondent*, pp. 118–20.
21. Ibid., pp. 121–2.
22. *Natal Mercury*, Zulu War Supplement, July 1879: report published 19 July dated 'From our War Correspondent, Magnum Bonum Camp, 7th July 1879'.
23. *Daily News*, 21 August 1879.
24. Prior, *Campaigns of a War Correspondent*, p. 123.

Surrender

While the 2nd Division and the Flying Column were inexorably advancing on the Mahlabathini Plain for the final battle of the war on 4 July, the 1st Division continued laboriously to push up the coast, getting no further north than the Mhlathuze River. Its lack of progress meant that it was quite unsuccessful in its primary purpose, which was to cooperate with the other two columns and force Cetshwayo to divide his forces. By the beginning of July it was encamped at Port Durnford and sending out patrols. A correspondent of the *Illustrated London News* based at Port Durnford sent home an account of a major raid beyond the Mhlathuze and of increasing Zulu submissions:

> Yesterday [4 July], at three in the morning, the cavalry, consisting of the Natal Guides, the mounted infantry, Cook's Horse and four troops of Lonsdale's Horse, and two hundred of John Dunn's scouts, with several mounted Basutos, started from the camp. . . . At four o'clock we off-saddled for an hour, not far from Emangwene [emaNgweni], where a military kraal [*ikhanda*], the head-quarters of a young regiment, was situated. At half-past five we reached the hill overlooking the kraal. A plan of attack was formed; two flanks were thrown out, and the centre advanced, in which were the mounted Basutos. These galloped up to the kraal, but found it was deserted. There were three or four hundred huts, placed around that of the chief in regular form. Two of the huts had doors and windows, and all the comfort of an English cottage.
>
> The chief's hut was surrounded with an intricate palisade, which would have been serviceable against the assault of a savage foe. At half-past six the kraal was set on fire, while the cavalry, at a hand-gallop, scoured the country around for cattle. . . . The spoils of the day were six or seven hundred cattle, eleven asses bred by Cetewayo, and about thirty goats. Major Barrow, who commands the cavalry, was apprehensive that the Zulus might assemble and endeavour to recapture the cattle. But they did not make the slightest attempt to oppose us. As usual, some Zulu women and children were brought in. It was strange to see a Kaffir woman in tears. Most likely, she had had her home burnt, and all that she cared for was scattered.
>
> A Zulu chief, with two hundred warriors, and a very large number of women and children, came to the camp here [on 3 July]. The men surrendered and gave up their arms. Our troops, mustering about five hundred, were paraded, with flags unfurled, which made an imposing appearance. Only twenty-five old guns and

two hundred assegais were delivered up by the Zulus. Such arms, indeed, are but a poor defence against the modern breechloaders. There is but little fight left among the Zulus now. Our vast preparations have terrified them, and their summer crops cannot be sown this year. The only fear is that Cetewayo has retreated into the bush; and, so long as he remains free, he will be a standing menace to Natal.

The 91st Highlanders had a large bonfire on Wednesday [4 July], while the pipers played some lively strains, and several of the men sang excellent songs. During the evening, two or three officers danced a highland reel. It must have appeared a strange sight to the natives.

July 8

Unusual activity has been shown lately, in the way of reconnaissances by the cavalry. These were formerly kept in camp, employed in stuffing saddles or other work. . . . But now it is different. The Zulus evidently see that they are overpowered [news of the battle of Ulundi reached the coast by 5 July], and have made but a feeble resistence, firing only few shots at long ranges at our mounted men, who have driven off their cattle.

Since it was made known to Zulus what favourable terms of surrender would be allowed, district after district has made its submission, preferring to keep their cattle rather than support a tottering King. The Zulus have been no losers by this campaign. The greater number of their kraals are left intact, and the same remark applies to their cattle. They care little for losing their men in battle. But since the battle of Gingihlovo not one man has fallen in fighting in this column of our army. Meantime, death by disease, though not by the hands of the enemy in the field, has made sad havoc with our troops. . . .[1]

A *Natal Witness* occasional correspondent at Port Durnford witnessed the formal submission on 5 July of most of the coastal chiefs at an impressive general parade of the 1st Division got up to overawe them:

> . . . The troops paraded and went out with the General to meet the larger gang; the band and pipers played, the troops presented arms, and the General and his numerous Staff smiled and looked pleasant, and, altogether, it was a very pretty and edifying spectacle, and it is to be hoped was duly appreciated by the Zulus and their families, for whose special entertainment it appeared to have been got up. After some few formalities had been gone through, the men marched up and laid down their guns, and were presented with small slips of paper, bearing the word 'pass,' by John Dunn, and which they at once stuck in their ears. After being photographed by an officer, and interrogated and admired by a numerous crowd, they slowly dispersed. Strict orders have been given that Zulus with these passes are, on no account, to be interfered with. . . .[2]

Among the Zulu leaders who began to give themselves up shortly after the battle of Ulundi was Dabulamanzi. As the Zulu commander at Rorke's Drift he was particularly notorious in British eyes, and the *Natal Witness* special correspondent described him on 13 July in fascinated detail:

BRAVO, CHELMSFORD!

Cetswayo :—"OH, CHELMY, CHELMY! I DIDN'T EXPECT THIS OF YOU."

'Oh, Chelmy, Chelmy!', cries a battered Cetshwayo in this cartoon by *Fun* satirizing
Chelmsford's victory at Ulundi, 'I didn't expect this of *you*!'. (Ian Knight)

I confess I had considerable curiosity to look on one whose name has been prominently before us since the commencement of this war, whose courage all admit and whose generalship in leading on savages has been highly spoken of by his bitterest foes. . . . [Dabulamanzi] arrived to-day on horseback with a mounted escort. He appears of medium height, the upper part of his burly form being incased in a pea jacket which was given to him at the Tugela. Like all the chiefs of Zululand that I have met he is very corpulent, so much so that no inexpressibles I have ever seen could be pulled on his form. Yet though obese, on his large feet he is wiry and active. His forehead is high and commanding, the face long and lit up by the light of two quick eyes of a yellowish hue. The nose is small and pretty. The lips are broad, much after the Negro type, but do not take away from a face I must call handsome. I noticed Dabalumanzi wears a whisker and moustachios which look as if they receive no small share of his attention. He cannot speak English. For any little act of kindness he will simply nod his head and show his white teeth. It appears to me that his disposition is most taciturn. . . . I may mention that Dabalumanzi has a bullet wound above the left knee, received at the battle of Ginginhlovu. It is a slight fleshy one.[3]

Chelmsford resigned his command on 9 July and Wolseley was determined to achieve peace without any further hostilities. In order to put the earlier submissions by the coastal chiefs on a more formal basis, he met them on 19 July at his camp near the emaNgweni *ikhanda*, which Major Barrow had burned on 4 July. Wolseley announced the end of the Zulu kingdom and his intention to break it up into a number of districts to be ruled by chiefs whose names he would announce later. The surrendered chiefs expressed their satisfaction with such easy terms. The *Natal Witness* correspondent present at the ceremony reflected on the condition of Zululand now that the war was over:

. . . Riding through the country one is struck by the marked contrast between the appearance of the country at the present time and a few weeks ago. Not long since the neighbouring fertile lands were the scenes of battle, desolation, and other evils attending war, no matter where or how conducted. Now everything presents a peaceful aspect, and those who until very recently were anxious to meet the invading forces of the white man in battle, are now industriously engaged rebuilding their old kraals, which have been fired and otherwise destroyed by the invading army, which now rests well satisfied with the results of its late conflict in the country of its late enemy. A stranger passing the knots of busy people would [not] suspect that a few months since these very same people were the cause of so many and vast preparations, and that their name was a bye-word in thousands of families both in South Africa and England, and, indeed, in every country of Europe. Now, how changed is the state of affairs. . . . Visits are repeatedly paid to camp by these Zulus, and in some cases returned, as if war had never disturbed him, or the fire from our guns created havoc among his own and neighbours' homes.

The war will long be remembered among the Zulu people, as fully one half of their young men have been killed since the outbreak of hostilities. There is

Wiping out the stains of defeat: Chelmsford's critics, led by Disraeli himself, clean his boots in the aftermath of Ulundi. (Ian Knight)

scarcely a family which has not lost one of its members, while numbers of them
have lost some of their cattle, which is the Zulus' treasure; and many have even
felt the pangs of hunger, which has probably hastened their surrender, – which
none regret, but one and all agree that it would have been wise to have
submitted before. . . .[4]

With pacification seemingly assured, the British began to evacuate most of their forces
from Zululand. The 2nd Division and units of the Flying Column marched out of the
subdued territory by the way they had come. The *Natal Witness* correspondent at
Landman's Drift described their invalids passing through the sleepy depot on 21 July:

There has been nothing to relieve the moral dulness of this place since the advent
of Mr. Archibald Forbes on the 5th inst., until yesterday, when we were
awakened from our lassitude by the arrival from the front of the sick and
wounded, with a strong escort of infantry . . . and some natives. The severe cases
were carried by Kafirs in bearers or stretchers, and the others, whose state would
permit, were in ambulance and other wagons adapted for the purpose. I have not
heard of any exceptionally bad cases, although some are serious enough. . . .[5]

The listless 1st Division began to break up from 10 July, and by the end of the month
only a few depleted garrisons remained in the coastal plain. Supplies landed at Port
Durnford for the troops remaining in Zululand still required handling, however, and
Wolseley adopted the not very successful expedient of raising a carrier corps for the
purpose. The *Times of Natal* correspondent commented critically on 28 July:

The starting point for the 2nd Division during the second invasion of Zululand: the camp at
Landman's Drift. (Ian Knight)

. . . There are now only between 200 and 300 men to protect the landing place here [Port Durnford], and about the same number on the Umlatoosi [Mhlathuze]. The formation of a carrier corps does not appear to be attended with such successful results as might have been anticipated. The natives are very dissatisfied at being employed in such a manner – assisting in discharge of cargoes – and say they are soldiers, not cattle; they have also been ridiculed by their brethren of the Native Contingent, who have treated them as very inferior beings, and so increased their dislike to their duties. Some of them, however, appear content at the change; they all receive pay at the rate of 1s per diem, and are rationed as well. Altogether, however, the corps is not such a benefit as it was thought it would be. . . .[6]

The various units of the Natal Mounted Volunteers returned home to rapturous welcomes. A *Natal Mercury* correspondent fulsomely described the scene on 30 July in Verulam, similar to so many others in the towns and villages of the colony:

The Victoria Mounted Rifles returned to-day, Wednesday. A large number of ladies and gentlemen met them on Fuller's Flat. The men all looked very hearty, and were in high glee. When they reached the main street . . . a large party of young ladies gave them welcome by a shower of flowers and bouquets of roses, whilst all the population of Verulam united in outbursts of cheering during their whole course through the town.

  The town was gaily decorated with flags and mottoes – 'Welcome Home our Volunteers,' 'Happy Day,' 'Peace and Happiness,' and other designs expressive of the one joyous feeling shared in by every hearth and home in Verulam. One sentiment was specially uppermost – 'Thank God they have all returned.'

  Captain Saner, in a few feeling and appropriate words, dismissed his men, briefly touching upon the work they had performed at Inyezane, Ginginhlovo, Etshowe, and in the defence of the colony at Thring's Post, thanking them for their services, of which he felt proud. He expressed his determination to obtain a just remuneration for all they lost at Etshowe, and as pay during the eight months of their irksome, arduous, but effective campaign. . . .

  This little town was never the scene of such general gladness as this return of the V.M.R.'s produced.[7]

On 30 July Wolseley passed through Greytown on his way north to oversee the final pacification of Zululand. He impressed the townsfolk (and the *Natal Witness* correspondent) with his habitual energy and decisiveness:

General Sir Garnet Wolseley and Staff passed through here last Wednesday, *en route* for Ulundi, staying one night in the village. With his usual thoughtfulness in such matters, he lost no time before visiting the soldiers' hospital, where orders were give that the patients should have a more liberal and judiciously selected diet than had hitherto been supplied, also that a better site should be found, for the tents were too much enclosed by gum-tree plantations. They have since been moved to the south side of the village. Five deaths in a month is a serious percentage from a detachment of 200 men, and shows the necessity of prompt action.[8]

While Wolseley was critically inspecting the hospital in Greytown, various units of the dispersing 1st Division were crossing the Lower Thukela into Natal. Now his services were no longer required, the special correspondent of the *Natal Witness* reflected in elevated and elegiac vein on the campaign and the hardships he had shared with the soldiers:

> Once more in following the movements of the coast column, I find myself on the banks of the Tugela. The 99th Regiment, to the merry strain of their Band, crossed into Natal yesterday [3 August], and as 'The Buffs' are following in their wake *en route* to Pinetown, I write for the last time from this inhospitable place, the duty of correspondent with this column being completed. I shall take my departure too, and, after a seven months' separation from civilization, shall be happy once more to find myself in more congenial society than Zulus. How long ago it seems since that January morning when I first wrote to you of our crossing the Tugela, and how various are the incidents which since then befel our arms. Starvation, cold, and hardships have had to be encountered, but it enlivens the prospects when side by side with them we place the victories achieved over the foe, and which, there can be no question, have such an effect on the Zulu mind that there is every reason to expect that not for many years shall the inhabitants of Natal be again placed in fear for their homes and lives by 'hunting excursions' of Cetywayo on the banks from which I write.
>
> With the exception of a few companies of the 99th Regiment and the 91st Regiment, placed in the forts from here to the Umlalazi, all the 'pomp and circumstance' of war are gone. The Tugela banks are now quite deserted, the same quiet and calm reigns over them as when the British troops had not yet reached here. The large camps of armed men, the prancing horses, the hundreds of wagons, the heavy artillery, are all gone, and their place is at this moment occupied by a few naked Kafirs, prowling round the camp ground, gathering up such articles as have been left behind. Fort Tenedos looks wild in its desolation, three soldiers being the only occupants, while Fort Pearson can only boast of a company. The Kafirs that made the night hideous with their shouting in transporting goods into Zululand, seem to have gone home to their kraals, the ponts have ceased to ply their trade, but in their place a good stout bridge spans the river. As the regiments marched out to-day, even the traffic seems to have ceased; all around looks dreary and deserted, and, with bitter recollection of my stay in the country, I turn my back upon it, and from the place where I sent you my first letter at the commencement of hostilities now post my last on their termination.[9]

More prosaically, the *Natal Mercury*'s Utrecht correspondent who, like many other settlers, had sustained heavy losses as a result of the war, acidly enquired on 7 August who was to pay them recompense:

> The Great question in England is, Who is to pay for the War? With European nations it is the rule to saddle the conquered with the war costs, but when England has to deal with savages in defence of the colonies, the conquerors have been asked to pay the piper, for the sympathy of the Aborigines Protection

Society is always in proportion to the subtleness and barbarity of the white man's foe. . . . Great outcry is made in the House of Commons about burning Zulu straw huts, which had been abandoned by their inmates, and sheltered the enemy's soldiers, but I have not seen a word about the white men's valuable and costly homesteads which had been built at the expense of years of toil and labour, and destroyed before the war commenced, and since; or of the sufferings of Christian British subjects and families from the aggressions of barbarous Zulus for the last ten years, to the entire ruin of a great many. I have been driven from my farm for two years, and deprived of the means of earning the means of existence for my family, and since the commencement of the war have had to pay famine prices for food. . . . This with losses of stock could not be compensated by £2000, exclusive of loss by the destruction of buildings and furniture, agricultural implements, &c. And still my loss is small in proportion to many of my neighbours, who are now called upon to pay for the weapon which knocked them down. If the colonists were the subjects of any foreign state they would have Mansion House subscriptions, and British sympathy would help us out of our misfortune, in place of calling upon us to pay expenses – incurred principally through blunders, and neglect, and wilful waste committed by the columns of Pearson and Crealock, for the thousands of pounds worth of wagons lying on the road between the Etshowe and the Inyezani Drift, and the hundreds of tons of food and stores carried from Durban to forts on the coast, and pitched off in the grass to rot, without covering above or drainage below. . . .[10]

Though the cost of the war was beginning to be counted, hostilities had not yet come to a complete end. Wolseley detailed a column under Lieutenant-Colonel Baker Russell (made up of portions of the disbanded Flying Column), to ensure the pacification of north-western Zululand where he feared the abaQulusi and Manyonyoba might attempt a last-ditch resistance. He ordered troops stationed in the Transvaal under Lieutenant-Colonel the Hon. G. Villiers to cooperate in the operation. Hamu and his men were expected to act as auxiliaries to Villiers' force, but proved reluctant, as the *Natal Mercury* correspondent in Utrecht reported on 10 August with considerable scorn:

There is not much stirring here. Oham has come back to his kraal, he only followed Colonel Villiers as far as the top of the Burghers' Pass, where he began to complain of a pain in his stomach, and returned to his kraal, where he still remains, and refuses to stir.

Colonel Villiers is now in Luneberg, and has raised a burgher corps and band of natives, with which he intends to enter Zululand should hostilities be renewed.

The Swazis, I learn, are uncertain in their movements, and it is not at all sure they will enter Zululand, even if allowed to do so.

The Zulus are reported to be gathering in force in the Entombi Valley, but the rumour of their concentration in the Pongolo Bush is denied, and the road to Luneburg, which passes close to it, is open.[11]

While Russell's column moved north-west, Wolseley detailed another column under Lieutenant-Colonel C.M. Clarke (formed out of the disbanded 1st Division) to re-occupy the Mahlabathini Plain and send out patrols to capture the fugitive Cetshwayo. The *Natal Witness* correspondent accompanied Clarke's column and wrote with considerable empathy on 11 August concerning the plight of the defeated Zulu:

> . . . In campaigns of this kind one is apt to look lightly on the suffering of the enemy who, happening to be of a darker hue, is often supposed to be utterly devoid of the gentler feelings possessed by the superior white man. Although not so highly cultured as their more favoured fellow-men, the paternal feeling is strong in many. . . . The love of country and home is also hereditary to nearly, if not all, the human race, and the loss of personal property is felt acutely by every one, no matter of what colour. A little sympathy should not be denied our late enemy as they have undoubtedly suffered severely, their relatives being dead, homes burnt or otherwise destroyed with their crops, cattle lost, and the pangs of hunger felt by many. Let us hope, however, that they will, as a compensation for these disasters, gain a freedom which will prove a means of success to them as a people dependent on the English nation. . . . Cetywayo has proved himself a tyrant whose rule they will tolerate no longer, he is in hiding about a day's march from this place, and, it is said, with but a dozen or two followers. . . .[12]

Patrols sent out from Wolseley's camp near oNdini, where he was waiting to receive the submissions of the leading men of Zululand, made some satisfying finds in the vicinity. The *Times of Natal*'s Ulundi correspondent reported:

> A cavalry patrol . . . returned on the 11th [August] with numerous articles of war, found hidden in various kraals and buried in the earth. Among the articles found were rockets, rocket tubes, shells, shrapnel, &c., rifles of modern and antique design, shot, and other things too numerous to enumerate. The party, after a diligent search for valuables, were returning with their spoil when, at a short distance they espied the gun-carriages with the two guns, of which so much has been heard, they having been taken from the Imperial forces on the memorable battle-field of Isandhlwana. One was found to be loaded with shell, which was extracted; and it was found that they were not spiked, but that rifle nipples had been placed in their vents which had never been extracted, consequently the guns were harmless. They were in a good state of preservation, and could be soon made fit for service again. They were brought into camp and placed close to the flag-staff, where they now remain in solemn grandeur, relics of a disaster scarcely ever known to our arms, and objects of interest to each one of us, and of every Englishman. The Zulus in their flight entirely overlooked these guns, upon which they set such value, and which, from their long detention by the enemy, have become historical objects which will be viewed by future generations as interesting relics of a war which has proved so deplorable to many. . . .[13]

On 14 August Mnyamana and a considerable number of chiefs presented themselves at Wolseley's camp. They had come to sue for terms of peace on the king's behalf, but after a lengthy interview decided to surrender themselves. The *Times of Natal* correspondent acutely described the proceedings which left Cetshwayo effectively isolated:

I noticed after breakfast on the 15th [sic for 14th] that John Dunn, with a few of his men, rode out of camp away over the hills, and thinking something important was going to happen, I went after him later on; and had not ridden very far, when I saw coming over the mountains from Amhlabatini [Mahlabathini] large numbers of cattle and Zulus. On meeting them, Dunn explained to me that he had been out to bring in the Prime Minister and other celebrated chiefs, who had been collecting theirs and the King's cattle to bring in. When the cattle, which were very fat, were herded in the valley, about two miles from our camp, the lot of Zulus formed single file, and, headed by John Dunn and his trusty sable followers, marched down solemnly to our camp. I counted 107 of them, not including many others, who remained herding the cattle. They all looked in excellent condition, and not in any way bearing evidence of having suffered any privations. They consisted of men of all ages and sizes, but all, except about ten, wore the india-rubber head-dress. . . . The five principal chiefs walked in front, but had no distinguishing mark whatever to the others. Nearly all were naked, wearing only the customary skins hanging from the waist; one or two had skins over their shoulders, and all had sticks of some sort or another. Preparations had been made to receive them, and the camp turned out *en masse* to see their entry. They were brought into our headquarter square, and squatted down in a semi-circle, two or three deep at the ends, but nine or ten in the centre, the Prime Minister Imanyamana [Mnyamana] being seated in the front row, exactly in the centre, with the celebrated general, his bosom friend, Tshingwayo [Ntshingwayo] on his right. . . . Just in front of them, four chairs had been placed, upon which, beginning from right to left, sat Colonel Brackenbury, General Colley, John Shepstone, and John Dunn. . . . After the names of the principal ones had been taken down, the *durbar* was opened by John Shepstone, who asked why they had not come in before, and had brought in only cattle, leaving their guns and assegais, which they were told especially to bring. The old chief Mnanyamana answered that after the battle of Ulundi they were so scattered that they had even now not had sufficient time to get all the cattle together. They had however, thought it best to come in at once with what they could get, and that as they were sincere in their desire for peace, they would go back and get together all the guns, assegais and rest of the cattle – both theirs and the King's. Upon being asked whether there were not some royal herds of white cattle to come in, they replied, No, that they had all been taken away by the King, but that plenty of others still remained to brought in. The cunning old fellow then turned to Dunn, and said that he would, he knew, bear him out in the statement that the King and nation had lost lots of oxen, &c., by lung-sickness. . . . He was then asked whether he got the messages sent to him lately about surrendering, &c., and whether that did not mention about guns and assegais especially. Several of them then began to talk at once – evidently apologising – but mixed up the purport of every message which had been sent them since the war commenced. . . . This ended the first part of the *indaba*, Shepstone informing them that the five principal chiefs would have to remain here until the guns, assegais, and rest of the cattle were brought in. This gave rise to a lot of talk and objection, as they said that they could not exercise their authority so well here as if they were allowed to go again; neither could they remain here, as the water was all polluted by the dead bodies of their comrades. These objections were, however, overruled, and so the matter ended. In the meantime, Dunn and Shepstone went off to witness the counting of the cattle, which numbered nearly 700, and among which was a span from Isandhlwana. . . . Shepstone, on his return, gave them a short history of the war, its causes and results, and reproached them for not having overruled the younger men, and advised Cetywayo to submit. They, of course, all blamed Cetywayo, and he doubtless would throw the blame on others. They now understood that he was no longer king, and the country would be left free under tribal supervision. The King, he hoped, would be captured in a few days. . . . This speech lasted half an hour, and being most impressively and distinctly given, seemed to attract their attention thoroughly, and pleased most of them. . . . I noticed Dr. Glanville was again able to get excellent sketches of the whole scene, so that the public at home will not only be able to read but also to see what took place at this most interesting and important meeting. I had plenty of leisure to carefully observe them all during the talk, and I must confess I think they earnestly now desire peace, and are very much cut up about their heavy losses, and thoroughly admit the supremacy of England. The Prime Minister is a tall thin man, about sixty-five, with an intelligent head, and slight, peaked beard, with a little whiskers and moustache now just becoming grey. Tshingwayo, one of Cetywayo's best Generals, and a leader at Isandhlwana, is much shorter, fatter, and more grey, but has a sharp intelligent look about him, and greater powers of speech than the minister. The two always have been, and still are, like brothers. Of the other chiefs, many had signs of old wounds on them, and in several instances I noticed stiff legs and arms, and other effects which will never go away. Cetywayo's two brothers are both fine-looking men. . . . None of the men would or could say anything about Cetywayo or his whereabouts, and they were not pressed.[14]

The hunt for the king intensified throughout August. Despite the resistance still continuing in some parts of the country, the search seemed to many among the British to be the last real objective of the war, and their patrols swept through vast areas of country which they had hitherto not penetrated. To an officer class for whom field sports were a traditional pastime, the hunt offered all the thrill of a sporting chase, and the patrols vied with one another for the honour of running their quarry to ground. The exhausted king was finally captured in a remote homestead in the Ngome forest on 28 August by a party of the 1st Dragoon Guards under the command of Major Marter, and the *Times of Natal*'s 'special war correspondent' at oNdini gleaned the details of the capture from Marter himself:

It appears that [Marter] was with Colonel Clarke at the Black Umvolosy [Mfolozi], and having received a message from General Colley to the effect that the King had gone towards the Ingomi [Ngome], started off in that direction on Wednesday, the 26th of August, taking two troops of the King's Dragoon Guards, under Captains Gibbings and Godsden, one company of Barton's Natives, under

Captain Plesh, and ten Mounted Irregulars, under Lieutenant Wurgh. Young Oftebro accompanied them as interpreter, and they had four guides. He passed several kraals during the day, and at each enquired for information, but could get none. . . . That evening they stayed at a kraal of Umkojanea's, and got some information and guides, and next day they went on, and during the morning were met by another Zulu, who said he had been sent by Umbovo to inform the white people that he had heard that 'the wind blew their way', pointing to the S.W.; but in order to get there they must go up north. . . . Following his guide and the hint he had received, Marter worked his way steadily up the side of the mountain ridge, and, when near the top, reached another kraal. Here the interpreter had another talk with the inhabitants, asking whether they knew the troops were in the neighbourhood, and if so, that they wanted guides and information. Without answering, two men got up, and quietly led the Major further up the hill, until near the top they reached an open space. Here they put up their hands and stopped. Then crawling on their hands, knees and stomachs, and followed only by Marter and his interpreter, they got through the grass patch, and they looked over the side of the mountain, which was nearly precipitous. Below in the valley, about 1500 feet down, Marter saw a small stockaded kraal of about twenty huts, and it was situated on a slight rise in the middle of a semi-circular glade, surrounded on three sides by thickly covered, bushy, precipitous rocks, and only exposed on the fourth. This was guarded by several spies who, however, never thought of watching the mountains behind. A very short time was needed to plan and surround it, and while the natives were sent down naked, with only their arms, to cut off the escape in front, the Major having found a ravine less difficult than any other, dismounted his men, at great risk, and losing two horses, and having several men injured, he managed to reach the bottom at three p.m., having been an hour and a quarter coming down. The trees were all interlaced with thick creepers, and here and there were boulders, and ledges of rocks, which necessitated a clean drop of four or five feet. How they got down at all is a wonder. Luckily when there they found that a slight hill intervened between them and the kraal, which was only 500 yards off, so they were able to wait the last man's arrival, and then mount. Orders were given for Captain Gibbing's troop to make for the right of the kraal, and Captain Godsden's for the left. When all were ready they galloped in single file, and, before the astonished Zulus knew what was up, they were surrounded on all sides, the Native Contingent just getting across the open space at the front at the right time to co-operate. The Zulus were all around with guns and assegais, but they were told that if a shot was fired the kraal would be set alight, and they would be blazed at from all round. However, no resistance was offered, and Major Marter dismounted, and, followed by the interpreter and some of his men, entered the kraal and enquired where Cetywayo was. Umkozana [Mkhosana], the last chief who remained and fled with the King, pointed out a hut at the other end, to which they went, but the King refused to come out, saying that they must come in to him, and wanting to know what rank was the officer. He also requested to be shot, but was assured of the perfect safety of his life. Talking being of no avail, threats were used, and, just as they were about to set fire to the hut, out he came, and looking around him haughtily, said they would never have caught him fairly, and that he had never expected troops could get down from the mountains at the back. The rest of the prisoners were then secured and brought out, and the King was told he must also come with them.[15]

With Cetshwayo now a prisoner and on his way to exile in the Cape, the chiefs were relieved of their embarrassing moral obligation to stand by their defeated king. On 1 September they publicly accepted Wolseley's terms for a final settlement. The Zulu monarchy was abolished, and the former kingdom fragmented into thirteen pieces, each under an appointed chief. Although these were nominally independent, they had to submit to the arbitration of a British resident. Wolseley hoped thereby to stifle any residual royal influence and to ensure that the *amabutho* system would not be resuscitated. Thus, although Britain would avoid the responsibility and expense of a direct annexation, an emasculated Zululand would no longer pose any sort of threat to the neighbouring British colonies. The special war correspondent of the *Times of Natal* witnessed the ceremonial proceedings:

. . . Notice had been sent out throughout the land that on this occasion the General would announce to the assembled Chiefs our terms for the settlement of the future Government of this country and this, of course, coupled with the fact of the King's capture, sufficed to bring all that could come. From early morning until past noon troops of them kept arriving from all directions, until, at three o'clock, there were nearly three hundred present. We had been having horse races on the day since noon, but when the hour drew near for the time fixed, the course was deserted, and the last three races left till after the indaba was over. An order had been previously sent round requesting the presence of every officer in uniform, with swords, punctually at four. All the Staff were ready, and arranged things for business. The scene was the square formed by the Head Quarters encampment, in the centre of which flew the Union Jack on a pole, around which was a camp table and several chairs, and at the lower end all the Zulus were placed in rows across from one side to another, and were when all seated about ten deep; Umgamana [Mnyamana], his Prime Minister, and Tshingwana being again prominent in the centre, while other notable Chiefs were scattered about in the front row, being immediately backed up in all cases by their head indunas and councillors. Our officers, of which there were many of almost every branch of the service, formed a semicircle at the upper end, merely leaving a small passage to Sir Garnet's tent as [at] the centre. Jantje's mounted natives were also present, and some of Captain Barton's Native Contingent. When all was ready, Sir Garnet came out, and all the Zulus unanimously and immediately rose and saluted him with loud hurrahs! pronounced very harshly. All then seated themselves; and Sir Garnet, having John Shepstone and Colonel Clarke on his left, while still further away, on a chair by himself, sat John Dunn; behind were Colonel Blackenbury [Brackenbury], General Colley, and Mr. St. Ledger Herberg, Private Secretary; and at the table which was very kindly placed at our disposal sat the representative of the *Telegraph* and myself. Standing behind these again, were the rest of the Personal and Head-quarter Staff. Silence was instantaneous; then Sir Garnet delivered an excellent speech, which lasted over an hour; it was interpreted sentence by sentence by the Hon. John Shepstone. . . . Sir Garnet finished his speech by saying that there were some chiefs not present to whom he had given districts, and that, therefore, they could not have their signed papers until they came personally. A copy of the terms and conditions of their accepting the chieftainship of the various thirteen districts having been read out and translated to them, and made distinctly understood, copies, in a book, for the use of the British Government, and others loose, for the chiefs to keep as titles, were then signed by the chiefs appointed, two indunas as witnesses, Sir Garnet as Her Majesty's representative, and, lastly, John Shepstone, as having interpreted it to them. . . . It was further stated that the boundaries were to be, wherever possible, banks of rivers, and that when they were fixed by a council of officers who were being appointed to go round with the different chiefs and settle them in accordance with the General's rough plan, inhabitants not liking to stay in the new district were to have full power to move to any other one which they might choose. Altogether the meeting was a grand success, and a brilliant finish to the whole question; all seemed satisfied. . . .[16]

NOTES

1. *Illustrated London News*, 23 August 1879: correspondent with General Hope Crealock's division.
2. *Natal Witness*, 15 July 1879: occasional correspondent with General Crealock's column, Umlalazi Plains, 7 July 1879.
3. *Natal Witness*, 19 July 1879: special correspondent with General Crealock's column, Umlalazi Plains, 13 July 1879.
4. *Natal Witness*, 29 July 1879: Port Durnford correspondent, 20 July 1879.
5. Ibid.: Landman's Drift correspondent, 22 July 1879.
6. *Times of Natal*, 4 August 1879: Port Durnford correspondent, 28 July 1879.
7. *Natal Mercury*, 1 August 1879: Verulam correspondent, 30 July 1879.
8. *Natal Witness*, 7 August 1879: Greytown correspondent, 4 August 1879.
9. *Natal Witness*, 12 August 1879: special correspondent, Lower Tugela Drift, 4 August 1879.
10. *Natal Mercury*, 22 August 1879: Utrecht correspondent, Tongaat, 7 August 1879.
11. *Natal Mercury*, 15 August 1879: Utrecht correspondent, 10 August 1879.
12. *Natal Witness*, 23 August 1879: Ulundi correspondent, 11 August 1879.
13. *Times of Natal*, 25 August 1879: Ulundi correspondent, 13 August 1879.
14. *Natal Mercury*, 29 August 1879: *Times of Natal* correspondent.
15. *Natal Mercury*, Zulu War Supplement, September 1879, quoting the *Times of Natal*, account by 'our Special War Correspondent, Headquarters, Usiswhili Valley, near Ulundi, September 3rd 1879'.
16. *Times of Natal*, 8 September 1879: special war correspondent, Ulundi, Tuesday morning, 2 September 1879.

Pacification

On 21 August the captive Cetshwayo proceeded under escort from Wolseley's camp to Port Durnford, whence he was taken off by sea on 4 September for the Cape and exile. A correspondent who accompanied him described the journey and the former king's illuminating conversation on military and political matters:

. . . The strictest surveillance was maintained the whole way from Ulundi to Port Durnford, which journey was accomplished in five days, leaving Ulundi at 2 p.m. on the 31st August, and arriving at Port Durnford on the 4th September. Cetywayo travelled the whole distance in an ambulance drawn by mules, which are most trying for cavalry to keep pace with, as it is only down hill they put on any pace, whilst the necessity of the mounted escort keeping close to the ambulance containing the King obliged the cavalry to trot at a most trying rate. . . . But little opportunity for communication whilst travelling presented itself, but of an evening Cetywayo was very pleased to have a few in his tent, more especially so if accompanied by a bottle of 'square face,' i.e. Hollands gin, to which he seems partial, though he is by no means a drunkard. I believe he would really have rather had some 'tyuala,' [*utshwala*] or beer, of the royal brew, which I can answer for as being very different to the usual stuff presented to you at the minor chiefs' kraals. Whilst squatted, sipping his 'square face,' and with a very gorgeous rainbow-hued rug thrown over his shoulders, which he exchanged at night for the damask tablecloth worn during the heat of the day, Cetywayo would enter most affably into conversation, behaving at all times with perfect courtesy and good breeding, being most particular not to interrupt any one who was speaking, and evincing considerable annoyance at the way some of the officers repeated the same question over and over again, often asking another question in the middle of the King's answer to a former one. A question that was frequently put to him was, what did he think of the battle of Ulundi? This was a standing dish, and both the King and officers of his escort seemed thoroughly sick of hearing it put, especially as the King was not present at it, but had already begun his flight towards the Black Umvolosi; having told his brother Umswetu [Ziwedu] that the white soldiers would be sure to win, and that his men were fighting without his wish or advise. He also spoke of the herd of cattle he had sent to ratify his peaceful intention, but which his young men had turned back again, refusing the men driving them permission to hand them over to Lord Chelmsford, and taking the question of more fighting completely out of the King's hands. Kambula was his fight, he said, the one in which he had given the most minute directions to the various commanders of his regiments how to attack and what ground to occupy, which regiments were to form the horns, which the main body – in fact he planned the whole of that battle. The others, he said, were not under his immediate supervision, and with Ulundi he distinctly declared he had nothing to do. Cetywayo was anxious to know which of his regiments we thought the best and bravest, he himself holding his Ingobomakosi [iNgobamakhosi] regiment in the highest estimation, and refusing to believe our cavalry had scattered half of this particular regiment which formed a horn of the Zulu host at the battle of Kambula, under the command of Dabulamanzi. . . . Cetywayo on several occasions tried to lead the conversation into a political channel, but was invariably told that no political discussion would be permitted; that the people he was with were only soldiers, whose business it was to fight. Yes, replied the King, I know, and I like the soldiers, they behave well to me; it is not they that drive me out of my country, but Shepstone; he wants to get rid of me quietly and quickly, as I could tell things he would not like to hear: in fact, Cetywayo laid the whole blame of the war on Shepstone's shoulders, saying: 'He was the man that set light to the fire that has burnt up Zululand.' This being too political a conversation, was put a stop to, though it was almost impossible to prevent the King constantly recurring to the same theme. His idea, when he heard of the death of the poor Prince Imperial, was that a nephew of the Queen had been slain, and he gave orders at once for the sword to be returned. To show how nearly caught he must have been more than once, he pointed out one person who had passed with a party close by the bush he was hiding in, within ten or fifteen yards in fact; and Cetywayo was able to describe the movements of the men patrolling in search of him minutely, from his personal observation.

The King evinced great uneasiness each time that they came to a cross road, saying that they were not going the proper road towards Natal, but were going towards the sea. He was not, however, enlightened as to his destination, but seemed perfectly aware that he was being taken to the sea, and grew more and more dejected at his worst fears being thus realised. He maintained that from the first he was aware that the English would in the end defeat him, but he said: 'I was not a child to let anyone come and take my country, which, as you have seen, is so large and beautiful, without my fighting for it. No nation,' he continued, 'could have done it but the English, and so thought his ancestors.' The ambulance was taken up close to the surf boat, and as he stepped into the boat, leaving his last foot-print on the sand of his recent kingdom, a feeling of pity was not wanting for a King among his brethren.[1]

With the signing of Wolseley's settlement on 1 September and the despatching of Cetshwayo into exile, it remained only to clear out the last few pockets of possible resistance. The *Natal Mercury's* special correspondent at Utrecht wired a report on 6 September of mopping-up operations in the Ntombe Valley:

Villiers' force paraded across the Pongolo to foot of Dumbi [Dumbe Mountain] on 29th [August], and on the 30th attacked Maqulisin [abaQulusi people]. Kafirs took 250 cattle and burnt all kraals in neighbourhood of Dumbi. This raid doubtless expedited the surrender of Mahobolin [Mahubulwana] and other Maqulisin Chiefs to Russell's column. . . . Manyonyoba asked terms of the Commanding Officer at Luneberg; and was promised safety till sunset of the 4th [September]. On the same day the natives of Russell's column [Teteleku's Mounted Natives] by mistake killed eight of his men. Negotiations have not been renewed. It is believed he has fled. Russell advanced against him on the 5th; result not known.[2]

Russell's patrols attacked Manyonyoba's caves in the Ntombe Valley on 5 September and again three days later, ending all last flickers of resistance. Russell marched his column north on 10 September for the Transvaal in order to take part in operations against the Pedi. On its way the column was halted, still in sight of Luneburg and the Ntombe Valley, for the Victoria Cross to be conferred on Private Samuel Wassall of the 80th Regiment. During the flight from Isandlwana on 22 January, he had dismounted on the Zulu side of the flooded Mzinyathi River to rescue Private Thomas Westwood who was in difficulties. He had then remounted his horse and dragged Westwood across the river under a heavy shower of bullets.[3] The *Times of Natal* correspondent witnessed the ceremony on 11 September and recorded Lieutenant-Colonel S. Malthus's peroration:

. . . At 9.30 a.m. this morning the troops, consisting of the 94th Regt. and Mounted Infantry, were formed into hollow square. The morning was cloudy,

The presentation of the Victoria Cross to James Langley Dalton, one of the heroes of Rorke's Drift, at Fort Napier, Pietermaritzburg, on 16 January 1880. (Killie Campbell Africana Library)

but on the troops 'forming up' a brilliant ray of sunshine, lit up the scene, which was, certainly, picturesque. Beneath us lay the Intombi, winding slowly through the deserted plains, which once swarmed with the dusky sons of Zululand, the majority of whom now tranquilly sleep beneath the sward. Far away in the distance the blue peaks of the mountains rose till they were lost in the clouds. The clustering trees of the Mission Station [Myer's], covered with blossoms, sent a balmy odour through the morning air – so pleasant and invigorating. But here in the wilds, remote from public view, was performed that interesting ceremony, which, let us hope, will ever grace our country's arms. Colonel Mallthus [Malthus], in pinning the decoration on the breast of the fortunate possessor, warmy congratulated him on the distinguished honour which he (Private Wassell) had achieved, which was highly creditable both to himself and the Regiment to which he belonged to – the 80th. Colonel Mallthus then proceeded to say that this should be the ambition of every soldier, from the highest to the lowest, and pointed out that nothing but the most conspicuous gallantry would entitle any soldier to this enviable distinction. In the course of his remarks, he pointed out the advantages to be derived by a steady application to one's profession, and as all could not possibly gain the Victoria Cross, there was one honour which was within the reach of every soldier, and that was the good conduct medal. Colonel Mallthus, in concluding, again warmly congratulated Private Wassell, and trusted he would live long to enjoy the proud distinction he had so gallantly earned.[4]

Not all the combatants on the British side had their services properly recognized, and were indeed left with feelings of considerable bitterness. Such a one was Chief Mqawe of the amaQadi people in the Inanda Location. When the Natal Native Contingent was being raised, he enthusiastically called out nearly a thousand of his young men who were mustered as the 2nd Battalion of the 2nd Regiment NNC. Chief Mqawe accompanied them when they marched with the No. 1 Column to Eshowe, fighting their way through at Nyezane. When the Eshowe garrison was reduced on 29 January, the 2/2nd Regiment NNC marched through the night back to the Thukela, repeatedly halting to allow white stragglers on foot (who had been abandoned by the Natal Mounted Volunteers) to catch up. Chief Mqawe felt strongly that his services had not been sufficiently recognized, and was particularly angered that the anticipated reward of captured Zulu cattle was not forthcoming. He shocked Colonial opinion by roundly declaring to a *Natal Witness* correspondent that he would never again fight for the ungrateful British:

The loyalty of Umqawe (one of our leading chiefs) during the Zulu war was well-known and frequently commented on. This personage has now given expression to sentiments the reverse of friendly to the power on whose side he fought. . . .

After commenting on colonial affairs in general, Umqawe, speaking bitterly, said:– 'Never more will I fight for the white man. Why should I? I was called out with my people to help in the punishment of a common and dangerous enemy. Here have I, the son of Dabeju, and of royal race, been lying in ditches

'Home from the war': Henry Francis Fynn Jnr, son of one of the most famous of the early settlers in Natal, and magistrate for Umsinga on the Zulu border, photographed with members of his Border Guard at the close of hostilities. (Ian Knight)

and in mud, nipped by frosts at night, drenched by rain and scorched by noon-day marches. I have stood out in the fight with my men; I have seen my favourite councillors, my relatives, my headmen, and my young men drop by my side shot by men whose whole life is evil. I have accepted the dispensation of the *Mashloze* [*amadlozi*] (spirits or fates) thinking I was assisting in removing the incubus of generations and felling the tree saturated with the blood of my fathers and my people's fathers, and now I find that we have been fighting for nothing, for a shadow. We are wholly losers by the campaign; the Zulus are wholly gainers. Nothing has been done to them to show them they are punished conquered; not a head of cattle taken. I come, out of the fight unrequited in any sense. Well, so be it. You are not human beings, you white people, but phenomena. Your missionaries talk platitudes about a man giving his left cheek to be smitten by the man who has already hit his right. It is all very well as a platitude, but it won't do with us black people, Zulu or no Zulu. My heart is angry, and never again will I respond to the call of your Government.'[5]

By early October the last faint eddies of the Zululand campaign were receding through Natal. Clarke's column, which marched out of Zululand by way of Middle Drift, enforcing submissions and exacting cattle fines as it went, had passed through Greytown on the cold, rainy 28 September. No field forces remained in the conquered territory, and only a few scattered garrisons had still to make their way back. On 8 October six companies of the 2/24th Regiment, which had reassembled at Utrecht from their various posts, marched through Greytown on their way to Pietermaritzburg under the command of Colonel H.J. Degacher. The *Times of Natal* correspondent could not but reflect sadly on the regiment's jaunty advance to the front during December 1878 before Isandlwana cast its tragic pall:

> . . . The pipe-and-drum band played merrily as they passed. The men are about the finest and healthiest looking of any that have come down from the front. The Colonel is said to be a severe disciplinarian, but it is as well known that he sees well to the health of his men. Mr. Chalklin [J. Chalkden, the schoolteacher] turned out his boys (about sixty), and with these and a few of the inhabitants, we were able to raise a good cheer for the men, for the band, for Major Bromhead an extra, and for the Colonel. The circumstance painfully reminded us of the 24th men, especially the bandsmen, who eight months ago [ten, in fact] charmed the whole village so often by their strains of music, but who now lie where they fell on that field of massacre, Isandhlwana. . . .
>
> There is no further news here of any importance.[6]

NOTES

1. *Natal Mercury*, 18 September 1879.
2. *Natal Witness*, 9 September 1879; *Mercury* Special Correspondent, Utrecht, 6 September 1879.
3. *Illustrated London News*, 20 September 1879.
4. *Times of Natal*, 19 September 1879: correspondent, 11 September 1879.
5. *Natal Witness*, 2 October 1879: Extraordinary statement by Umqawe.
6. *Natal Mercury*, 17 October 1879: from the *Times of Natal*, Greytown, 9 October 1879.

Index

Individual military units have been entered under **British campaign formations; British units;** *amaButho*; **Colonial units; Imp[…] units.** Fortifications have been entered under **Forts, laagers, camps and posts**. In accordance with modern practice, Zulu word[…] entered under the stem and not under the prefix. Zulu names are all spelled in the current, standard fashion.